Management's
Self-Inflicted Wounds

MANAGEMENT'S SELF-INFLICTED WOUNDS

A formula for executive self-analysis

Charles F. Austin

Colonel, Infantry, United States Army.

Doctor of Business Administration, Harvard.

Associate Professor of Organizational Behavior and Business Administration, The American University, Washington, D.C.

Professorial Lecturer in Behavioral Sciences, The George Washington University, Washington, D.C.

Graduate and former member of the faculty, The Industrial College of the Armed Forces, Washington, D.C.

Lecturer in Human Relations, The American University, Washington, D.C.

First Chief, Personnel Research Division, Directorate of Personnel Studies and Research, Office of the Deputy Chief of Staff for Personnel, United States Army, Washington, D.C.

Former member, Faculty, United States Army Management School.

Illustrated by Thomas M. Hickson

Holt, Rinehart and Winston, Inc.

New York   Chicago   San Francisco   Toronto   London

Grateful acknowledgment is made to the following for permission to reprint excerpts from their copyrighted works:

American Management Association, New York, N.Y., for excerpts from *Personnel* Magazine; from the article "The Quality of Leadership" by Cameron Hawley, copyrighted, 1960, by Cameron Hawley.

McGraw-Hill Book Company, New York, N.Y., for excerpts from *New Patterns in Management* by Dr. Rensis Likert, copyrighted, 1961, by the McGraw-Hill Book Co., Inc.

Harper & Row, Publishers, New York, N.Y., for an excerpt from *The Elements of Administration* by Lieutenant Colonel L. F. Urwick, O.B.E., M.C., copyrighted, 1943, by Sir I. Pitman & Sons, Ltd., London.

Mr. J. Lewis Powell, for excerpts from his lecture, "The Collapse of Time." Copyrighted, 1959, by J. Lewis Powell.

Preface

Why Should YOU Read This Book?

The appalling truth is that, generally speaking, with increase in importance of position held, there is a corresponding decrease in demonstrated leadership.

Sixty to ninety percent of all bosses are not regarded as organizational assets by their peers and their subordinates.

More than half of *YOUR* bosses were not regarded as organizational assets.

Your bosses were *TYPICAL* bosses.

YOU are a typical boss; therefore,

YOU are probably not regarded as an organizational asset by your peers and your subordinates; however,

YOU WILL BE A BETTER BOSS A FEW HOURS FROM NOW IF YOU WILL READ THIS BOOK.

The foregoing is not a typical beginning to a preface. It is not intended to be. This is not a typical book. However, this preface will attempt to satisfy two of the typical purposes of a book preface: to suggest values and uses of the book and to explain how the author came to write it.

First, however, let us pursue further the introductory comments, which are designed to motivate you to read this book.

v

Like many books, it began with the development of a lecture, which was later published into articles, and then followed by feedback in the form of mail and re-publication of the articles, all of which convinced the author (and the publisher) of the desirability for publication of a book along the same lines to perform the same function: to help a boss examine and analyze himself as a boss.

The beginning of this preface, like that to the lecture, is intended to convince the reader that the book is worth his while to read, in preference to reading another of the few books he has time to read in this busy life. The beginning to the lecture reflected the speaker's belief that, if he could not capture the minds of his listeners in the first three or four minutes of the lecture, the value of the remaining portion of the lecture was quite limited. Likewise, if the preface is not convincing, you will not read the book, or you will do so half-heartedly and defeat its purpose.

First, let us accomplish something you have done every day of your life as a *subordinate,* and which *your* subordinates do every day of their lives with *you as a boss: Let us prepare a performance appraisal of the bosses you have had along the way, including the present one.* This is a bit unconventional, and it may make you a bit uncomfortable. The conventional approach is to prepare appraisals of our *subordinates,* rather than of our bosses. Even the appraisal of subordinates makes us uncomfortable, particularly if we are required to show the appraisal to the subordinate on whom we prepare it, for this requires a kind of courage that is best recognized by its demonstrated absence in most bosses.

Uncomfortable or not, let's rate your bosses. First of all, let us throw out the word *like* and NOT use it in the ratings. That one word has clouded more performance appraisals of people in organizational life than a high-speed computer could calculate. I *am not* saying that it is not important whether you *like* your boss or not. I *am* saying that your *like* or *dislike* or your *respect* of your boss is based on facts or factors which we shall use as measurements, but that we shall not use *liking* itself as a measurement. We shall use the following five measurements, developed for the lecture, which have had wide acceptance, and which I have reason to believe you will accept as valid measures of the worth of a boss:

On Rating Your Boss

1. As a professional person (did he know his job?).
2. As a human being (did he behave like a human being and did he seem to recognize that *you* were also a human being?).
3. Did the organization make progress *because of him* or in *spite of him?* (No explanation needed on this measurement)
4. Did you learn from him more *bad things to avoid doing* or more *good things to copy* in *your own* behavior as a boss?
5. When you refer to him in retrospect, are those references primarily *positive* or *negative?* (He was better than, worse than, etc.)

In applying this rating to the bosses you have had along the way, please give equal weight to the ratings. It is helpful if you will select an *odd* number (3, 5, 7, and so forth) of bosses, placing plus or minus signs beside each of these ratings for each boss. Then total the plus and minus signs and arrive at a *net negative* or *net positive* figure for each boss. This makes the scoring process relatively simple in that each boss comes out with either a net negative or net positive score, and each *group* of bosses is similarly identified. *Please do not read further here until you have performed this rating process.*

Having prepared these ratings of your bosses, if your bosses have been typical, of that ghostly parade which has passed in review all too clearly in your mind's eye, 60 to 90 percent now have a minus sign beside their images. If you are one of the fortunate few whose bosses scored a *net positive* rating, do not get comfortable, for all bosses rated by all readers could be categorized as typical bosses. Most readers who rated their bosses are also bosses in their own right. Those readers can also be validly categorized as typical bosses. This leads us to the inescapable conclusion that, *of the readers of this book who are bosses, 60 to 90 percent are not regarded as organizational assets by their peers and their subordinates.* Perhaps this is reason enough for you to read this book, especially when coupled with the guarantee that, YOU WILL BE A BETTER BOSS A FEW HOURS FROM NOW, if you do read this book.

How is this guarantee possible? I have a friend who thinks it is *not* possible. A good administrator for twenty-five years, who has been bossed by many bosses during that time, he is very pessimistic and not at all hopeful that there will ever be any improvement in the present low state of the art of bossing. He said to me recently, "Chuck, you're wasting your time. I refuse to believe that bosses will ever be any better than they are now. Most of them are not good bosses now, and the bosses after you are dead and gone won't be any better. I don't know why this is true, but I believe it. Most bosses get the job done, but they certainly are not regarded as organizational assets by their peers and their subordinates."

If most bosses are not good bosses, why aren't they? The answer is not simple, but we could conjecture two reasons, or a combination of them:

1. We have not yet learned to educate for leadership.
2. The boss system of organization is not the best way to organize.

While we could spend a long time arguing the second item, this book is devoted to the former, that we have not yet learned to educate for leadership. In choosing the word *educate* I am using it in its broadest sense, to include self-education. Galileo once stated, "You cannot *teach* a man anything—you can only help him to find it within himself." In today's world of executive-developmental education, the most accepted truth is, "Executive development is self-development." Another widely-held belief in the field of boss education is that "developing requires action," postulating that human behavior stems from attitudes; that behavior will not change unless attitudes change; that attitudes will not change unless the individual becomes emotionally involved in the subject he is studying; that this involvement can best be brought about by experiences which induce or cause the individual to *act* or *react* mentally or physically, or both. This method of learning has been dubbed *gut-level* learning because of the belief that you are not truly involved in something unless you can "feel it in your guts."

What This Book Will Do for You

This book accepts that belief and attempts to give the reader a gut-level opportunity to examine himself as a boss, first by looking at the behavior of other bosses (particularly the bosses *he* has had along the way), and then determining whether he himself is guilty of the same type of undesirable boss behavior. Having identified these *self-inflicted wounds,* the book then hopes to prescribe therapy geared to bring about improvement.

However, the uniqueness of this book is its devotion to identifying the *wrong* way of doing things. As such, it reflects the author's belief that there is something fundamental about the human animal that makes it easier for him to *avoid doing wrong things* than it is to *remember to do right* things. He believes that it is no accident of theological history that eight of the Ten Commandments contain the words, *"Thou Shalt Not."* He further believes that, as a method of education, the *parable* method of education adopted by The Great Teacher two thousand years ago has not been improved upon as an educational device. Jesus of Nazareth chose as subjects of his parables stories whose common denominator was the fact that they were capable of being understood by the rich man, the poor man, the educated man, and the ignorant man. *This* book (claiming no divine origin) has as its common denominator the most universally known and recognized (though not most understood) relationship in the world today, second only to the husband and wife relationship of marriage. That relationship is the one between the boss and the bossed; the superior and the subordinate; the supervisor and the supervised; the generals and the colonels; the president and the vice presidents; the corporal and the privates; the foreman and the workers.

This book is a collection of parables describing this boss/ bossed relationship in many ways, involving many situations, in all of which the boss behaved in the "wrong" manner. This "wrong" manner is easily identified in the same manner that it has been said that few men can define *justice,* but any man can define *injustice.* In the words of a friend of mine, "I may not know anything about management, but I sure know how I don't like to be managed." The parables cut evenly across business, industry, education, government, and the military.

These parables are contained in, and form the primary description of, each of the self-inflicted wounds which are the central theme of the book. Following the description of each wound, and after securing your agreement that it is a "wrong" rather than "right" method of leadership, you are asked to look in the mirror to determine if you bear that wound. To assist you in accomplishing this, there is a brief "Self-Analysis" formula and, having diagnosed your wound, there is a "Heal the Wound" prescription for your self-medication.

How This Book Came to Be Written

In the past thirty years of my organizational life, which has ranged from companies of the Civilian Conservation Corps (CCC), to banks, to various kinds of government and military headquarters, to tactical organizations such as infantry companies and battle groups, to foreign organizations, and to American business industry and education, I have interviewed thousands of bosses and subordinates on the subject of boss behavior, or leadership if you prefer the word. In the seven years from 1953 to 1960 which began with two years as a student at the Harvard Graduate School of Business Administration (and the study of 1500 actual cases), followed by five years on the Faculty of the United States Army's executive development school, known as the Command Management School, I had the good fortune to associate with thousands of people in organizational life, including hundreds of executives who were students in courses such as those conducted by the American Management Association and the National Training Laboratory for Group Development. The parables are stories culled from the many conversations, observations, interviews, and research efforts of those years.

When a few of the parables were first put together in lecture form, the response was favorable and I was encouraged to put them into article form. This was done, with the first version of "Management's Self-Inflicted Wounds" appearing in *Army Magazine* in April, 1959. The fan mail was most encouraging, (the editor states the most prolonged in the history of his periodical) with many business, governmental, and military organizations requesting permission to reproduce the article and give it to supervisory personnel at all levels of the organizational hierarchies. As the chief executive of one organization stated, "We plan to give copies of it to every boss, supervisor, and executive in the organization."

I think the event which encouraged and inspired me most was the day, in the same mail, that I received letters from a semi-literate supervisor who misspelled a few words and from a Ph.D. Director of Executive Development for a large corporation. While the wording of the two letters was different, the message was the same: They agreed with the article and wanted to use the material for supervisory and executive development. This convinced me that the parable approach, plus the universally understood boss/bossed relationship, was the common denominator I needed to make a contribution to the little-developed state of the art of bossing, management, leadership, command, or whatever word you choose to use for the function.

Encouraged by these responses, including use of the articles by two foreign armies, I put the material in book form, prepared a sales talk and headed for the big city for the quick sale—which turned out to be not so quick. In my first interview with a book editor of an internationally-known publishing concern, the first question he asked me was, "How big will the book be?" I answered, "About three hundred pages." He responded, "Oh, my goodness, my company never publishes a book with less than five hundred pages." I responded, "Do you mean to tell me, Mr. ——, in this day and age when busy executives have so little time to read, that books are still selling by the *pound* like manure, instead of by the *ounce,* like gold?" He shook his head sadly, glancing at the stacks of manuscripts on his desk, and said, "I'm afraid the answer is yes."

Notwithstanding this exchange, he wanted to know more about the book. I took him through several self-inflicted wounds and, as I did so, I noticed him looking through his glass windows at his subordinates, muttering to himself. As I concluded my presentation I said, "At about this point the reader or listener has quite a feeling of guilt." He exploded, "You're telling me! I'm doing everything wrong! I'm no damned good as a boss." I did my best to calm him down, and have told friends that I missed two planes from New York while I helped him get control of himself.

To this day, however, I do not know if he ever realized that my little presentation had accomplished with him exactly what it was intended to accomplish with its readers: to get him to examine himself as a boss at the *gut level.* He wrote me later that he tried to buy the book, but that his policy committee had said the book "did not weigh enough" (did not have enough pages) for them to publish. Fortunately, my present publisher does not buy manuscripts by the pound.

What You Will Find in this Book

In any event, that is the story of how I came to write this book, and my hopes and dreams for it are clearly implied in the story. The book is as its title indicates, a formula for executive self-analysis, or boss self-analysis, if you prefer the term. It contains descriptions of seventy-six self-inflicted wounds which may exist on *any* executive or supervisory anatomy. It contains a diagnostic procedure for you to employ in checking your own executive anatomy to determine whether you bear any or all of those wounds. Finally, it contains a prescription to aid you in healing each of those wounds. Like the "Spirit of '76" which sparked the American Revolution, it is hoped this book will spark a revolt against executive ineffectiveness. The book hopes to be an answer to Robert Burns' and our own wish for the "giftie gie us to see ourselves as others see us," particularly through the eyes of our peers and our subordinates.

When the late Mr. C. D. Jackson, Publisher of *Life* magazine, introduced Mr. Ralph Cordiner, famed past President of the General Electric Company, to the 80-odd nation gathering of hundreds of delegates to the International Management Congress in New York City in the Fall of 1963, he stated that the latter would talk on the role of the chief executive, a subject which everyone knew a lot about, but which no one performed well. He was saying, I believe, that many people know a lot *about* leadership and management, but not many people *lead* well and *manage* well. At the same International Management Congress Louis Armand, the famed European industrialist stated,

"Authority today is based on competence and efficiency of bosses more than on organizational charts."

My hope is that this book will help bosses at all supervisory levels improve their effectiveness as bosses to the degree that they will be regarded as organizational assets by their peers and their subordinates.

Finally, I hope this book will be a boon to subordinates whose bosses bear these self-inflicted wounds, but are doing nothing to heal them. There is the story of the midwestern farmer who frequently received many pamphlets from the Department of Agriculture giving him suggestions and recommendations on how to farm better. After many months and many pamphlets, he wrote a letter to the Secretary of Agriculture, stating, "Please stop sending me your damned pamphlets telling me how to farm better. For your information, I ain't farming as well as I know how to now." Similarly, many bosses know how to be better bosses than they are, but they do not try to improve. I hope the subordinates of those bosses will obtain this book, identify the pages depicting those wounds their bosses bear, and present the book to those bosses, either openly or secretly. Perhaps the knowledge that their subordinates are aware of their self-inflicted wounds will motivate these bosses to improve. This has happened with some of the articles. If this does not do the job, I suggest you give the book to the *boss of your boss,* along with the information on your boss's deficiencies. (It may be well to do this in a more or less surreptitious manner, however, since there is an element of risk in such actions.) If you do it, you can expect early improvement in your boss's behavior. As the analysts say, he will have been motivated.

After You Read this Book

If this book is successful, the trend line on the following chart may change. Discouraging as it may seem, and unwilling as we may be to admit it, there seems to be an inverse correlation between increased position or rank in organizational hierarchy, and the amount and quality of demonstrated leadership. With the state of the art of leadership, command and management in the undeveloped state that it is today, the chart looks like this:

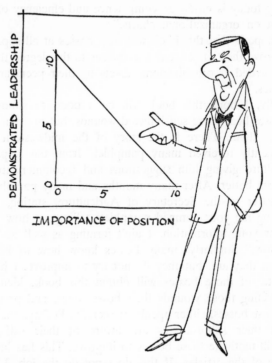

I hope you share with me the view that the trend line on this chart *can* and *must* be changed; that with this book and its seventy-six self-inflicted wounds we can spark a new Spirit of '76 which will rise in successful revolt against executive ineffectiveness (and *not* against the ineffective executives) with the result that the trend line of the practice of leadership will, some time in the future, reverse itself in the way we all think it ought to be: that with increasing age, knowledge and experience, our individual leadership ability will increase accordingly. It will not happen overnight, and it may not happen to a marked degree in the three hours of my guarantee to you. But now is the time to initiate the change. It will never happen unless you start the action to bring about the change. In the words made immortal by the late President John F. Kennedy in his inaugural address, *"Let us begin!"*

Washington, D.C. U.S.A.   Charles F. Austin
July 3, 1966

Contents

Management's
Self-Inflicted Wounds

To my
wife and daughter
for their help and inspiration

The Executive's Most Difficult Task

Some scholars and practitioners regard management as an art, others as a science. Whether it is one or the other or both, ancient and modern history leave no doubt that the capability of individuals in positions of authority to get results with and through people is the most valuable art and science of all. Some call this capability *leadership,* others call it *command,* others call it *management.* Regardless of what it is called, it has a common denominator: the exercise of authority. The *individual* who exercises this authority is the key to the success or failure of the organizational element—large, small or medium-sized—of which he is the head.

If you had the time (or through some miracle could get six months off) to read all of the countless books and articles that are written on leadership, command, and management, your mind would become cluttered with such terms as: *Manage by exception* (but don't neglect the nonexceptional areas); *Delegate—don't deputize* (but in delegating do not lose control); *Staffs may approve but can never disapprove a line proposal* (except where the line proposal is obviously stupid); *Consider your span of control* (but don't let the numbers restrict you); *Recognize the importance of group dynamics* (except when individual considerations outweigh them); *Practice decentralization* (except where centralization will result in better management); and so, drearily, on and on.

As a matter of fact, many writings about management do have considerable value, and throughout this book I have cited some that have struck me as especially valuable in the subject areas discussed. Most books and articles about management, however, are of greater use to the student of the subject than to the practitioner, who is daily subjected to the stress and strain of meeting conflicting requirements under difficult circumstances which are the rule rather than the exception. For the working executive, existing literature is of value chiefly for *mind-stretching.* When it comes to his day-to-day work he needs something more practical.

3

There are dozens of rules, principles or guidelines, or whatever you may choose to call them, available to today's executive. He can memorize them, print them on signs hung in conspicuous places, put them under his glass desk top, and/or circulate them to his subordinates. He can even require his subordinates to certify periodically that they have read, understand, and will practice them.

Frankly, I can't help wondering how much good comes from all this. Somehow it smacks of the things I try to remember when I am playing tennis or golf. More often than not, by the time I've remembered to keep my eye on the ball, to keep my arm stiff, and to plan a graceful follow-through, I've missed the ball completely. It's something like the "cook book" formulas for leadership contained in some books and articles. You or I can take a conventional examination in leadership, and score a perfect 100 percent —and ten minutes later, in one difficult human situation, violate every one of those rules and principles. In other words, when the chips are down, we revert to type and act like the same so-and-so we've always been.

The examples I have quoted (such as *management by exception*) and most that I have read and heard of, are couched in *positive* terms. That is, they urge you to *do* something (such as managing by exception). As a student of management for a number of years, I have come to believe in a radically different approach which is difficult to categorize. For lack of a better name and because it is rather accurately descriptive, I have invented the term, *management's self-inflicted wounds.*

What do I mean? I do *not* mean the undesirable situations which are directly attributable to those *above* you, your immediate superior or the next higher organization. I *am* pointing the accusing finger at those undesirable situations presently existing in *your own* organization, under *your own* roof; conditions which *you* have caused directly or indirectly, which *you* begot, or which you inherited and have allowed to exist or even worsen. You may not even know they exist. You, and you alone, are responsible.

I have catalogued the more typical *wounds* into categories and parables to enable you to perform the most difficult executive task of all: the task of self-analysis. To assist you in this self-analysis, there is a brief diagnostic procedure at the end of the description of each wound. Following that, there is a prescription offered to you to aid you in the healing of the wound.

So let's take a look at each of these self-inflicted wounds and as we do, ask yourself if *you* bear any of these wounds. This will require careful examination because you are now your own doctor,

so to speak. So look in a mirror. But don't do it the way the mountaineer and his wife did the first time they saw a mirror. He found it in the woods, looked in it and remarked, "Well, if it ain't a picture of my old dad. I never knew he had a picture took." His wife saw him hide the mirror under the mattress, took it out later, looked in it and remarked, "So that's the hussy he's been playing around with!" Don't do it that way. When you look in the mirror, look at *yourself!*

So let's turn the page and begin that long look in that mirror!

On
Wounding Yourself

The self-inflicted wounds that you will find in this section are a direct result of your own wrong behavior that hurts yourself. You, the boss, suffer the primary impact from the wrong kind of management discussed in each one of the chapters. It goes without saying, of course, that your people and your organization will also suffer, but you are the one upon which these wounds exact their highest toll.

You procrastinate decisions until they no longer are decisions. You are a *NO-DECISION BOSS.*

35

You feel personal contact with your employees doesn't befit your position as a manager. You are an *UNNECESSARILY-LONELY BOSS.*

38

Your door is open but you are guarded from contact with your employees by a series of complex procedures. You are an *OPEN-DOOR BOSS.*

41

You only want to see your subordinates when you choose to do so. You are a *CLOSED-DOOR BOSS.*

44

Many of your important but not pressing projects seem to get lost in the press of daily business. You are a *BOSS WHO DOES NOT PRACTICE THE PRINCIPLE OF CALCULATED NEGLECT.*

47

You are often surprised by events that you have not anticipated. You are a *BOSS WHO DOES NOT EXPECT THE UNEXPECTED.*

50

Somehow you never accomplish what you set out to do when inspection time comes. You are a *BOSS WHO CONDUCTS INEFFECTIVE INSPECTIONS.*

53

You have never matched your body schedule with your work schedule. You are a *BOSS WHO IGNORES HIS METABOLISM.*

56

You have not identified your inadequacies. You are a *BOSS WHO DOESN'T KNOW WHAT HE DOESN'T KNOW.*

59

When you have a leadership problem, you refer to a handful of *tried and true* rules. You are a *BOSS WHO MANAGES BY PRINCIPLES AND TRAITS.*

62

When something goes wrong, you waste time wishing it hadn't. You are a *BOSS WHO WISHES THINGS WERE DIFFERENT.*

66

You divide your thoughts: business from 9 to 5; social before and after. You are a *BOSS WHO FAILS TO UTILIZE HIS SUBCONSCIOUS MIND.*

69

You believe that the cliché "one thing at a time" has merit in problem solving. You are a *ONE-THING-AT-A-TIME BOSS.*

73

Members of a committee that you appoint always seem to endorse your ideas. You are a *BOSS WHO SABOTAGES HIS COMMITTEES.*

77

You do not know the detailed characteristics of highly effective groups. You are an *UNAWARE-OF-GROUPS BOSS.*

80

You frequently veto a younger man's suggestion for your own with the words: "Experience is the best teacher." You are a *HANDICAPPED-BY-EXPERIENCE BOSS.*

88

You really believe that all problems can be solved by mathematical equations. You are a *SLIDE-RULE MANAGER.*

91

You can never catch-up with the work load. You are an *AFTER-THE-FACT MANAGER.*

95

Integrity is only a word that you define to suit your immediate needs. You are a *SHADES-OF-INTEGRITY BOSS.*

99

the

CRISIS MANAGER

What I call the Crisis Manager hardly needs definition. In the Pentagon his behavior is called "flapping." But it isn't limited to the "Concrete Carousel" as its many riders refer to it. It can exist anywhere—even in your own organization. One of the symptoms stated, overpolitely, is: "The boss sneezes and everyone runs for a Kleenex." The importance of his need is overstated, as well as its urgency.

Tension is rampant under the Crisis Manager. People are always putting out brush fires, and the smoldering forest fire goes unnoticed. There is no time for calm, considered action. Back-up deadlines defeat themselves, and the man on the end of the line never stops running, with results that you could predict.

This kind of management breeds fatigue and animosity among the subordinates who must operate in its environment. The finished products are consistently poor. The man who first said, "When you want it bad you get it bad!" really knew what he was talking about. "CYA" [1] documents are very prevalent and very necessary. Under this false kind of management by exception, *nothing receives attention unless it is involved in a crisis.* These symptoms are not new to you—you know a lot of people who have caused them. My question is, do you see a Crisis Manager when you shave?

It has been well established by observation and research that extreme or unique behavior of the top executive is emulated by most of the bosses below him, and the type of behavior which causes crisis management, which can be referred to politely as *emotional instability,* is no exception to this rule. In his article, "What Makes an 'Emotionally Stable' Executive?" Perrin Stryker describes and analyzes a survey on this subject made by *Fortune* magazine.[2] The survey sought from a large number of executives

[1] Pentagon slang. The first two words are "Cover Your."
[2] Perrin Stryker, "What Makes an 'Emotionally Stable' Executive?," *Fortune,* (July, 1958).

their individual opinions on emotional stability. Their definitions ranged all the way from complete, continuous control of the emotions to sympathetic expression of feelings about others in the organization.

Whatever literature or other help he may seek on the subject,

each Crisis Manager owes to himself, to his subordinates, and to his organization a responsibility to make an honest effort to reduce the emotional instability which contributes so heavily to this *wrong* kind of management.

SELF-ANALYSIS

Examine your last five important decisions. How much time did you allow your staff to complete each delegated task? Was each job completed in the allotted time—in the best possible fashion? If none had been completed before the deadline, you are becoming a Crisis Manager. If more than one had to be done over, you are becoming a Crisis Manager.

HEAL THE WOUND

In future tasks, work out a reasonable schedule. Then add some extra time for each. Mark only urgent tasks "urgent." Try to schedule your work better.

the

TOTAL MANAGER

You know several Total Managers, and you know the symptoms: (1) the boss must approve everything first, and you get dressed down the first time you use initiative and act for him (2) the boss must change every paper you send him or you'll think he wasn't competent to handle it. Subordinates soon learn this and see no need to make sound recommendations. Incomplete staff work is actually encouraged in this climate. The boss' desk is a bottleneck and the wheels completely stop when he is away, even for short periods of time.

Subordinates are punished by the Total Manager when they make mistakes. I know a corporation president who says proudly, "My subordinates have a *right* to make mistakes. In fact, I want the mistakes in my corporation to be made at the lower levels of management. If they are postponed until they get to me in consolidated form, they become million-dollar bloopers." You could list a

lot of Total Managers in the next five minutes. What I would like to know is: Do you see a Total Manager when you tie your tie?

There is probably no better advice for the Total Manager than that given to Moses by his father-in-law, Jethro, after he had watched Moses struggling with his *executive workload* of acting as judge and arbitrator for his people. Jethro, who could be called the first management consultant in history, said to Moses, "You are not acting wisely. You will surely wear yourself out, and not only yourself but also these people with you. The task is too heavy for you; you cannot do it alone. Now, listen to me, and I will give you some advice, that God may be with you. Act as the people's representative before God, bringing to him whatever they have to say. Enlighten them in regard to the decisions and regulations, showing them how they are to live and what they are to do. But you should also look among all the people for able and God-fearing men, trustworthy men who hate dishonest gain, and set them as officers over groups of thousands, of hundreds, of fifties, and of tens. Let these men render decisions for the people in all ordinary cases. More important cases they should refer to you, but all the lesser cases they can settle themselves. Thus, your burden will be lightened, since they will bear it with you. If you do this, when God gives you orders you will be able to stand the strain, and all these people will go home satisfied." (Exod. 18:17–23.)

The wisdom of Jethro's advice and the success of its implementation is shown in the following diagrams, often used in lectures by Dr. Ernest Dale, recognized authority on organization and author of *The Great Organizers* (New York, McGraw-Hill, 1960). The first (Figure 1) shows Moses' organizational chart at the time of Jethro's advice (Figure 2). Figure 3 shows Moses' revised organization chart, while Figure 4 shows the successful results of the reorganization.

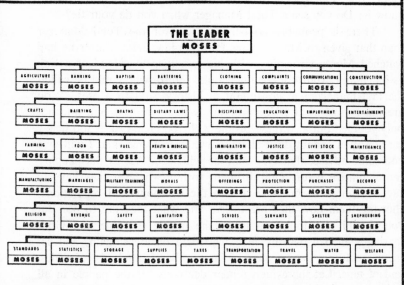

Figure 1

Figure 2

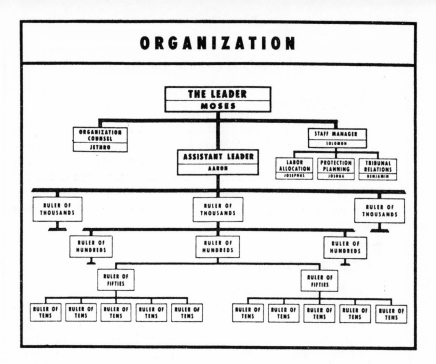

The result of reorganization: Delegation and accomplishment of goal

Figure 3

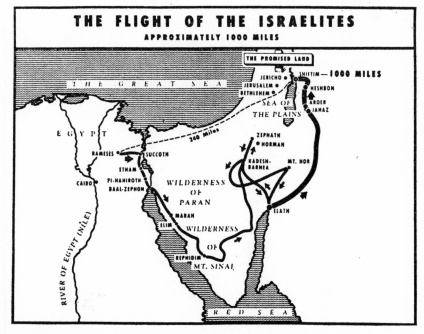

It took the Israelites 39 years to get from Egypt to Elath. After the reorganization, the remainder of the journey to the Promised Land was accomplished in nine months.

Figure 4

SELF-ANALYSIS

(1) Look into your files for the last ten memos you have received. If at least three of these don't advocate new ideas (and I mean new ones, not merely rehashes of your old suggestions) you are acting as a Total Manager. (2) Re-examine those ten memos. On any of them, have you made needless changes merely to put your supervisory mark on them. If so, you are acting as a Total Manager.

HEAL THE WOUND

(1) Pull your staff together and explain how interested you are in new ideas. Encourage them to put their thoughts on paper and send them on to you. Explain that even the most "far-out" suggestions will get a fair hearing—with no criticism if they're rejected. (2) Resist that impulse to change memos. See how many papers can pass through your hands without additions any more than your initials. Compliment your staff on papers which do not need revision by you.

SUGGESTIONS FOR FURTHER READING

Urwick, Lyndall F., "The Manager's Span of Control." *The Harvard Business Review* (May–June, 1956).

the

PAROCHIAL MANAGER

There are several definitions of the word *parochial*. Here I mean the Oxford Dictionary definition of "narrow, provincial, confined to a narrow area or domain." I'm talking about the manager (and his subordinates) who "doesn't see the big picture." I'm thinking of the production man who knows only the *production* business; the man in the sales division who knows only the *sales* business. And if it's true of the boss, it's true of his subordinates.

This manager doesn't have one organization composed of parts —he has a *collection* of *small* organizations. He doesn't have a team, he has a collection of individual players. One cause of this fragmentation is the prevalent vertical system of communication, which prohibits the wonderfully effective horizontal peer channels from functioning. I strongly feel that parochialism of this type is one of the greatest ills in management today, and the finger of blame can only be pointed to the boss at each level of supervision.

This *wound* is different from others in that you don't need to check to see if you have it. You've *got* it. It was built into each organization the day it was set up. All you can do is wage a continuing war against it. The well-conducted periodic staff meeting is a valuable weapon to use in this war. An executive told me recently he had put a stop to the custom of periodic staff meetings in the organization he had inherited! He said meetings were a waste of time! I didn't have time to *heal* him, but he has a self-inflicted wound!

You know many Parochial Managers. *Is the name of one of them on your personnel file?*

Mary Parker Follett in 1925 attacked parochialism with great perception in her paper, "Business as an Integrative Unity," by saying, "We have been so delighted with what has sometimes been called the functional theory, that is, the division of work so that each can do what he is best fitted for, that we have tended to forget that our responsibility does not end with doing conscientiously and

19

well our particular piece of the whole, *but that we are also respon-sible for the whole. A business should be so organized that all will feel this responsibility.*" [1] [My italics] She later pursued this same line of thought in her paper, "The Psychology of Control."

I am afraid that her writings, and those of others on the same subject, though widely read, are little followed. The military long ago invented the title and rank of "general" to describe an officer qualified to handle all matters, even though some of them had

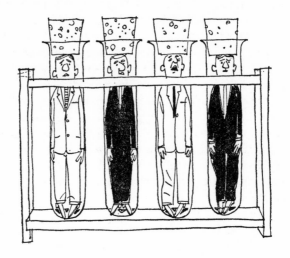

specialized aspects. Most general officers, however, are known by reputation through the specialized fields they came up through, and the executive behavior of some of them is parochial in nature, with excessive weight given to those areas with which they are most familiar.

A continuing awareness of the built-in problem of parochial-ism, combined with an untiring and ceaseless war against it, is the best treatment I know for this illness.

SELF-ANALYSIS

When was the last time that you: (1) listened to a lecture or discus-sion by someone who worked in a different responsibility area from

---

[1] Henry C. Metcalf and L. Urwick, "Business as an Integrated Unity," *Dynamic Administration, The Collected Papers of Mary Parker Follett.* (New York, Harper and Brothers, 1940) pp. 71–94.

yours (2) read an article in a trade magazine that might concern your company, but not your specific area of responsibility (3) bought —and read—a book about a different aspect of business beyond your own responsibility area (4) held a staff meeting in which you encouraged a discussion of general company policy and procedures (5) held a staff meeting in which you invited a speaker from a different area within the company. If you are not in the practice of enlarging your own and your staff's knowledge by doing the above, you are a Parochial Manager.

HEAL THE WOUND

Merely adopt at least three of the above procedures. The staff meetings are probably the most important since they will aid in broadening your own outlook and keeping you on your toes.

the

DEFAULTING MANAGER

Of all the sad and sorry categories of mismanagement, this type is probably the worst. I'm talking about management which takes place by itself, with no conscious decision having been made, or if a decision was made, it was made at too low or too high a level. Or perhaps a decision was delayed so long the problem disappeared or was absorbed by a bigger problem.

This type of management is best described by examples such as the *One-Sheet-of-Paper Boss*. He won't even entertain or receive something that hasn't been reduced to one sheet of paper. As a famous corporation president once said: "What the poor fool doesn't realize is that the decision is being made by the subordinate who decides what to omit from that one sheet of paper."

And then there's the major commander who had apparently heard or read somewhere that executives shouldn't spend time reading papers, so he had his chief of staff stand at attention and read paper after paper to him, literally dozens of pages, so he could take "executive action" on them! How about that? And how do you reduce your reading requirements?

You will laugh at this one until you take a look under your own roof. I refer to the "support" organization discovered overseas late in World War II. Totalling twenty thousand personnel, it was composed of laundries, motor pool, port facilities, and many other supporting elements. But one day someone (a visitor from outside) discovered that *they were supporting each other*—and no one else. They were taking in each other's laundry, so to speak. My eyewitness tells me that everyone was working hard, however, and they were doing a very good job. Try that one for size. But before you die laughing, how much laundry are your own people doing for each other?

And before you put a stop to this practice in your organization, ponder this fact: There is an island in the Southwest Pacific where the natives do each other's laundry—they never do their own. On that island a researcher has found the quality of the laundry to be the highest in the entire area! So, now what do you do? I suggest you see to it that your people do each other's laundry only when it results in a better over-all job being done. Then, at least, it will be a calculated action, and not one by default.

SELF-ANALYSIS

At random, take out and examine three recent decision-making memos from your files. Ask your secretary to get together all the correspondence that resulted in these decisions. If you can't come up with a file for each—a file containing depth examinations of the situation, and pro and con arguments—you are becoming a Defaulting Manager.

HEAL THE WOUND

Ask your subordinates for full reports when decisions must be made. Make certain they include pro and con arguments along with their recommendations. Ask them to outline briefly what—in their estimations—will be the most important problems in their areas of responsibility during the next six months. Winnow the wheat from the chaff and make a rough schedule of decisions to be made in the future.

the

HIDDEN-AGENDA BOSS

I won't dwell long on this boss. I would get too emotional if I did. This man uses the well-known and despised *hidden-agenda*

manipulation technique on his subordinates to motivate them. This man's subordinates often find they have to use the same sort of subterfuge on him in order to get anything accomplished.

A quick example. A boss decided to pull away or remove a particular function from an organizational element under his overall control. He called in the chief of that element and informed him he was removing that particular function from his supervision and direction. He then stated further that he was also removing *still another* function from the chief and his organizational element (which the boss had not the slightest intention of doing). He knew the second function he listed for removal was dear to the heart of his subordinate and vital to his status and to his other functions. When he mentioned the second function to his subordinate, the subordinate became alarmed and expended his entire efforts defending the retention of the *second* function, and decided not even to fight for the *first*. The conference ended with the subordinate giving up the first function without a fight or argument and thinking he had retained the second through his defensive efforts. The boss was well pleased with himself, notwithstanding the fact that he had been plenty guilty of duplicity, insincerity, and downright dishonesty. This story makes you mad, doesn't it? Of course it does! But wait a minute! How visible have *your* agendas been lately?

SELF-ANALYSIS

Consider the last time you called a man into your office to discuss management problems. Consider your last important staff meeting. Did you frankly discuss—at the beginning—all the topics you wished to cover; all the decisions you wished to examine? Did you have to manipulate the discussion to cover your hidden aims? If you answer no to the first question or yes to the second, you've become a Hidden-Agenda Boss.

HEAL THE WOUND

This primarily involves a mental turnabout—the determination to be frank and honest with your subordinates. However, besides a continual self-examination of your own actual motives, you can aid the situation by reducing your objectives to rough notes in advance of a meeting—then making certain you discuss those notes in the meeting, freely and frankly.

the

BOSS with the DEPUTY COMPLEX

This manager is best described by the expression: "All that I need is a deputy." I'm sure this communicates, but I'm talking specifically about the boss who feels that he just can't operate without a *number-two* man to *run the show* for him (or to unload his problems on, or to hold responsible, or to do his thinking for him).

It is a very prevalent practice and the reasons behind it are not easy to define. I asked a profound student of executive behavior about it recently and he gave his opinion that it stemmed from (1) insecurity on the part of the boss—a fear that he was not competent to do the job himself, and (2) a desire to unload his problems on a principal assistant and to harass him and to hold him responsible for their solution.

Regardless of the reason for the use of a number-two man, it exists and is very prevalent, and it is detrimental to the overall effectiveness of the organization. The department or division chiefs are placed in situations of conflicting loyalties—they wonder whether they are working for the boss or his *number-two* man— and the executive skills of the boss in the way of supervision and development are not available to the division chiefs. A few years ago the president of a well-known, large and progressive corporation, Mr. George Decker of Corning Glass, was distinguished by the fact that he used *no number-two* man to help him direct or supervise the fourteen vice presidents and staff chiefs who reported to him. I asked him why he did not use a *number-two* man. He replied, "I would not want anyone diluting the very fine supervision that I as president give them four hours a day. I also play golf and travel quite a bit. You see, I give them a job to do and then *I let them do it.*"

You'd give your right arm to work for such a boss. If you're the typical executive, your present subordinates would also! You don't *really* need a deputy, do you? (And if you think you've disguised your *wound* by having an Executive Officer or Administra-

26

tive Assistant or an Assistant To—instead of a deputy, you are only fooling yourself!)

I know of no more classical and typical example of the effect of the use of a deputy than the following example used by the noted British authority on organization, Urwick, in his book *The Elements of Administration* (his writer is Sir Ian Hamilton, a British Army Officer):

In 1896 I was Deputy Quartermaster-General at Simla; then, perhaps still, one of the hardest-worked billets in Asia. After a long office day, I used to get back home to dinner pursued by a pile of files three or four feet high. The Quartermaster-General, my boss, was a clever, delightful work-glutton. So we sweated and ran together for a while a neck-and-neck race with our piles of files, but I was the younger, and he was the first to be ordered off by the doctors to Europe. Then I, at the age of forty-three, stepped into his shoes and became officiating Quartermaster-General in India. Unluckily, the Government at that moment was in a very stingy mood. They refused to provide pay to fill the post I was vacating and Sir George White, the C.-in-C., asked me to duplicate myself and do the double work. My heart sank, but there was nothing for it but to have a try. The day came; the Q.M.G. went home *and with him went the whole of his share of the work.* As for my own share, the hard twelve hours' task melted by some magic into the Socialists' dream of a six hours' day. How was that? Because when a question came up from one of the Departments, I had formerly been forced to compose a long minute upon it, explaining the case, putting my own views, and endeavouring to persuade the Quartermaster-General to accept them. He was a highly conscientious man and if he differed from me he liked to put on record his reasons—several pages of reasons. Or, if he agreed with me, still he liked to agree in his own words and "put them on record." Now, when I became Q.M.G. and D.Q.M.G. rolled into one, I studied the case as formerly, but there my work ended: I had not to persuade my own subordinates; I had no superior except the Commander-in-Chief, who was delighted to be left alone: I just gave an order—quite a simple matter unless a man's afraid: "Yes," I said, or "No!" [1]

Writers and researchers in this important management area have experienced considerable difficulty coming to grips with the subject, some by self-admission and others by implication, especially on the knotty question of the optimum span of control. There are many hoary, but seldom tested, notions about the num-

[1] L. Urwick, *The Elements of Administration.* (New York, Harper and Brothers, 1943), p. 51, 52.

ber of subordinates a manager of any kind can control. In his *span of attention* theory, for instance, V. A. Graicunas wrote, in 1933, that the amount of attention required of a supervisor by his subordinates is proportionate to the number of possible relationships between himself and his subordinates, and among his subordinates. He computed the number of relationships using the usual formulas for permutations and combinations. Among many other things, he computed that the amount of attention required by eight subordinates is twenty-six times the amount required by four subordinates.

Alvin Brown attacks this theory with learned sarcasm in his book, *The Armor of Organization.* Any student of *delegation* and *span of control* will do well to ponder Mr. Brown's comments on these subjects. I particularly like the statement he makes toward the end of his analysis: "There is no rule or formula that will compute the proper number of delegations. Like most important questions, it is not that easy. It requires judgment." [2] At which point the honest, searching reader feels he is right back where he started.

Dr. Ernest Dale conducted a huge and thorough research project on organization, which he reports in his book, *Planning and Developing the Company Organization Structure.* While he was doing this research, he interviewed Dwight D. Eisenhower, then president of Columbia University and former commander-in-chief of the successful Crusade in Europe. Mr. Eisenhower made quite a point with Dr. Dale in stressing his belief that most executives could and should use a much wider span of control, with many more executives reporting directly to him, thereby benefiting them (and the organization) from the supervisory and developmental talents of the principal executive.

While researchers have not as yet described in detail Mr. Eisenhower's method of operation as United States President, there is a general feeling that he used a very narrow span of control, far less than the actual number of cabinet members, let alone the many executive departments. Many observers have felt that the President's use of an Assistant President affected his leadership image in the eyes of many. Among these observers was Stan Opotowsky,

[2] Alvin Brown, *The Armor of Organization.* (New York, Hibbert Printing Company, 1953).

who described the White House operating methods of Adams in a New York *Post* article.[3] These same observers have since noted with interest that one of President-elect Kennedy's earliest statements was to the effect that there would be *no* assistant president nor White House Chief of Staff.

I am personally as well as professionally neutral about United States politics, but I am convinced that the statement was made by an astute young student of human relations and group psychology as he considered the task of recruiting the ablest executives in the country to assist him—men who had read and heard about (and detested) the assistant president concept and wanted none of it. In studying Kennedy's executive behavior these same observers were impressed with his strong individual leadership which simultaneously maximized the use of teams in getting the job done. I have no doubt that the President-elect knew that the men he selected to assist him would want to work for him and him alone, and not for a deputy. The principal subordinates in any-sized organization feel the same way. They want to work for—and be judged by—the boss, not by a deputy.

I feel that the art of delegation requires a degree of finesse which makes it a will-of-the-wisp for most executives, eagerly and sincerely pursued but seldom achieved. And among those who feel they have accomplished it, a careful analysis will usually indicate that instead of delegating they have abdicated. In fact, the executive who can truly distinguish between delegation and abdication—and practice the former—is rare indeed. And it is almost impossible for the executive himself to evaluate his situation, for the *apparent* situation is more important than the *real* one. For example, I researched very carefully the behavior and relationships of a major general who commanded an infantry division and the large post it was located on, with his chief of staff, a full colonel. At the completion of my research, I came to two inescapable conclusions: (1) the commanding general had truly delegated, not abdicated, in getting organizational missions accomplished, and (2) only he and the chief of staff knew this; everyone else in the command felt the chief of staff was truly running the show, doing so by usurpation on his part and abdication on the part of the commanding general.

[3] Stan Opotowsky, "Eisenhower, Inc. Adams & Hagerty, Mgrs," New York *Post* (April 7, 1958).

Because of this belief, all of the negative products and by-products of such a situation had resulted. *Facts* were not the controlling factors while *attitudes* were, insofar as the effect on the organization was concerned.

Any student of delegation and span of control would be remiss if he did not study the Sears Roebuck Organization, which

prides itself on its "flat" (nonhierarchial) organization, and that of the Roman Catholic Church, which for most of its long life has had only one supervisory executive (the bishop) between the parish priest and the Pope.

Until you have completed your own study and analysis and come up with your own solution, tailored to the capabilities and limitations of yourself and your principal subordinates, your author recommends Mr. Decker's approach.

SELF-ANALYSIS

Here's a simple one: do you have a deputy—no matter what title he goes by? If you do, you are wounding yourself by shutting your own function away in a box and consequently lowering both the morale of your staff and your powers of control.

HEAL THE WOUND

Again, simple; eliminate the deputy's function. If he's really getting the job done (a job you should be doing, remember) he's certainly ready to move out and up in your own or a similar company. If he is not getting the job done (and this reflects on you no matter how much you've made your deputy into your fall guy), you don't need him in any case. Remember: This practice may well convince your superiors that your deputy is actually doing the work while you receive the credit—and how long will that situation be allowed to continue?

SUGGESTIONS FOR FURTHER READING

Dale, Ernest, *Planning and Developing the Company Organization Structure.* New York, American Management Association, 1952.
————, *The Great Organizers.* New York, McGraw-Hill Book Company, 1960.
Graicunas, V.A., *"Relationship in Organization, 1933."* Reprinted in Luther Gulick and L. Urwick, eds., *Papers on the Science of Administration.* New York, Institute of Public Administration, 1937, pp. 181–187.
Lawrence, David, "White House Burdens—They Are Older Than Kennedy." *U.S. News and World Report* (November 13, 1961).
Suojanen, Waino W., "The Span of Control—Fact or Fable?" *Advanced Management* (November, 1954).
Urwick, Lt. Colonel Lyndall F., "The Span of Control—Some Facts about The Fables." *Advanced Management* (November, 1956).
————, *The Elements of Administration.* New York, Harper and Brothers, 1943.
"How Kennedy Runs the White House." *U.S. News & World Report* (November 13, 1961).

the

ONE-WAY-LOYALTY BOSS

Any treatise on executive misbehavior would be remiss if it omitted the boss who demands *loyalty up* from his subordinates, but who does not demonstrate *loyalty down* to them. He hasn't heard, or doesn't believe, or doesn't have the courage to practice *loyalty down* by going to bat for his subordinates when the chips are down in one way or another.

A case in point: This man was a branch chief in a division. In the course of events, a new division chief was assigned and became the new supervisor of the branch chief and of the other branch chiefs. The new division chief soon held a staff meeting and instructed all branch chiefs that his policy was to run a *business-like shop* and that he would tolerate no foolishness. Specifically, he wanted people to *work* the full working day. Coffee breaks, informal visits or conversations, newspaper reading, and so forth, would be eliminated or strictly controlled. *Our* branch chief's office had an outstanding reputation for work and had very high morale. It was also noted for its informality. Individuals came and went as they pleased, drank coffee at frequent intervals, and engaged in long conversations. The office had the highest percentage of effectiveness of any in the division. What happened when "our hero" came back from the staff meeting? Did he call his subordinates together and tell them about the new division chief's *policy* and then tell them he wanted them to maintain the *status quo* and that he would describe their branch and their method of operation to the new division chief and get his permission to continue? He did not! He ordered immediate implementation of the new division chief's policy to the letter, down the line. You can imagine what happened to the effectiveness of that branch, the morale of its personnel, and the attitudes they felt toward their branch chief! Before you castigate the *gutless* one, please take a look at your own behavior in the *loyalty down* department and see how you stack up.

And as you make this analysis, you would do well to ponder

the words of Simon Bolivar, the Liberator, unquestionably one of the truly great and able leaders in history: "The first requirement of a military leader is to know one's specialty, and the second, *to be loyal to one's subordinates.*" It seems to me that General Maxwell

D. Taylor said the same thing in remarking, "The badge or rank which an officer wears on his coat is really a symbol of servitude —servitude to his men."

All of us believe this, it seems, until the stress and pressures of the situation come into play. The acid test occurs when we must choose between loyalty to subordinates and loyalty to bosses. Our subordinates soon know our batting average—in fact they post that average. We start off with their loyalty, but our behavior on the job determines how long we can keep it.

Question: What is *your* score with *your* subordinates?

SELF-ANALYSIS

When was the last time you went to bat for a subordinate? The last time you took the responsibility for a subordinate's mistake in front of a superior? In the average organization a case like this should come up periodically. If it doesn't in yours, it's probable you've become a boss with one-way loyalty.

HEAL THE WOUND

Remember, loyalty—as everything in life—is a two-way street and you can only take out what you're willing to put in. Try maintaining loyalty to your subordinate even if it means an occasional battle with your own boss. He'll be impressed with your integrity. The work of your organization will improve as its morale improves —and you'll sleep better at night.

the

NO-DECISION BOSS

We now come to the No-Decision Boss. This executive just won't (or can't) make a decision, no matter how hard his subordinates press him. Often he delays the decision so long that time itself eliminates all courses of action but one!

Some time ago, a well-known senior executive retired. I asked his principal subordinates for a profile of him as an executive in action. They sketched it for me willingly and in great detail. One behavior pattern stood out more prominently than all the rest. As one subordinate executive put it, "He just couldn't make a decision. He would delay the decision hour after hour, day after day, and week after week. Actually, he didn't really make any decisions, although he always announced that he did. By the time he announced his "decision," it was no longer a decision. It was the only alternative left that the hands of the clock had not eliminated. The clock and the calendar made his decisions for him."

Now, I am not saying that decision-making is easy, or that some decisions should not be delayed. In fact, the decision to make *no decision* for the moment is a difficult and challenging one to make in this fast-moving world. What I *am* asking is this: *Are you or your calendar making the decisions in your organization?*

Much has been written and spoken about the decision-making process and the effects of good and bad decisions on the organizations in which they were made or upon which they were forced or foisted. As a delegate to the National Training Laboratory in Group Development at Bethel, Maine a few years ago, I heard Professor Howard Baumgartel of the University of Kansas School of Business make the statement: "An organization is the sum total of the decisions which have been made in that organization in the past." My reaction at the time was that he was stretching a point rather far, but I have since changed my mind. I am now convinced that an organization is a dynamic, living, breathing organism which is never quite the same from one hour to the next or, more specifically, from one decision to the next. And it *is* the sum total of past decisions.

And certainly the timeliness of decision-making is as important as any other single aspect of this vital executive function. In his article, "The Managerial Mind," Charles E. Summer, Jr. states:

Top executives, in addition to desiring to change things in the real world, should have a predisposition for timely action. John L. Burns, president of Radio Corporation of America, a man with a doctorate in physical science, has put the attitude this way: "I'd rather be president than right"—by which he means simply that when timeliness and speed of decision are necessary, truth and validity must sometimes rank secondary. There seem to be at least two ways in which an executive can fail to demonstrate this vital quality of timeliness:

1. He can insist on a deluge of facts without any forthright conclusion. Examples of this are familiar to most businessmen (although seldom recorded). It is also interesting to note that military history is full of cases where commanders refused to act because they de-

manded more facts. General McClellan, for instance, made this mistake when he followed Lee into Virginia.

2. The executive can postpone action for a long time on the grounds that we have to wait and see. What he may really mean is that he is afraid to make a move until all the facts are in. By the time they are in, of course, it will probably be too late to accomplish much.[1]

Once again I have no magic solution for you. Somehow, though, I like Mr. Burns' statement, "I'd rather be president than be right." Please remember it the next time you get ready to delay a decision.

SELF-ANALYSIS

Consider the last two major decisions you made. How far in advance of the final possible hour were they actually made? If there wasn't a significant time lag between the time they were actually made and the time they had to be made, you are probably a No-Decision Boss.

HEAL THE WOUND

I have said, there is no magic way to make decisions. However, it may help if you schedule a certain time, a certain hour and day, each week to outline those problems that need to be solved and to make actual—if only tentative—decisions. This may still be using the clock and the calendar to make decisions, but at least you are making them, making them in advance, and giving yourself time to re-consider them. At the very least you'll get a reputation as a boss who can make decisions—and that's a reputation worth having.

SUGGESTIONS FOR FURTHER READING

Calkins, Robert D., "The Decision Process in Administration." *Business Horizons* (Fall, 1959).

Drucker, Peter F., "Making Decisions," Chapter 28, in *The Practice of Management*. New York, Harper and Brothers, 1954.

Kepner, Charles H. and Tregoe, Benjamin B., "Developing Decision Makers." *Harvard Business Review* (September–October, 1960).

[1] *Harvard Business Review* (January–February, 1959) p. 69.

the

UNNECESSARILY-LONELY BOSS

I've been unable to determine who first used the expression "loneliness of command," but I wish he had defined it in such a way as to prevent the distortion of its meaning through countless generations of military progression and business enterprises. It no doubt originated in the military and I'm also sure it was meant to describe the necessary (and somewhat lonely) lot of the commander who, in the final analysis, must personally make the important decisions and be held responsible for them. It has been sometimes stated that "a commander is responsible for all that his organizational unit does or fails to do." Certainly there is nothing wrong in this description. However, today's interpretation of the phrase seems to be that the *boss* (manager, leader, or commander) must take overt and covert steps to seal himself off from his subordinates, among other reasons, to prevent them from *taking advantage* of him. He takes these steps in complete or feigned ignorance of the recognized psychological and cultural *fact* that the status of just being a *boss* creates an invisible wall between him and his subordinates which is more impenetrable than concrete and steel.

A colonel I know (Colonel A) served in the Pentagon not so long ago with two other colonels (Colonels B and C) who were long-time friends of his. One of these two colonels had been Colonel A's immediate subordinate in an organization on an earlier tour. In the course of the current Pentagon tour, the three colonels saw each other often and continued their longstanding first-name friendship. Then one day Colonels B and C were each promoted to the rank of brigadier general. Colonel A congratulated them but was quite puzzled in the weeks that followed by their *treatment* of their old friend (Colonel A). General B and General C were very aloof and cool with him. They no longer called him by his first name. Instead, they used his last name and at times in groups seemed to be unaware of his presence. Instead of realizing that the stars on their shoulders had created an invisible wall around them, they had set about thickening and reinforcing that wall!

You have been role-playing Colonel A and are angry, aren't you, even if you feel the generals may not have been typical? Let's leave the generals with *their* problem, and look at *yours. What are*

you doing to tear down that invisible wall between yourself and your subordinates?

Recently, during a talk on this subject to a group of senior-civilian executives, one of them could hardly wait to challenge me during the discussion period with the question, "You mean you feel I should *fraternize* with people under me in my organization?" His question communicated his feelings so strongly that instead of responding, I got him into an argument with a few fellow delegates, also chief executives of their organizations. These men had seen the light, and tried to convince him that his organization would be more effective if he would occasionally circulate among his personnel, get to know them, and show a *sincere* interest in them. I won't say they converted him, but I'll bet he has done a lot of thinking on the subject since then. Won't you please give it a little thought yourself?

The *status* problem will probably always exist, but merely recognizing it is progress. A few years ago a research study examined status-seeking in three types of organizations, business, military, and educational. The study included behavior of wives. The results may or may not surprise you: Listing from "most-status conscious" to "least-status conscious," the study showed that educational institutions were most-status conscious followed by business organizations, and then military organizations.

SELF-ANALYSIS

When is the last time you spent at least a few moments during the business day informally speaking to your subordinates about business—or preferably—non-business matters? The right answer should be "yesterday at the latest," but I'll allow you the benefit of the doubt—this may have been an exceptionally busy week—and stretch the right answer to "only last week." If it's been any longer, you're an Unnecessarily-Lonely Boss.

HEAL THE WOUND

First of all you must make a change in mental attitude: remember, the words "all men are created equal" are not just words; you have something in common with all your subordinates—even the boy in the mailroom—if only the fact that you are all working for the same company. Now, go out there and meet them; I think you'll find that the quality of work produced will improve—and you'll even get to like the experience.

the

OPEN-DOOR BOSS

The Open-Door Boss is the executive who *thinks* he has an open-door policy, but in the eyes of his subordinates his door is anything *but* open. He goes out of his way to announce that his door is wide open—that any member of his organization can walk in any time of the day or night that he (the boss) is in his office.

However, one fact puzzles him (when he takes the time to notice it and think about it). Nobody comes in. He doesn't know why; there is no one he can ask about this, for he is the boss, and he has boasted many times about his *successful* open-door policy. He alternates between complimenting himself on the apparent health of his organization, since no one comes to him with problems, but in the small hours he wonders if, somehow, something is wrong with his system.

I once called on a senior executive who was head of an organization of several thousand employees. We had known each other before but were now living in different parts of the country. He welcomed me cordially and, although it was a normal business day, he insisted that I stay in his office three hours as we discussed various philosophies of leadership and management. While we had several bases for the discussion, one was that several months prior to this we had spent a week together in a course in executive development.

I knew his lifelong behavior pattern well. He was described by his peers and subordinates alike (what better judges?) as having been outright mean and ruthless as he climbed the ladder of success from promotion to promotion and from one position to another of increasing importance and prestige. The remark was often made that he had climbed the ladder of success by trampling over the bruised and battered bodies of his contemporaries and had left in his wake a trail of burned out and exploited subordinates.

As our conversation progressed on this particular day he became quite serious as he said, "I'm very pleased with the way things are going, Chuck, and I'm especially proud of my *open-door* policy. It's a policy I've had from the day I took over this organization. I announced it in my opening address to the organization, and I've repeated it at almost every opportunity since then. I've said over and over again that my office door is open and that I *want* my people to walk in. In fact, as you can see (pointing to it), that door is always open. However, one thing worries me. No one

ever comes in. Usually, I figure it's because I have a happy, healthy organization, and my people are taking their problems to their immediate supervisors for solution, and getting satisfaction. However, I'm not completely satisfied. I have the usual indicators in looking at my organization, and for some time now most of them have not been good. For example, absenteesim has been high, including absences for short, self-diagnosed illnesses. Resignations and voluntary transfers have also been high. Where we have measured production, it has been on the decline, and where we have no finite measurement, I have the feeling that it is also lower than it should be.

"I have always believed that most organization problems can be identified and solved through an effective open-door policy. My question is, Chuck, *why in the hell don't people walk in that door?"*

The door he spoke of was a massive one, in keeping with his huge office, his massive desk, and the huge chairs, all on a heavy carpet. As I had approached his office that day, I had reached it by successfully encountering and eventually getting by a phalanx of *palace guards* and *assistants to* to whom I had been required to state my business and purpose in life. My friend's open door was at the far end of a long rectangular room, with these *guards* spaced at even intervals, like a military obstacle course. As he talked, I felt sure that even the most difficult of such military obstacle courses would seem like a walk in the park to my friend's subordinates as they looked at the path to his door.

Do you have an open-door policy? If so, how do you measure the effectiveness of your open-door policy?

SELF-ANALYSIS

Stand up, walk to the door of your office, look out, and count the number of guardians an employee with a suggestion or complaint has to face before he can see you. If there's *any* guard at all, you're an Open-Door Boss.

HEAL THE WOUND

There is no reason your subordinates should not feel free to walk in on you—whenever your door is open. Believe me, you can rely on their good sense not to barge in on you when your door is closed. In personal conversations, staff meetings, and even memos, if necessary, get that fact across. Close the door when you want to be undisturbed, but make it apparent that no appointments are necessary when the door is open. Remember, that door is a *door* —not another wall shutting you off from the problems and needs of your organization.

the

CLOSED-DOOR BOSS

The Closed-Door Boss is the executive who, either by calculation or default, secludes himself behind a closed door, which is usually guarded by at least one secretary and by some other kind of subordinate. I use the word *guarded,* for there might as well be fixed bayonets and drawn pistols, for they are just as effective as if there were guards, and the results are the same.

There is something basic in the inner makeup of the American male (and female) which makes him very resentful of the Closed-Door Boss. I'm not sure what it is, but I think it has its roots in the origin of our country, the foundations of which are so aptly described in the belief, expressed in the Declaration of Independence, "that all men are created equal, that they are endowed by their Creator with certain unalienable Rights. . . ."

While it is not listed in so many words, I firmly believe that one of those rights is the right to meet your boss face-to-face when you desire, without being forced to go through the degrading and devious process of entering progressive caves ominously guarded by successive ranks of assistants who might as well be successive ranks of spear-tipped Macedonian Phalanx, insofar as your chances of penetrating into the inner recesses are concerned.

The natural American reaction to the Closed-Door Boss is best described by the words "To hell with him—he's not worth it!" This describes better than any scholarly words I know the attitude and frustrations of the subordinate who has such a boss. So, the net result is he doesn't try to see his boss, and all the wonderfully beneficial effects, direct and indirect, which accrue from face-to-face relationships and all those wonderful ideas the subordinate had, go down the drain. Some subordinates settle for writing a memorandum to the boss, but most of them either dismiss the reasons they had for seeing their boss from their mind or postpone them for the next boss after they have outlasted the present one (and they *will* outlast the Closed-Door Boss).

44

As you have read these lines, if you are a normal American and have not been behind your own closed door too long, you have been reminded of some very uncomfortable and unhappy emotions and experiences which you as a subordinate have felt along the

way. You must admit this is true. It is. You know it is. Then, why in the hell have you got *your own* door closed, flanked by *your own* Macedonian Phalanx?

SELF-ANALYSIS

When is the last time you spoke to a subordinate in your office when he just came to see you—without being summoned? If it's been longer than a week, either you're that impossible boss whose subordinates never have personal and business problems—or more probably—you're a Closed-Door Boss.

HEAL THE WOUND

My words of the previous section apply equally well here. I would add this: how can you expect to manage properly when you don't know what's going on—and how do you expect to find out what's really going on when your subordinates don't—can't—come to see you?

the

BOSS WHO DOES NOT PRACTICE
the PRINCIPLE
of CALCULATED NEGLECT

The Boss Who Does Not Practice the Principle of Calculated Neglect is the executive who sets priorities at the top of his priority list, but who ignores or blindly neglects those projects and programs for which he feels he has no time. He does this without analyzing them periodically (daily, if necessary) so that at a minimum he makes a *calculated* decision to neglect them. The net result is that he incurs a self-inflicted wound similar to that of the Horizontal-Priority-List Boss (*See page* 213).

The nature of the wound is that half or more of his continuing projects or programs, which as a fact of life must be neglected in this busy world, are not treated in the same calculating manner as the other half of those projects and programs that are receiving assigned priorities.

As I write these lines, I have the distinct feeling that this *wound* is more easily described in lectures or conversations than in writing. What I am trying to say is this: The effective setting of priorities requires the careful consideration of *all* projects and programs, not merely those which keep bobbing to the surface, or those which are pushed there by the inevitable small number of subordinates who are riding their favorite hobby horses. However, the tendency is too bunch those which are not on the upper half of the priority scale, and to ignore or neglect them for days and weeks on end under the defaulting assumption that they command no attention. The very nature of any dynamic organization—and most organizations deserve that name today—is such that the true importance or criticality of incremental elements of production, sales, programs, and projects is constantly changing. Yesterday's low-priority item can well be, and often should be, on the upper half of tomorrow's total-priority list. It will not be so placed, however, unless the boss practices the *principle of calculated neglect* in assigning his priorities.

I first heard this principle expounded by Don Schoeller of Don Schoeller Associates in the summer of 1960 when he and I appeared on the program of the American Management Association's seminar, "Human Factors in Decision-Making." I believe he deserves credit for coming up with the best descriptive phrase for a

very important executive function. His thesis was that the executive who did not practice this principle was injecting an undesirable human factor into his decision-making process. I agree completely, and I suspect you do also. My question is, what kind of neglect are *you* practicing with the lower half of *your* priority list?

SELF-ANALYSIS

Check your In-basket and Hold-basket periodically and analyze the items which are not receiving attention. Give yourself an honest answer to the question: Has my failure to act on these been the result of a calculated decision on each individual item, or has my failure to act on them been merely because I didn't get to them because I was working on more important items? If the latter is true, you are a Boss Who Does Not Practice the Principle of Calculated Neglect.

HEAL THE WOUND

From now on, make it a regular practice, either as the *first* thing you do each day, or the *last* thing you do each day, to go through all the items awaiting your attention, setting up a *current* priority of sequence of action each day. You'd be surprised how their relative priorities change from day to day. If you have many items which have not been acted upon, you need not handle the papers themselves; instead, you can note each of them on a small card and rearrange the cards in priority order. For years I have used a "floor-priority" system—putting the hottest items for each day on the floor, where they will have my attention, and where they will not go away until I do something about them. Of course, you'll have to indoctrinate your assistants to this system, or they will pick them up, put them back upon your desk among the low-priority items, and thereby foul up your priority system!

the

BOSS WHO DOES NOT EXPECT
the UNEXPECTED

The Boss Who Does Not Expect the Unexpected has existed for many decades, but with the increasing complexity of the executive function, the number of executives with this particular *wound* has increased geometrically with the passing of the more recent ten-year spans. This man is the boss who does not recognize today's basic fact of life that it is the *unexpected* event, action, development, behavior, and so on which tends to decide or dictate the outcome of events which shape the lives of organizations. In other words, it is not the *expected* things in life which control and influence events—it is the *unexpected* things which perform this function, and the boss who does not recognize this and prepare for it has a chronic self-inflicted wound which will seriously impair his executive effectiveness.

In discussing this thesis with an able executive recently, I received this immediate response: "I couldn't agree with you more. It is no longer enough to prepare for the expected events in order to be a successful executive. It seems to me that most people do this more or less adequately today. But the issues are never decided by the *expected* events. If they were, countless studies and conferences would not even be necessary, and life would become routine. When I *win* in a conference, staff action, or management problem, it is because I have been better prepared for the unexpected developments and have coped with them better than have my adversaries or competitors. When I lose, it is because the reverse has been the case. In recent years, after I have completed my routine planning and preparation, I try to devote the final minutes or hours to asking myself, 'Now, what unexpected or startling developments can happen in this situation, and how can I prepare for them?' I have learned the hard way that this is absolutely necessary, and I have developed some skill at it, although admittedly with me it is an inexact science. But so are management, adminis-

50

tration, command, and leadership. This concept is just one more way of refining my executive performance."

A humorous but highly perceptive dissertation on this subject by Francis P. Chisholm appeared in the April 1959 issue of *Mo-*

tive. In it he postulated Chisholm's Laws, which consisted of the following truths:

1. If anything can go wrong, it will.
2. If anything just can't go wrong, it will anyway.
3. When things are going well, something will go wrong.
4. When things can't get any worse, they will.
5. Any time things appear to be going better, you have over-looked something.

The expression, "This will separate the men from the boys," is quite appropriate here. If this measurement alone were used to segregate executives into those two categories, the boys would out-number the men by at least ten to one. While there is some diffi-culty in self-application of this yardstick, most honest and analyti-cal executives can accomplish it by examining the outcome of past efforts and events to determine the primary cause of success or failure. If you will do this with care, you can categorize yourself with reasonable certainty in this vital area of executive perform-ance.

SELF-ANALYSIS

At the end of a day, or at the end of a week—if your memory is that good—analyze the events of that time period and pin-point the incremental events which directly affected or brought about the outcome of conferences, staff actions, committee meetings, and the like. Having done so, ask yourself if you had *anticipated* those events through the mental process of "expecting the unexpected." If your score is high, you are probably doing all right. However, you can't afford even a few failures. So . . . if your score is less than 80 percent or 90 percent you're guilty of not expecting the unexpected.

HEAL THE WOUND

Before each event of the type outlined above, as the last item of preparation for it, sit back and ask yourself: Now, what can hap-pen here that I am not prepared for? What motivates the individu-als I will be dealing with? What are *their* vested interests, compul-sions, or that of their organizations and/or their bosses? If possi-ble, get an associate to role-play those individuals, or have them role-play you and you play the roles of the other individuals.

the

BOSS WHO CONDUCTS
INEFFECTIVE INSPECTIONS

The term *command inspection* is well known in the military, and civilian executives use such terms as field inspections, plant inspections, and the like. The military definition of command inspection

is simply, "inspection of equipment and personnel by a commander." My research indicates that a much more accurate definition would be: "A carefully planned, organized, directed, coordinated, and controlled effort by groups of people at different echelons of command designed for the purpose of creating an artificial and unnatural situation, which is facetiously regarded as *real* before, during, and after the exercise." The purpose of a command inspection is commendable, for it is intended to contribute to the managerial function of control. Like many other things, however, the purpose too often is lost in the doing thereof, and practically everything else but the purpose gets accomplished. The net result is often lost production, harassment, resentment, and a great deal of unproductive effort. My question is: Which definition describes the command inspections *you* have been performing in *your* organization?

A highly important facet of this command and managerial function is the need of the executive performing the function to determine the validity or typicality of the situation as he sees it. He must determine what is whitewash and what is not; what was created for his benefit and what was not. One effective way to accomplish this is the *unscheduled* inspection or visit, which tends to reveal the organizations and operations as they typically exist. Not long ago, in a large organization I know of, a series of scheduled inspections were followed by a series of the non-scheduled or surprise variety. You guessed it. The scheduled, expected inspections resulted in ratings of *superior,* while the unexpected inspections resulted in ratings of *unsatisfactory*. While there are many factors at play here, careful attention to this managerial function will pay tremendous dividends and help you determine whether your present performance in this area represents an asset or liability to the organization.

SELF-ANALYSIS

Reflect upon your last several inspections. Were they planned in a way to insure that you observed the normal situation, or do you think you were taken on a conducted tour? Did the people and/or facility know you were coming? Did you examine areas or samples of your own selection, or were they selected by the subordinate official whose activities you were inspecting and evaluating? Compare the number of unannounced visits with announced visits. If the former does not exceed the latter, you are probably deficient.

HEAL THE WOUND

The cure for this wound is predicted from the self-analysis above. I would add that it will not be healed until you reach the point where your inspections and evaluations are *planned* events, asking and deciding in advance the self-analysis questions above. If you find you should inaugurate a new system after doing it the wrong way for some time, it would be a good idea to announce in advance to your entire organization your philosophy of inspections; that they are to be valid efforts to observe normal operations and normal situations; that whitewash will be identified as such and punished, not rewarded, and so on. This policy will then become one of the norms of your organization and will be accepted as such, and you, your organization, and the people in it will be the beneficiaries.

the

BOSS WHO IGNORES
HIS METABOLISM

This very serious self-inflicted wound is based on a premise which I believe to be entirely true, but I am not able to state the medical or biological bases, even though I have validated it to my own satisfaction through discussions with a large number of executives and a significant number of members of the medical profession. My premise is: During any twenty-four-hour cycle the human body and brain enjoy or reflect differing capabilities to cope with differing types of executive tasks. My thesis is: Most executives are either ignorant of this or, being aware of it, do not select a timetable for the various types of executive tasks which will enable them to maximize their personal performance of those tasks.

For example, I believe there is a time frame during each day when an executive can be more creative than at any other time period. Further, I believe there is a time frame during each day when an executive is most capable of deep and perceptive thought. Obviously, that executive should use the former time period for tackling problems requiring innovation and creativity; he should utilize the latter time period for tackling his most difficult problems, and for planning, particularly long-range planning, that most neglected of executive functions. As a final example, there is undoubtedly a time frame during each day when an executive is best equipped mentally and physically for handling routine matters and problems, which may be a way of saying he is *least* equipped for creativity and deep thought.

Unfortunately, it is a rare executive who recognizes this, and an even rarer boss who does something about it in terms of scheduling his daily activities. His scheduling is more often done by default by his subordinates, his secretary and/or the volume of papers awaiting action in his In-basket, and that's usually stacked in sequence of arrival rather than in terms of importance or priority. Of course, every boss has a boss, which complicates the matter

56

somewhat. Your boss tends at times to schedule *your* timing of your own work, but even this is subject to your own influence if you know how to go about it.

I happen to know that my most creative time of the day is from six to ten in the mornings. Once upon a Sunday morning I took my pen in hand at six o'clock (after a good breakfast) and at ten awakened my wife and handed her a completed article, which was later accepted immediately for publication, without rewrite or revision. If these pages had been written during those hours, this

book would not have taken nearly as long to write as it did. Unfortunately, since it was written on an off-duty "hobby" basis, most of it was written after dark, with the exception of weekend writing. I use this personal example for a purpose. My evening hours are typically *not* my best hours for creating, but I have tried to combat that with an early evening nap for the purpose of charging my battery, or more specifically, charging my metabolism. As an actual fact, *this* chapter is being written after midnight.

The practice of taking a daytime nap to combat mental and physical fatigue is commented on by Sam Blum in excellent fashion in his article, *"Ssh! The Boss is Asleep!"* (*This Week* Magazine, May 27, 1962.) He states that the number of bosses who do that is growing, but also points out that many of them are embarrassed or ashamed of it, and often keep it a secret. The implication is, of course, that even those bosses who take naps would not let their subordinate bosses do it. The ideal combination, of course, would be rest and naps as needed, but to use them in conjunction with the more important need to schedule executive tasks to make them compatible with the timing of the various states of mental and physical capabilities during the day. The boss who does not do this has a self-inflicted wound which if not healed will definitely keep him far short of his potential executive effectiveness. *How is your metabolism these days?*

SELF-ANALYSIS

Have you identified the varying portions of your metabolism cycle to the extent that you know your most creative hours, your deepest-thinking hours, your shallow-thinking hours, and the like? If not, you have a self-inflicted wound. Further, even if you have, and are not scheduling your activities in accord with your metabolism cycle, you are similarly wounded.

HEAL THE WOUND

For several days in a row, keep a timed record of *what* you did, and when you did it, and *how* you felt when you did it. If you do this carefully, you should be able to identify your varying "ability" periods and schedule yourself accordingly. This is not the easiest thing in the world to do, so you may have to make this analysis over a period of time, but you *can* do it.

the

BOSS WHO DOESN'T KNOW
WHAT HE DOESN'T KNOW

The Boss Who Doesn't Know What He Doesn't Know has a very serious self-inflicted wound. I mean by this descriptive title the boss who has not determined what it is about his job that he has not yet learned, or has not learned adequately. In this day and age of complexities surrounding the overall executive task, it is a rare executive who is adequately qualified to make decisions in all of the substantive areas in which he must exercise direction, supervision, and control. This in itself is not fatal or even necessarily damaging, if the boss is aware of his deficient areas and takes action to compensate for them. He can do this by greater concentration in these areas, more research prior to taking action, heavier reliance on experts or subordinates whom he respects, and any of a number of additional valuable methods.

This boss is far more prevalent than need be, partly because of the overall backward state of the art of executive ability, but probably even more so because of the psychology of the situation. In this respect the boss is at least, in part, a victim of today's climate and environment in which there is a myth that the able executive is such a well-rounded boss that he has no glaring weak spots, no chinks in his armor of ability. In actual fact, it is a rare executive of whom this can be said. Most of them have come up through one or at most two lines of specialized endeavor in the organization or the industry, such as sales, production, personnel, intelligence, operations, or the like. They have both strong and weak areas of substantive knowledge and ability. If they have been rotated rapidly on the way up the development ladder from one line of activity to another, the old description, "jack of all trades and master of none," has a wide basis.

The Boss Who Doesn't Know What He Doesn't Know proceeds in a pseudo-confident manner on all problems, whether he truly feels that way or not. He has read or heard that it is a sign of

59

weakness to show deficiencies in any areas. This tends to cause him to fool himself, and he makes no real effort to identify his deficiencies and to do something about them. It is frequently said about him that he is "often in error but never in doubt."

I think you will agree that the Boss Who Doesn't Know What He Doesn't Know suffers from a grievous self-inflicted wound. The question is, are *you* such a boss?

SELF-ANALYSIS

Can you, right now, take a couple of hours and list in detail the portions of your job responsibilities that you are well-grounded and confident in; those that you are only partially confident about; and those areas in which you definitely lack enough confidence and knowledge to perform effectively? If not, you are a Boss Who Doesn't Know What He Doesn't Know. Further, the only way you can answer these questions is to actually go through the process of analysis—*in writing*. Just thinking about them is not enough.

HEAL THE WOUND

A good way to heal this wound is to break your job down into responsibility and functional areas, and those areas in turn into project, program, and task areas. This must be done in enough detail so that nothing is overlooked, and so that the parts add up to the whole. Having done this, you should then score each item as to your knowledge and confidence in each, and then act accordingly in your day-to-day functions, getting competent help in those areas where you need it. And don't be afraid to admit to a subordinate your lack of knowledge in these areas. He will respect you more for doing so because *he already is aware of your deficiency!*

the

BOSS WHO MANAGES
by PRINCIPLES and TRAITS

The Boss Who Manages by Principles and Traits is the modern result of the centuries-old seeking for the magic formula of leadership, the quest for the five "handy-dandy" rules by which to guide one's personal leadership and executive behavior. Unfortunately, he is usually so preoccupied with principles and rules that he is unable to perform effectively.

Down through the decades of study of personal leadership and executive behavior, there have been much analysis and argument as to principles and traits of leadership, their uses and their value. Many contend that they are valid and useful; a growing number question their validity and their usefulness, and those who do not fit into these two categories yearn for an agreed-upon solution to the problem. Personally, I am afraid the hoped-for agreement will never happen.

This book could be devoted entirely to statements of principles and traits, and the analysis and evaluation thereof. However, I shall leave that to other scholars and practitioners, for I belong to the group who questions the validity and usefulness of these principles and traits of leadership. Perhaps I question their usefulness more than I question their validity, but it seems to me that to question the former is to question the latter. As Victor A. Thompson states, "Although social psychologists have generally concluded by now that there are no leadership traits, that leadership is a function of the situation, including the kind of people, the kind of problem, the kind of group, etc., such studies are continued by business schools and individuals who seek the traits of successful executives." [1] In addition, he cites research studies which support his statement.

Somehow, when I read or hear about a principle or trait, the

[1] Victor A. Thompson, *Modern Organization* (New York, Albert A. Knopf, 1961) p. 118.

62

huge and difficult word, *"How?"* pops into my mind. Take, for example the principle: *Make sound and timely decisions.* This is pure gold. The question is, how? One dissertation on leadership traits in a current military manual [2] urges the leader to have, among others, physical and moral courage, decisiveness, dependability, endurance, enthusiasm, initiative, integrity, judgment, justice, knowledge, loyalty, tact, and unselfishness. Once again, pure gold. The question is, *how?* What about the following: *Principle of effective human relations: To be truly effective our human relations practices must be based on the recognition of the individual as a person and must take into account the moral, the managerial, and the psychological factors in any situation.* Very good. No one would quarrel with this. But how? How? *How? How? How?* I challenge you—*How?*

The Harvard Graduate School of Business Administration developed the *case* method of instruction and education, which de-emphasized the *principles* and *traits* approach to leadership. In so doing, it concentrated on the *substance* of the management problems, including the human aspects of them. Typically, the nearest thing to a *principle* which evolved was referred to as a "currently useful generality," which is a pretty good way of describing the nature and life of a method of analysis of a management or leadership problem, or, as is more often the case, a combination of the two.

The inescapable truth about the use of principles is the fact that for each principle there is an opposite or contrary one, and therein lies the rub. For example, the principle of decentralized management sounds ridiculous when stated as follows: *We should practice decentralized management unless centralized management gets the job done better.* Once again we have a nugget of pure gold. Or have we?

The most profound and learned dissertation on this subject that your author is aware of is a small one entitled *Conflicts of Principle* by A. Lawrence Lowell, which he wrote toward the end of his long and distinguished career that included a lengthy service as president of Harvard. I commend it to your reading, and quote the following which is the first paragraph of his introduction:

[2] *Military Leadership.* United States Department of the Army Field Manual No. FM 22-100 (June, 1961).

What appears as a universal principle is in fact often true only within the limits of the conditions in which it is properly applied, and becomes partially true, or altogether inapplicable, under new and unfamiliar circumstances. Yet we find a difficulty in emancipating ourselves from a conviction of its absoluteness and tend to rely upon it as an infallible guide where it is so no longer.[3]

My research question here is not an easy one to phrase. Perhaps it is best to say: *In what way do you use principles and traits of leadership in getting the job done? What is your basis for this? Do you understand the value and use of traits and principles? How do you know?*

SELF-ANALYSIS

This one is not easy, for it requires you to look at your behavior, or to have others such as peers and subordinates do so, to try to divine the basic philosophical foundational source of your behavior. What do you really believe in? Does your behavior reflect those beliefs? Do you find yourself, as you face a problem or

[3] A. Lawrence Lowell, *Conflicts of Principle* (Cambridge, Mass., Harvard University Press, 1956) p. 3.

a difficult situation, groping for something to base your action upon, such as grasping for some principle or conjuring up some trait which will help you? If so, you probably bear this wound.

HEAL THE WOUND

I know only one good prescription here. You *must* define, in writing, your basic philosophy of life, and from that derive your basic philosophy of life in organizational settings. Such questions as: What do I really believe? How do *I* like to be treated? Do my subordinates and peers like to be treated in the same manner? What are my personal values? What do I respect? Disrespect? Having done this, you must still perform the difficult task of insuring that your day-to-day actions reflect these beliefs and values. As you do this, however, over a period of time it will become somewhat routine. I like to say that I bounce each problem against my private matrix of personal beliefs and values, and that when the problem bounces back, the only solutions which survive are those that are acceptable within my personal code of conduct. It is easier said than done, but it can be done. Do it.

the

BOSS WHO WISHES
THINGS WERE DIFFERENT

The Boss Who Wishes Things Were Different—and this includes most bosses at one time or another—is not only wasting every minute, hour or day that he spends in this fruitless wishing, but he is also guilty of using that time in such a manner that it has a "net negative" effect upon himself and on his organization. The thought process he indulges in clouds and confuses the issues as they are, rather than clarifies them.

I am the first to understand this wishful thinking and the psychological bases from which it stems, but this understanding will serve no purpose here unless it assists my readers in identifying this negative use of executive time and provides some help in reducing the amount of it or eliminating it entirely. Once again, there is no magic formula, but it should help to periodically call a halt in the middle of the problem-solving or decision-making processes and ask yourself a point-blank question: *Am I wasting time wishing things were different?* Further, you must subject your answer to critical analysis, for you may think yourself into believing that you are just acquiring and analyzing *background* information, for this is sometimes useful, and it is often difficult to distinguish between the two.

The best single, concise, perceptive, and profound piece of philosophy on this subject I have ever read is the following passage from *Guard of Honor.*

In any human situation, even the simplest, there are more variables than any human mind can properly take account of. . . .

A great many people, maybe most people, confronted by a difficult situation, one in which they don't know what to do, get nowhere because they are so busy pointing out that the situation should be remade so they *will* know what to do. . . .

There are reasons for everything that is. . . . They're often interesting. Figuring them out increases our understanding. They may

66

arouse our indignation or our compassion. They add up to say that if things had been different, things might be different. That seems quite likely; but things aren't different, they are as they are. That's where we have to go on from.[1]

Thus endeth *my* therapy and *thine* beginneth, I trust.

---

[1] James Gould Cozzens, *Guard of Honor* (New York, Harcourt, Brace and Co., 1948), pp. 438–441.

SELF-ANALYSIS

This is partially indicated in the second paragraph of this wound, but it is easier said than done. Perhaps the best analysis is reflective thinking after each event: analyze the time you spent on it, and also *how* you spent it; be alert to detect any time you spent wishing things were different, before getting into action solving the problem.

HEAL THE WOUND

Make a calculated effort to *avoid* this self-inflicted wound, by determining *what* the problem is and then immediately getting on to solving it, without spending time wishing the problem hadn't happened at all.

the

BOSS WHO FAILS to UTILIZE HIS SUBCONSCIOUS MIND

When I tell you that an executive has a self-inflicted wound when he fails to utilize his subconscious mind in the solution to difficult problems, you may decide that I have suddenly gone "off my rocker," close the book, put it down, and never open it again. I hope you do not, for if you do you will have placed yourself at a competitive disadvantage with those executives who have discovered this wonderful aid to decision-making and problem-solving. And you can't afford that, for things are difficult enough as they are. As one harassed executive remarked to me recently, "I need all the help I can get!"

While I do not know of any scientific basis for this approach, I am not at all concerned over whether or not there actually is any. The proof of the pudding is in the eating, and there are people who are eating this particular pudding and enjoying it. In fact, they are savoring it. If Babe Ruth, Joe Dimaggio, Ted Williams or Mickey Mantle were to tell us their personal opinion for their successes in hitting a baseball, I think we would be inclined to accept it at face value without asking them to validate their opinions with scientific bases, other than the percentage columns to which we have already had access. Nor, it seems to me, should we ask for scientific proof if we find an executive of similar stature in the business world who utilizes his subconscious mind in problem-solving and decision-making. We should be content to obtain his best description of his *method* of so doing, and attempt to apply it to our own advantage. There is such a man, who happily shares his method with the fortunate few who have heard him give his talk on "What It Takes to Be a Manager." I was fortunate to have heard Mr. John M. "Jack" Fox give this talk. The outstandingly able past president of Minute Maid Corporation, who wasn't always successful and acquired most if not all of his executive abilities through self-development, commented as follows:

The ability to think creatively can be developed. One of the greatest aids to this worthwhile pursuit is the faculty of turning loose the tremendous thinking power that is latent in every one of us. This is the *use of our subconscious minds*. Those of you who have learned to tap this great human resource know its tremendous value. For those of you who have yet to experience the wonder of having the solution to a knotty problem reveal itself to you as you are shaving in the morning or at some other unheralded and unplanned moment, one of life's greatest thrills still lies ahead.

My own first such experience took place early in my sales career with I.B.M., and before I had heard or read anything about the subconscious mind. I had sold my first installation of tabulating equipment to a textile firm in New Bedford—the Wamsutta Mills. I'm afraid that in my great anxiety to make that ice-breaking sale I oversold the customer rather shamefully. It wasn't until the machines were delivered and the installation of the accounting system was under way that I awoke to the fact that I had promised results that the machines were not designed to produce. I spent several anxious, then panic-stricken, days trying to make the equipment live up to my claims.

Finally, nearly at the end of my rope, and quite seriously wondering if I would be fired when Wamsutta learned the truth and the machines were sent back, I spent one whole evening at the New Bedford Hotel recapitulating and reviewing the elements of the problem. With no glimmer of an answer, I went to bed—exhausted and completely discouraged.

The next morning as I was sitting in the bathtub, the answers to my problem started to come to me as clearly as if they were being written on the tile wall around the tub. I jumped out and without bothering to dry myself hastily wrote down the procedure that had seemingly just popped into my mind.

Without wasting time on breakfast, I tore down to the Wamsutta office—punched up the cards needed to test the program and started up the machines. It worked exactly as I had visualized it and exactly the way the Wamsutta people wanted it!

Many years later I learned that this was a demonstration of my subconscious mind at work. I learned that it is best to feed the elements of a problem to your mind just before you retire. Then while you are in repose that night or perhaps after several nights, the solutions will come to you—almost like magic. And, what is much more important, the solutions will represent clearer and sounder thinking than you can usually produce with your everyday conscious mind. The old axiom of *Let's sleep on it* is based on this power, and I heartily recommend it to you as a valuable tool in your management kit.

I ask you to try it, and you have wounded yourself if you do not. After all, you need all the help you can get.

SELF-ANALYSIS

Check up on the last three or four *big* problems you have struggled with, including the one in which you are now immersed (or submerged) (or enveloped). Did you put the elements of the problem into order just before you dropped off to sleep, or were they in a jumbled state of confusion? If the former were true, you probably got a good night's sleep and very likely arrived at a solution the next day. If the latter were the case, you probably woke up as tired as you went to bed, and may even have had a series of crazy dreams (or nightmares) in which the elements of the problem came alive to haunt you.

HEAL THE WOUND

Adopt the procedure advised by Mr. Fox in the last paragraph of his quoted statement, and . . . you will have one *less* self-inflicted wound.

the

ONE-THING-at-a-TIME BOSS

The "One-Thing-at-a-Time Boss has the completely mistaken impression that the human brain was designed with a *one-problem capacity,* and he refuses to entertain, work on, or consider more than one problem at a time. The net result is that he, his subordinates, and his organization are under-achievers and under-producers.

This boss would be the first to criticize an unused assembly line or an idle plant at a time when a company had a backlog of unfilled orders and was losing new business because of lack of customers' confidence in timely production and delivery. He would get excited and immediately issue the orders necessary to bring about better utilization of the company's production resources. But he refuses to realize and act on the fact that human brains (of which his is one) have such unlimited capacity that the outer limits of that capacity have not even been discovered.

Unfortunately this boss, and thousands like him who vary only by degree, are suffering from a sadly neglected state of the art of research. Woefully little research has been done in this area, and hardly any results or findings have been available to the honest, sincere, and hard-working boss (which includes most of us) who would welcome some sort of education or training courses on how he could more fully utilize his brain. In fact, I am unaware of any research findings which I can pass along to you here, but I do have a few observations which may be helpful.

I once read in a source which I have long since forgotten, that Lenin was very competent in utilizing his brain to deal simultaneously with a large number of problem areas or subjects. It was stated that he could read a document rapidly, listen to a detailed oral report on a complicated and important problem, carry on a telephone conversation, and give instructions to a continuing stream of subordinates, *all at the same time.* Concurrent with this, of course, he was thinking about and mentally coping with many other problems and conceiving detailed plans. I cannot prove that Lenin actually had this capability. In fact, I couldn't care less. What I do care about is the under-utilization of the human brain and the huge number of bosses and executives who are guilty of this sin.

Mr. John M. "Jack" Fox, whose outstanding executive ability no one questions, has expressed concern over this lack of utilization of existing brain power, and has stated, "It is well recognized now that the brain not only never tires, it actually becomes more productive and efficient with use. Moreover, no one has yet been able to utilize more than a small fraction of the potential in his brain."

The boss who feels he has reached the outer limits of the capacity of his brain by simultaneously handling a small number of problems would do well, it seems to me, to reflect on the executive position known as the Presidency of the United States. In doing this, he would accept without argument the fact that all the incumbents of this position have repeatedly demonstrated the ability to simultaneously think about and deal with a multitude of problems and problem areas and subject areas which require short-range and long-range planning. (Their manner of performance is not for discussion here.) He *must* accept as an historical fact that many if not most of these incumbents either had not held significant executive positions nor had significant amounts of executive experience prior to assuming the position of Chief Executive of the United States. I think we can further assume that they received only normal amounts of Divine Guidance—although you may wish to debate this—and that their Creator required them to process what guidance He gave them through their on-hand mental and physical facilities. If all this is so, then, how did they do it, and why can't you utilize *your* brain the same way? Remember, it is made of the same quality material and has the same wiring diagram as theirs.

The contents of the preceding paragraph could hardly be regarded as research, but it is probably as valid and as acceptable as any that exists today, and it *is* deductive reasoning, if you wish to call it that. And my examples *are* valid, I think you will agree. The presidential careers of Harry S. Truman and John F. Kennedy, who as Chief Executives used human brains in human bodies made of the same common clay from which yours was fashioned, are cases in point. Each proved thousands of times that executive experience is no prerequisite to able performance as Chief Executive. And there have been many, many like them in that position and positions of lesser, but great, importance.

This chapter must end here with one statement and two prayers: You are using only a small fraction of your brain. I pray that scientific research will soon be conducted to teach us how to use

our brains more effectively. I pray that you will not wait for that research to take place. Andrew Johnson, Chester A. Arthur, Theodore Roosevelt, Harry S. Truman, and Lyndon B. Johnson could not wait for such research. Why should you?

SELF-ANALYSIS

This will require rather careful introspection, for you may confuse the desired practice with an undesirable one. You may feel that you are thinking of all your problems at the same time, and you probably are—but by default rather than in a methodical manner.

In actual practice, you are probably unable to keep some problems from mingling with and confusing the issues of other problems. Or, you may be actually oblivious to all other problems as you work on one of them. Some executives proudly call this "concentration," whereas I call it under-utilization of their brains. If you find yourself doing either of these, you have this self-inflicted wound on your executive anatomy.

HEAL THE WOUND

My personal system is to keep my individual problems standing more or less alone, like blank pages in a book, with the pages having headings only, plus the major elements of the problem. Then, as the time progresses, and ideas concerning each of them come to mind, I quickly write a mental note on the pages, and go back to the immediate problem. Another method I use is to keep an "action" sheet on each problem readily available on my desk or nearby table, where I can quickly jot down the thought or idea on the problem. A final system is to keep three-by-five cards in my shirtpocket for quick notes. A portable dictaphone in your car and one by your bedside is also invaluable. These mechanical devices have become so simplified for use that they are practically as necessary as a pen to a boss or executive, and they help you avoid the loss of valuable ideas, which do not come to you by-the-clock.

the

BOSS WHO SABOTAGES
HIS COMMITTEES

This particular self-inflicted wound concerns the boss or executive who appoints a group of individuals to study an important problem, and then sabotages the entire effort before it gets off the ground by the *method* he uses in selecting or appointing the group. He does this by placing people in situations wherein they face continuing conflicts between loyalty to the larger organization and loyalty to the smaller organization of which they are ordinarily a member.

I have chosen the terms *ad hoc committee* and *task force* to describe the two most common types of temporary organizations which are used for this purpose. In the *ad hoc committee* situation, the individuals who serve on the committee do so with the understanding that they are doing so as a representative of their day-to-day organization, and their service on the committee reflects this situation. Their actions are more that of the "instructed delegate," even though they have been appointed to conduct an "objective" study.

In the *task force* situation, the individuals are divorced from their day-to-day organizations, told that their only loyalty is to the larger organization and the executive who appointed them, and their actions are those of "uninstructed delegates" who are generally free of conflict of loyalties as they serve on the temporary organization.

The Boss Who Sabotages His Committees is a very real danger in government and in the military, and is also prevalent in business and education. Human beings are just that, and they will be objective only when being such satisfies their greatest need. The example I should like to give here is too glaring to cite, but it placed several senior executives in positions of conflict of interest— conflict between loyalty to their present boss and present organization on the one hand, and loyalty to the temporary task of the tem-

77

porary group on the other. I needn't tell you which "loyalty" won out. It could be called the "bread and butter" one. And the boss who appointed the group had only himself to blame for the unsatisfactory results. In the case I'm speaking of, that boss didn't even know they were unsatisfactory. In fact, he proudly published the findings, and the study has been used as a concrete foundation

upon which other important decisions have been based! All this while many observers are laughing up their sleeves with the knowledge that the *concrete* foundation is in fact a very, very sandy one.

As you have read this chapter you may have felt with relief that this is one particular wound which you do not have, because you are the boss of a small organization, or organizational element. This may be the case; however, if you are in the habit of appointing groups of people to tackle problems for you, the fundamental problem exists in one form or another, and can only be coped with through an awareness of the subtleties of the situations and the conflicts involved.

SELF-ANALYSIS

Analyze directly the instances in which you as a boss have played a part in creating committees and study groups. One good measurement is to see who had the power of performance appraisal, efficiency report, fitness report, merit rating, and so forth during the period that the subordinate served on the committee or task force. This instrument means life or death to many people and therefore is a critical matter. Also, you should check to see whether the situation called for "instructed delegates" or "uninstructed delegates" in order for the best job to be done. If uninstructed delegates were desired, then the power of performance appraisal should be taken away from the man's present boss and given to the boss in charge of the task force or committee. If this is not done, you have deprived the subordinate of his objectivity. It is as simple as that, and you are guilty of this wound.

HEAL THE WOUND

Following the self-analysis above, take actions consistent with your findings, and make clear to all concerned what you are doing. If you do this, and the man comes up with findings contrary to those desired by his day-to-day associates, he will be admired as an honest man, rather than being branded by his peers and nominal boss as a traitor.

the

UNAWARE-of-GROUPS BOSS

If I were asked to list the most prevalent single serious deficiency of the American boss at all supervisory levels, it would be with no hesitation that I would list this self-inflicted wound. It can best be described, perhaps, by the simple statement that he is not aware of the nature of groups, how and why they function, why some groups are effective and others are not, how group goals and group standards are established, and the many and varied aspects of group life within organizational life. Not only is the boss unaware of the nature of groups, but he does not seem to be making any particular effort to further his understanding in this vital subject area, even though practically everything his organization does, *or fails to do,* is accomplished by collections of individuals functioning as groups.

If we accept this alleged deficiency as a fact, or as a hypothesis if you are reluctant to accept it as a fact, what is the reason for this state of affairs? Let us list first a partial alibi or, better stated, an obsolescent alibi. It is a fact that the research on this subject is relatively sparse and relatively recent. In commenting on this situation in his book, *New Patterns of Management,* Dr. Rensis Likert, one of the world's foremost authorities on the nature of groups, had this to say:

> The surprising thing about committees is not that many or most are ineffective, but that they accomplish as much as they do when, relatively speaking, we know so little about how to use them. There has been a lack of systematic study of ways to make committees effective. Far more is known about time-and-motion study, cost accounting, and similar aspects of management than is known about groups and group processes. Moreover, in spite of the demonstrated potentiality of groups, far less research is being devoted to learning the role of groups and group processes and how to make the most effective use of them in an organization than to most management practices. We know appreciably less about how to make groups and committees effective than we know about most matters of managing.[1]

[1] Dr. Renis Likert, *New Patterns in Management* (New York, McGraw-Hill, 1961), p. 163.

Our boss who is unaware of groups manifests this ignorance in many ways and, from my standpoint, the type who is merely ignorant and silently suffers is the least of the guilty. Probably the guiltiest is the boss who goes around mouthing anti-group remarks which are usually critical of committees. He likes to criticize the results of committees, particularly those on which he has served (unless he was the chairman). He is usually trying to cover up for his feelings of inadequacy in groups, either as a peer member of such or as the boss of a group. He would be far better off if he were to spend his time studying some of the elementary literature on the subject, reaping the benefits for his organization and himself.

Another type of boss who bears this wound is the boss who honestly believes, based on what he has heard and observed, that groups are ineffective and that committees are inefficient because of the mere fact that they exist as an organizational entity. The following single paragraph from Dr. Likert would help this boss:

Although we have stressed the great potential power of the group for building effective organizations, it is important to emphasize that this does *not* say that all groups and all committees are highly effective or are committed to desirable goals. Groups as groups can vary from poor to excellent. They can have desirable values and goals, or their objectives can be most destructive. They can accomplish much that is good, or they can do great harm. There is nothing *implicitly* good or bad, weak or strong, about a group.[2]

The hope for this boss is that he will read some of the research on the subject, or that he will observe or be part of an *effective* group, and then wonder why it was effective. Perhaps this will lead him into an understanding of the nature of groups.

The *anti-group* attitude can and does exist at all levels of organization. It is said that Harry Truman, prior to the outbreak of the Korean War, did not attend meetings of the National Security Council because he doubted that free discussion and argument would ensue within that body with the Chief Executive present. After the outbreak of that war, however, it is said that he started attending the meetings and was quite pleased to observe that healthy discussion and argument *did* ensue with him present. While it is said that there was a lack of such argument immediately

[2] *Ibid.*, p. 162.

after the late President Kennedy took office, up to and including the Bay of Pigs episode, there is wide agreement that the young President made outstanding use of groups, both of the standing and ad hoc variety, as he coped with crises *and* routine matters.

Executives who are unaware of the nature of groups often harbor unwavering prejudices against the use of groups. One is to the effect that the collective courage of a group is less than that required by, and possessed by, executives acting as individuals. Actually, the reverse should be the case, if for no other reason than the *risk* of the action is shared by the committee members, whereas by comparison the entire risk falls upon the single executive, and becomes a deterrent to the exercise of courage. Another myth is to the effect that voting in committee is somehow unsavory, and that groups which require unanimous agreement for action can't possibly be effective. Perhaps those who attach an unsavory nature to voting in committee are unconsciously reacting to the act of standing up to be counted in a gathering, which does require a bit of courage. Perhaps the concept runs counter to the leadership image which the critic carries, that of the decisive leader making all decisions in a quick and tidy manner, through some special grace from on high.

As to the unanimity of decisions, and the ineffectiveness thereof, the critic would do well to peruse the book, *Exploration in Management,* by Wilfred Brown. Written by the head of a large and successful British business organization, the entire book is well worth reading; however, I now refer to the chapter entitled, "The Legislative System," in which the author describes the most effective operation of an important "council" which contained fourteen members from all levels of the organization, including the managing director himself. His incisive description of the inner workings of the group, and the responsibilities demonstrated by its members, dispels many erroneous impressions of group action, including that of a group requiring unanimous decision never accomplishing anything. In Mr. Brown's own words, "In seventeen years of operation of this mechanism, the number of occasions when we have reached stalemate is trifling." [3]

This chapter could go on and on about the endless subject of groups, but space does not permit. It will close with the following

[3] Wilfred Brown, Exploration in Management (New York, Wiley, 1960), p. 237.

excerpt from the previously referred to book, *New Patterns of Management,* which is included here for the benefit of those readers, particularly in other countries, who may not have access to that splendid book. It should be of great value to anyone who honestly wants to maximize group effort.

THE NATURE OF HIGHLY EFFECTIVE WORK GROUPS

The highly effective group, as we shall define it, is always conceived as being a part of a larger organization. A substantial proportion of persons in a company are members of more than one work group, especially when both line and staff are considered. As a consequence, in such groups there are always linking functions to be performed and relationships to other groups to be maintained. Our highly effective group is not an isolated entity.

All the persons in a company also belong to groups and organizations outside of the company. For most persons, membership in several groups both within and outside the company is the rule rather than the exception. This means, of course, that no single group, even the highly effective work group, dominates the life of any member. Each member of the organization feels pressures from membership in several different groups and is not influenced solely by loyalty to any one group.

Since the different groups to which a person belongs are apt to have somewhat different and often inconsistent goals and values, corresponding conflicts and pressures are created within him. To minimize these conflicts and tensions, the individual seeks to influence the values and goals of each of the different groups to which he belongs and which are important to him so as to minimize the inconsistencies and conflicts in values and goals. In striving for this reconciliation, he is likely to press for the acceptance of those values most important to him.

The properties and performance characteristics of the ideal highly effective group are as follows:

1. The members are skilled in all the various leadership and membership roles and functions required for interaction between leaders and members and between members and other members.

2. The group has been in existence sufficiently long to have developed a well-established, relaxed working relationship among all its members.

3. The members of the group are attracted to it and are loyal to its members, including the leader.

4. The members and leaders have a high degree of confidence and trust in each other.

5. The values and goals of the group are a satisfactory integration and expression of the relevant values and needs of its members. They have helped shape these values and goals and are satisfied with them.

6. In so far as members of the group are performing linking functions, they endeavor to have the values and goals of the groups which they link in harmony, one with the other.

7. The more important a value seems to the group, the greater the likelihood that the individual member will accept it.

8. The members of the group are highly motivated to abide by the major values and to achieve the important goals of the group. Each member will do all that he reasonably can—and at times all in his power—to help the group achieve its central

objectives. He expects every other member to do the same. This high motivation springs, in part, from the basic motive to achieve and maintain a sense of personal worth and importance. Being valued by a group whose values he shares, and deriving a sense of significance and importance from this relationship, leads each member to do his best. He is eager not to let the other members down. He strives hard to do what he believes is expected of him.

9. All the interaction, problem-solving, decision-making activities of the group occur in a supportive atmosphere. Suggestions, comments, ideas, information, criticisms are all offered with a helpful orientation. Similarly, these contributions are received in the same spirit. Respect is shown for the point of view of others both in the way contributions are made and in the way they are received.

There are real and important differences of opinion, but the focus is on arriving at sound solutions and not on exacerbating and aggravating the conflict. Ego forces deriving from the desire to achieve and maintain a sense of personal worth and importance are channeled into constructive efforts. Care is taken not to let these ego forces disrupt important group tasks, such as problem-solving. Thus, for example, a statement of the problem, a condition which any solution must meet, a suggested solution, or an item of relevant fact are all treated as from the group as a whole. Care is taken so that one statement of the problem is not John's and another Bill's. A suggested solution is not referred to as Tom's and another Dick's. All the material contributed is treated as ours: "One of our proposed solutions is A, another is B." In all situations involving actual or potential differences or conflict among the members of the group, procedures are used to separate the ego of each member from his contribution. In this way, ego forces do not stimulate conflict between members. Instead, they are channeled into supporting the activities and efforts of the group.

The group atmosphere is sufficiently supportive for the members to be able to accept readily any criticism which is offered and to make the most constructive use of it. The criticisms may deal with any relevant topic such as operational problems, decisions, supervisory problems, interpersonal relationships, or group processes, but whatever their content, the member feels sufficiently secure in the supportive atmosphere of the group to be able to accept, test, examine, and benefit from the criticism offered. Also, he is able to be frank and candid, irrespective of the content of the discussion: technical, managerial, factual, cognitive, or emotional. The supportive atmosphere of the group, with the feeling of security it provides, contributes to a cooperative relationship between the members. And this cooperation itself contributes to and reinforces the supportive atmosphere.

10. The superior of each work group exerts a major influence in establishing the tone and atmosphere of that work group by his leadership principles and practices. In the highly effective group, consequently, the leader adheres to those principles of leadership which create a supportive atmosphere in the group and a cooperative rather than a competitive relationship among the members. For example, he shares information fully with the group and creates an atmosphere where the members are stimulated to behave similarly.

11. The group is eager to help each member develop to his full potential. It sees, for example, that relevant technical knowledge and training in interpersonal and group skills are made available to each member.

12. Each member accepts willingly and without resentment the goals and expectations that he and his group establish for themselves. The anxieties, fears, and emotional stresses produced by direct pressure for high performance from a boss in a hierarchical situation is not present. Groups seem capable of setting high performance goals for the group as a whole and for each member. These goals are high enough to stimulate each member to do his best, but not so high as to create anxieties

or fear of failure. In an effective group, each person can exert sufficient influence on the decisions of the group to prevent the group from setting unattainable goals for any member while setting high goals for all. The goals are adapted to the member's capacity to perform.

13. The leader and the members believe that each group member can accomplish "the impossible." These expectations stretch each member to the maximum and accelerate his growth. When necessary, the group tempers the expectation level so that the member is not broken by a feeling of failure or rejection.

14. When necessary or advisable, other members of the group will give a member the help he needs to accomplish successfully the goals set for him. Mutual help is a characteristic of highly effective groups.

15. The supportive atmosphere of the highly effective group stimulates creativity. The group does not demand narrow conformity as do the work groups under authoritarian leaders. No one has to "yes the boss," nor is he rewarded for such an attempt. The group attaches high value to new, creative approaches and solutions to its problems and to the problems of the organization of which it is a part. The motivation to be creative is high when one's work group prizes creativity.

16. The group knows the value of "constructive" conformity and knows when to use it and for what purposes. Although it does not permit conformity to affect adversely the creative efforts of its members, it does expect conformity on mechanical and administrative matters to save the time of members and to facilitate the group's activities. The group agrees, for example, on administrative forms and procedures, and once they have been established, it expects its members to abide by them until there is good reason to change them.

17. There is strong motivation on the part of each member to communicate fully and frankly to the group all the information which is relevant and of value to the group's activity. This stems directly from the member's desire to be valued by the group and to get the job done. The more important to the group a member feels an item of information is, the greater is his motivation to communicate it.

18. There is high motivation in the group to use the communication process so that it best serves the interests and goals of the group. Every item which a member feels is important, but which for some reason is being ignored, will be repeated until it receives the attention that it deserves. Members strive also to avoid communicating unimportant information so as not to waste the group's time.

19. Just as there is high motivation to communicate, there is correspondingly strong motivation to receive communications. Each member is genuinely interested in any information on any relevant matter that any member of the group can provide. This information is welcomed and trusted as being honestly and sincerely given. Members do not look "behind" the information item and attempt to interpret it in ways opposite to its purported intent. This interest of group members in information items and the treatment of such items as valid reinforces the motivation to communicate.

20. In the highly effective group, there are strong motivations to try to influence other members as well as to be receptive to influence by them. This applies to all the group's activities: technical matters, methods, organizational problems, interpersonal relationships, and group processes.

21. The group processes of the highly effective group enable the members to exert more influence on the leader and to communicate far more information to him, including suggestions as to what needs to be done and how he could do his job better, than is possible in a man-to-man relationship. By "tossing the ball" back and forth among its members, a group can communicate information to the leader which no single person on a man-to-man basis dare do. As a consequence, the boss receives all the information that the group possesses to help him perform his job effectively.

22. The ability of the members of a group to influence each other contributes to the flexibility and adaptability of the group. Ideas, goals, and attitudes do not become frozen if members are able to influence each other continuously.

Although the group is eager to examine any new ideas and methods which will help it do its job better and is willing to be influenced by its members, it is not easily shifted or swayed. Any change is undertaken only after rigorous examination of the evidence. This stability in the group's activities is due to the steadying influence of the common goals and values held by the group members.

23. In the highly effective group, individual members feel secure in making decisions which seem appropriate to them because the goals and philosophy of operation are clearly understood by each member and provide him with a solid base for his decisions. This unleashes initiative and pushes decisions down while still maintaining a coordinated and directed effort.

24. The leader of a highly effective group is selected carefully. His leadership ability is so evident that he would probably emerge as a leader in any unstructured situation. To increase the likelihood that persons of high leadership competence are selected, the organization is likely to use peer nominations and related methods in selecting group leaders.

An important aspect of the highly effective group is its extensive use of the principle of supportive relationships. An examination of the above material reveals that virtually every statement involves an application of this principle.[4]

As a final motivating factor to encourage your study of groups, the following statement, based directly on research, is contained on page 28 of the same book: "Supervisors who are evaluated highly by management make much more frequent use of group meetings to deal with work-related problems than do supervisors who receive a mediocre or poor rating."

Our end-of-chapter question could well be stated: what do you *really* know about groups?

SELF-ANALYSIS

This one is fairly simple. You can use Dr. Likert's listing of characteristics to check up on your group—*but wait!* Don't do this by yourself. Get your group together, give them the list to study, and then meet for a group diagnosis of your situation.

HEAL THE WOUND

As you carry out the group diagnosis on an item-by-item basis, reach agreement on what changes are necessary to heal the wounds. You will find it to be a wonderful experience—but not necessarily painless—in group therapy.

[4] Likert, *op. cit.*, pp. 165–169.

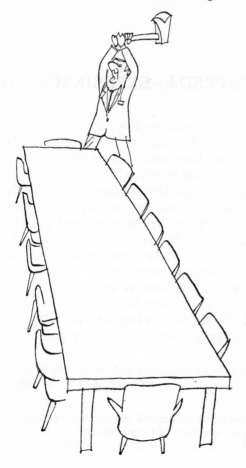

SUGGESTIONS FOR FURTHER READING

Olmstead, Michael S., *The Small Group*. New York, Random House, 1959.

Homans, George C., *The Human Group*. New York, Harcourt, Brace and Company, 1950.

the

HANDICAPPED-by-EXPERIENCE BOSS

The boss who is handicapped by experience is more prevalent today than at any other time or period in history. The expression "experience is the best teacher" is a very suspect saying in this world of organizational life which has changed so much in the past few years and which continues to change so rapidly. If today's executive is not very alert and very careful, what he regards as valuable experience can very well be a millstone around his neck, in the same manner that the younger executive's inexperience can be a great *asset* to him in that he has not yet learned to make the mistakes which our more experienced executives are making.

Of the writers and lecturers who have expounded this concept, none has done it better than J. Lewis Powell, management consultant, lecturer, writer, and orginator of the "Collapse of Time" lecture, who comments on the handicap of experience:

Everything now being done is, at best, being done by the most modern *obsolete* method known. Inevitably it will be replaced or improved. . . .

Just as business needs accelerated amortization to offset the accelerated obsolescence of equipment, so business needs a technique to offset the increasing obsolescence of executive experience. . . .

In his lecture, Mr. Powell pointed out how the typewriter industry did not invent electric typewriters; the steam locomotive industry did not invent diesel locomotives; the invention of the sewing machine was delayed for years by the assumption that the eye should be on the same end of the needle as in hand sewing; the use of the already invented iron plow was delayed for fifty years because of the belief that it would poison the ground; the invention of the steamship was delayed for years because it was conceived to be a mechanized rowboat; the dial telephone was invented by an undertaker, not the telephone industry; and other examples. He then developed the theme that *experience* is a handicap rather than an asset unless we learn how to cope with it.

The past experience of an executive should provide the power pack that propels his organization into expanded profits; unfortunately the past experience of some executives creates a prison that confines his organization to a brilliant past.

Capable executives are those who make progress by consistently replacing old experience with new and better experience. A prime function of an executive is to generate a forward motion, to spark-plug innovations and improvements.

Just as the performance of a computer depends on the current validity of inserted data, the value of past experience is dependent on the current validity of past experience, as applied to present conditions. To be useful a tool has to be maintained in good operating condition; experience can be a tool of value only if it is consistently up-dated and continuously related to current conditions.

Experience does not up-date itself automatically—it can and does become obsolete. Inherently, experience by itself usually provides only yesterday's answers to yesterday's problems. Unless the raw material of past experience is continually reprocessed by current thinking and refined by up-dated judgment, it is of doubtful current value.

Executives who can liberate their judgment from the bondage of past experience, can free their thinking from phantom limitations of bygone experience. The very problem that was a stumbling block when viewed from the restricted viewpoint of previous limitations, frequently becomes a stepping stone when viewed from the expanded viewpoint of more recent developments. The competent executive is the one who capitalizes on change, converts it to an asset and makes it work for him instead of against him.

SELF-ANALYSIS

As in many of our self-inflicted wounds, there is no magic way to diagnose this one, no simple way of labeling that part of our experience which is of value to us and that part which is a handicap. But then, practically none of the executive's tasks in today's world can be regarded as simple or easy. However, you must carry on a continuing program of assessment of your past experience to determine its value, or its danger, in today's environment. For example: Think of your solutions to your last three major problems, and the role played in those solutions by your past experience. A good rule of thumb on this is to accept as axiomatic that today's problem may be *similar* to yesterday's problem, *but it is never the same as yesterday's problem!* If you did not determine the uniqueness of the new problem, as you applied yesterday's solution to it, and then adjusted your solution accordingly, you bear this self-inflicted wound.

HEAL THE WOUND

Reverse the wording of the last sentence above. After your diagnosis, take the actions required by the uniqueness of your new situation when compared to the old, and deal with it accordingly, adding as a final ingredient a liberal dose of ingenuity and creativity, without which no solution to a problem is ever really effective.

the

SLIDE-RULE MANAGER

The Slide-Rule Manager belongs to that breed of bosses who thinks that all problems, including human ones, can be solved by mathematical equations of one kind or another. He goes on his merry way, managing by computation both the material and human resources at his disposal. As he "quantifies" the factors in his equations, the human factors always seem to come out with the lesser values; they are merely variables in the analysis.

This approach to management often seems to have its origins in the undergraduate and graduate education of men who later become executives. I was able to observe this in a most interesting way among my younger classmates at the Harvard Business School in the Master of Business Administration (MBA) program. The class included many students who had either majored in engineering and/or mathematics or had done graduate work in those fields. They seemed to do quite well in those case problems involving only quantitative analysis; however, they often ran into great trouble in the many case problems which involved human beings in organizational life. By using the slide-rule approach, they often arrived at quick solutions, fitting the human factors into neat and tidy compartments in much the same manner that they computed the break-even point of a new product. The returned examination papers caused many a traumatic shock in the form of unsatisfactory grades. Notwithstanding this feedback, it was often many months before the slide-rule approach could be "unlearned" enough to bring about the assignment of proper values to the human factors contained in the case problems.

A dramatic case in point was contained in the television play *Patterns,* previously referred to. The corporation president made a decision to purchase a company which was going in the direction of bankruptcy. The organization in trouble was in a company town, where the entire community relied in one way or another upon the company for its livelihood. The vice president for indus-

91

trial relations recommended that the company be purchased at once, in order to avoid the adverse impact upon the community which company bankruptcy would bring in the form of unemployment, poverty, and all their attendant ills. However, the ruthless president, a slide-rule manager if there ever was one, insisted upon letting the company go broke and then bought it for a song, and let the community lick its wounds and heal itself—and, hate the company's new owner and its president, for the remainder of their lives.

In all decision-making, of course, values must be assigned to the factors involved, either by calculation or default, or else a decision would never be made. Oftentimes, however, the values appropriate for assignment to the human factors in the problem do not lend themselves to quantification, and they can best be handled by the executive who postpones the assignment of those values until all other factors have been quantified and values assigned. This having been done, it is less difficult (but never easy) for him to assign values to the human factors in the situation, and to arrive at his decision. It is *not* the intent of this chapter to criticize the boss who quantifies the factors in his decision-making process; it *is* the purpose of this chapter to point the finger at the boss who uses the slide-rule approach to the solution of the human problems in his organization. In such an organization, the boss is not viewed as a human being walking around; rather, his subordinates see a giant slide rule with arms and legs walking around, and they fear this robot who makes decisions affecting their organizational lives.

Question: Are you a Slide-Rule Manager?

SELF-ANALYSIS

Reflect upon several past decisions, particularly those which had as factors a challenging mixture of "quantifiable" and "unquantifiable" items. Check to see if there is a pattern of decision-making which indicates that the nod always went in the direction of the *greater* quantifications (pro or con), regardless of the importance of the "unquantifiable" items. This should be a clear indication that you are a Slide-Rule Manager, for it could not be coincidence in this complicated world, where one intangible, almost unmeasurable item, when placed on the decision-making scale, often outweighs several easily quantified and easily measured ones.

HEAL THE WOUND

The preceding diagnostic formula predicts our prescription for healing this wound. Every decision you make in organizational life requires that you assign values to each of the elements in that problem, whether they are tangible or intangible. What you need is a system of assigning those values to the intangibles. This can be done in different ways, but one good way is to select—after you have assigned values to all the tangibles and intangibles—the *critical variable* which will tip the scale of decision-making one way or the other, depending upon the value you assign to it. You should then re-evaluate the weight you have given to this variable, giving it the appropriate attention demanded by its criticality, place it back on the decision-making scale, and the proper decision falls out of the process. *One caution here:* You *must* avoid subjectivity in this re-evaluation of the critical variable, or you may be guilty of assigning a value which will cause the decision to come out the way you had originally *felt* it would, or *hoped* that it would, or the way your boss had indicated he desired, or for some other unworthy reason.

the

AFTER-the-FACT MANAGER

It is easier to describe this boss than it is to heal his self-inflicted wound, for it is a deep one. His wound does not stem so much from his behavior pattern as it does from his environment or, more specifically, from his inability to cope successfully with that environment. He finds himself enveloped and almost smothered by his workload. In short, he is behind in his work and, to use the Pennsylvania Dutch term, the harder he works, the *behinder* he gets.

This boss is never in a position to *act,* because he is always *reacting* to events others have initiated. There is a military axiom to the effect that a commander must conduct himself so that he can "influence the action." Our After-the-Fact Manager never seems to be able to do this because, to use the midwestern expression, he is always "just one step ahead of the sheriff."

There is a philosophy of management which states that the manager of today must conduct himself in such a way that he *causes* the events of the future. The After-the-Fact Manager not only does not achieve this—he is a *part* of the events which have been caused by others. It has been said that the future belongs to those who plan for it. Not so with our boss. He cannot find the time for the *present,* let alone for the future. And working overtime doesn't seem to help; neither does bringing home a briefcase full of work every night and weekend. He never seems to catch up.

There is a poignancy about this boss, of whom there are tens of thousands in the world of organizational endeavor today. Somehow, he reminds me of the true story of a married couple described to me by a friend of mine. They have a garden, and they raise nice tomatoes. In fact, on the average, they seem to raise too many. The wife is a very dominant person. She refuses to let him eat any tomatoes fresh from the garden as long as there are any uneaten, less fresh tomatoes on hand. The net result—you've guessed it—is that the husband is always forced to eat the old tomatoes while the fresh tomatoes sit in the house and lose their freshness. The husband continues to hope that some day he will be able to eat a fresh tomato, but through the years he has grown somewhat pessimistic as he eats away at his backlog of aged tomatoes while his wife carefully safeguards the fresh ones. A sad but true story. And it describes our After-the-Fact Manager quite well.

I wish I had a solution for this boss, but all I can do is to suggest an approach to a possible solution. The diagnosis which you have probably already made is that this boss has not learned to *delegate* adequately to his subordinates. Actually, this is probably true, but how can he correct the situation? The art of delegation is one of the true hallmarks of executive ability, and the distinction between *delegation* and *abdication* is a very fine one indeed. Many bosses refrain from delegation because of their perceptions of the individual and collective abilities of their subordinates, which they regard as inadequate in terms of the requirements of the work to be done. Also, these bosses contend that it actually takes *more* of their own time when they do delegate, for they must go through a process of correcting inadequate work before it can be considered satisfactory. This contention is often a valid and true one.

A corollary problem which often exists in this situation is that the boss has high standards of performance, and will not permit himself or his organization to turn out work unless it is of high quality. He refuses to accept the fact that there is often a direct correlation between quality of work effort and time spent upon that effort.

About all this boss can do is to indulge in a two-part concurrent process (1) to lower standards to a minimum adequate level for the time being, and (2) to initiate a process of delegation and subordinate-training which, though costing him more time at the beginning, will gradually get him out of his dilemma. It will be a slow process, but it can be done.

If our After-the-Fact Manager does *not* take this action he will, like the husband just described, be doomed to eating stale tomatoes all his life, while the fresh tomatoes, in the form of unrealized opportunities, wither away on the vine or, more likely, will be gobbled up by his peer bosses in the organization.

Now for the tomato question—I mean the acid-test question:

Are you an After-the-Fact Manager? Are you eating stale tomatoes? If so, are you willing to delegate your work, help your subordinates develop, and look forward to someday obtaining the

benefits of the fresh fruits of opportunity? Or will you be content
for all eternity to eat the stale tomatoes, the only diet of the After-
the-Fact Manager? You, and you alone, can answer this question.

SELF-ANALYSIS

Somehow, get away from your office for a day, and take stock of
your situation. Take an inventory of the actions you have taken
lately, and make an honest identification of them as to whether

they are *actions which you have initiated,* or whether they are *reactions to actions which someone above or below you has initiated.* If the latter of the two is the case, you are an After-the-Fact Manager.

HEAL THE WOUND

With your inventory and diagnosis complete, you must somehow catch up with the situation; you must become an actor rather than a reactor. This is not easy, but it can be done. One way is to give short shrift to the reaction items which come your way for a few days, utilizing the saved time to become an actor—that is, to initiate some items yourself. This short shrift must be on a calculated basis, however, or you will become a Boss Who Does Not Practice the Principle of Calculated Neglect. (See p. 47) Having done this, keep a little score, and keep up the therapy until by actual count you are initiating more actions than those actions of others you are reacting to. You will like the taste of fresh tomatoes, and may never have to eat stale ones again.

the

SHADES-of-INTEGRITY BOSS

This boss defines integrity to suit himself, depending on his own selfish desires and/or the pressures he is subjected to at the time of decision. In describing this boss, we shall not waste time with dictionary definitions of the word *integrity*. Recently, I heard a comedian define the word as "not getting caught." I am afraid this attempted humor is all too true far more often than we like to believe. This chapter will not deal with honesty in the eyes of the law, such as stealing or not stealing. It will deal primarily with integrity of the *intellectual* kind, the practice of which seems to be more difficult because of the ease with which actions lacking integrity may be rationalized. In addition to easy rationalization, actions lacking integrity are often easy to conceal, because the individual is often the sole witness, judge, and jury. Two dramatic examples of this will now be described.

Several years ago in a speech at the Army's Command Management School, Mr. John M. "Jack" Fox, had this to say about the manager's need for integrity.

Managers must be men of high integrity. The quality of integrity— the honesty, sincerity, the moral posture of a top executive must be unquestionable. This is a common ingredient of all real leaders. . . . I race sailboats for a hobby—not well, I'm afraid, but enthusiastically. In sailboat racing we have a term known as "Corinthianism" that I believe illustrates this quality of integrity. I had the occasion to demonstrate "Corinthianism" to my children one day a couple of summers ago. The Foxes' boat by some strange fluke rounded the first mark well ahead of the fleet. This was the first time this had ever happened. By an even stranger fluke (the breezes on Long Island Sound are famous for their flukiness) we approached the second mark with our competitors out of sight under our stern. At this exultant moment, father goofed. In rounding this mark the main boom jibed over and struck the buoy a resounding thump—we had fouled out.

I turned the boat and started home for our mooring. The children who were crewing nearly had apoplexy. "Holy cow, Dad, what are you doing—the finish line is in the other direction!" I explained we had committed a foul and were required to withdraw from the race. "But no one saw us—not even in their glasses could they have seen us!" It took a little while to point out that since we had committed a foul that was all that counted. That is *"Corinthianism."* To be a manager a man must have the confidence of his superiors that his actions will be the same whether his deeds are subject to observation or not. *This is integrity.*

Our second example depicts an experience where tremendous pressure against intellectual integrity caused a crisis in the life of a rising executive, one which left its mark on his entire life. In describing his experience to a group of executives attending a well-known executive development course, this man, then executive vice president of a large corporation, listed it as the most difficult problem of his entire career. His remarks follow:

I've saved my most difficult problem of all for the last. I have had no difficulty remembering the details of this one, I can assure you. In fact, I've been reminded of this one every few months since it happened several years ago. There is no point in disguising the core of the problem. The one word, *integrity*, describes it. Perhaps it would be better described by four words, *The Shades of Integrity*, for that is what it is about.

It happened this way. One of the organizations in which I served was great on making *studies*, and then using the studies as the bases for decision-making. The individual study would be made either by a committee or by an individual. It was customary for the study to become known by the name of the individual who made the study, or by the name of the individual who was chairman of the committee who made the study. This seemed to give the studies added psychological and social significance, especially when the studies turned out to be regarded as particularly good or particularly poor. The studies when completed were usually subjected to executive and staff appraisal, but this was customarily in the form of separately written comments, rather than as amendments to the study report. The study report usually remained intact, and was always signed by the individual or individuals who made the study. Typically, the reports of the studies became a part of the permanent organizational files, and were never retired or destroyed, which also seemed to impart a uniqueness to the studies and to the frames of reference of the individuals making the studies.

My experience was as follows. At a point in time in my career, after being a member of five or six business, industrial and governmental organizations, I felt that I had found the organization with which I wanted to spend the remainder of my professional career (of which I hoped there were many years left). I was in a spot which my friends and I believed to be the last, or next-to-last, stepping-stone to a vice-presidency, which in turn should be a stepping-stone to bigger things.

One day I was called into the office of the vice president in whose department I served and was told the following. The corporation was considering a very important change in company-wide policy, one so important that it could make or break the company in the long run. The board of governors and the president of the company had decided that a study should be made to provide a basis for the decision on whether or not to adopt the proposed change in policy. The nature of the study had caused the president to decide that it should be a one-man study, rather than a committee study, and he had further decided that that one man making the study could ask for any resources he needed to make the study, in the form of statistics, interviews, travel, and the like. I was then informed that, after a careful selection process, I had been chosen to make the study. While my selection was news to me, I had heard rumors of the proposed policy change, and had heard that the proposed policy change was completely controversial, with executive personnel from the top down being about evenly divided on it, and with the union already having a strong, unofficial view on it, although I was not clear as to why the union was so interested in it.

In telling me that I was to make the study, my own vice president made some revealing statements. He stated that, while the proposed policy change would effect the entire corporation, he felt that it would have its greatest impact on that part of the company over which he was vice president, and that he had very strong feelings on the subject. He then went on to state those feelings, which consisted of a very strong, partly emotional endorsement of the status quo, and *against* the proposed policy change. He went on to say that the executive vice president would assign the study to me, along with giving me general instructions. He also told me, and asked me to keep it in confidence, that he happened to know that the executive vice president felt the same way that he did about the proposed policy change. He closed off the discussion by reminding me of his opinion that the proposed policy change would have greatest impact on his area of authority and responsibility, that he expected to be consulted in detail on it, that he expected to be advised of anyone under his authority with whom I would wish to consult, and closed by reminding me that he had been very pleased with my work and was considering making me his principal assistant when that position became vacant through retirement of his present deputy in about six months.

You can imagine my feelings as I walked from the office of my vice president to the office of the executive vice president, to receive my charter. I can assure you I was anything but happy. Not that there was anything wrong with the study. It was a most challenging one, but I liked challenges, and I already knew enough about the problem to have confidence that I was capable of making a good study. It wasn't that that worried me.

It was an open secret among executive personnel that the company president and the executive vice president did not see eye to eye on a significant number of subjects; however, the president always publicly prevailed, even though there was some suspicion that the executive vice president was often less than enthusiastic as he implemented the decisions of his superior. It was also common knowledge that my vice president and the executive vice president were close friends and were often together socially.

I was greeted cordially upon entering, and it was soon made clear to me where the executive vice president stood on the subject of the study. He was very much against the proposed policy change, he said, but that he wanted me to make a good study and, laughing, one that would lay the idea to rest for good. He stated that it would be regarded as a one-man study, and that only I would sign it. Further, he stated that he would like to be kept informed on the progress of the study, which I could tell to him, or to my vice president whom, he reminded me, he often saw in the evenings.

As I walked out of his office I found myself wishing that the selection process which chose me to make the study had not been so discriminating, I can assure you. For several hours I tried to figure out how to *get out* of making the study, rather than how to begin it. Hard as I tried, I couldn't find any way out of it. To be selected to make the study was a high compliment. Making the study, and doing it well, was quite within my capabilities, even though it would be difficult and challenging. But, I wondered, how in the name of heaven can I make an objective, honest study with my own vice president and the executive vice president so violently opposed to the proposal, and with them breathing down my neck every step of the way? Well, without going into detail here, I can assure you that I made a good study. I must admit that I withheld information from the two VP's as the study progressed, and was as general as I could get away with when they would interrogate me on the progress of the study. I sought the information I needed, much of which was partly opinion, partly emotions and partly fact. I used the best research techniques I could learn about, including consultation of this type of research with a firm of well-known management consultants. Actually, the study progressed very well.

The trouble was, the logic and facts soon started pointing strongly toward the conclusion that the proposed change in policy should be adopted—the conclusion opposite to the one desired by my vice president and the executive vice president. Although I tried to ignore this, I found myself thinking about it more and more. I think the two VP's sensed my dilemma, for they increased their pressure upon me to make my findings fit their preconceived conclusions.

My research was completed, and I was ready to write the report.

I don't suppose I should admit this to you gentlemen, but I found my-self becoming very disturbed, and not sleeping very well. My family noticed my condition, for it began to spill over on them. Normally, for example, I might have one cocktail before dinner or I might have none at all. As the study progressed, I started having two or three before dinner and later after-dinner brandy, which I had never indulged in before. I became irritable and was very cross with my wife and fine young children, some of whom were approaching teenage.

I found myself writing first one, then two, then three versions of the report of my study, then trying to choose one of them as the final one. When I first started this story, I used the expression, *shades of integrity*. That was exactly what my three reports represented. One was

honest. One was half-honest. One was downright dishonest. However, I had the feeling that they were written in such a way that no reader other than myself could detect these shades of integrity. I became convinced that I could submit any one of the three reports and get away with it, in so far as the report itself went. It was the probable consequences that caused me sleepless nights. If I submitted the *honest* report, recommending and justifying the proposed major policy change, my goose would be cooked as far as my vice president and executive vice president were concerned. I would have had my last promotion in the company with which I had hoped to spend the rest of my executive career. If I submitted the half-honest report, which recommended a gray compromise between the unlike black or white proposals of changing or not changing a major policy, my goose would be half-cooked. If I submitted the dishonest report, recommending *against* the proposed policy change, the company would probably go along with it and my vice president and executive vice president would be very pleased with me, and would probably promote me, but I was sure the corporation would suffer. Further, I had so shaded the dishonest report that, being the sole researcher, probably no one other than myself would ever know the truth. This was my situation as the deadline for submission of my report approached.

Well, all three reports were typed in final form. (I had hired three commercial typists in different parts of the city to type them, for obvious reasons.) The day before I was to submit my report, I walked around as though I had an anvil on my shoulders. That evening, at home, I had several martinis before dinner, and was so cross at dinner that finally my favorite daughter ran crying from the table. I left the house for a long walk and, though I had never been a particularly religious man, I stopped into a church to pray for guidance. . .

As I drove to the office the next morning, I still did not know which report I would turn in. All I will tell you today is that I made a decision and submitted a report. Rather than telling you what it was, I will only say that *that problem,* and *that decision,* had a profound effect upon my life, an effect that is continuing today, as I sometimes ask myself what I am and what I am not.

It should not be necessary to list any more examples of the need for, and the pressures against intellectual integrity. The sad fact of the story, however, is that most of the choices are usually not as clear cut and defined as they were in the examples given, difficult as they were. The two expressions, "You can't fight city hall" and, "Discretion is the better part of valor," are used over and over again as basis for or rationalization of intellectual dishonesty. Pressure from a boss has often caused a subordinate to decide that it is more important to keep one's boss happy than to do a good job as one sees it. The continuing conflict between loyalty to one's subordinates, loyalty to one's bosses, and loyalty to one's organization, can drain the intellectual integrity from a man in organization life, unless he carries on a continuing, vigorous and courageous effort to prevent it.

What is *your* score on intellectual integrity? The next time you say, "discretion is the better part of valor," will you also ask yourself the question, "discretion or cowardice—what *is* the difference?"

SELF-ANALYSIS

This is a difficult one, for it requires absolute honesty with one's self, plus a good memory. Look back upon the times in recent weeks or months when you found youself in situations where there was pressure against your intellectual integrity, along with its ever-present corollary of opportunity or room to rationalize intellectual dishonesty. These incidents may not be so difficult to remember, unless they were followed by the psychological process of wiping them from your mind as though they had never happened. Having done this, subject the incidents to very critical analysis to determine your manner of performance in the integrity department. You should soon be able to come up with a score for yourself, and to determine whether you have shaded your definitions of integrity in order to cope with the situation. If you have done so a few times, you have incurred the wound, for you have either exercised integrity or you have not. Integrity is a lot like pregnancy, it seems. It is difficult to be only a little bit dishonest, just as it is impossible to be a little bit pregnant: either you are or you are not.

HEAL THE WOUND

It would be easy for you to decide, after finding yourself guilty of incurring this self-inflicted wound, that there is no hope for the future—that you have compromised your integrity so many times there is no hope of recovery. This is not so. You *can* turn over a new leaf. Just like the taxi driver who worked out the perfect system of doctoring his meter so that he could steal with impunity, but who later quit the practice because, in his words, "I didn't like the way it made me feel," so can you also regain your self-respect. And, having done so, one honest action gives you additional strength for the next until, like a rolling snowball, you will build up the strength to maintain your intellectual integrity under the most difficult circumstances.

On

Wounding Your People

In this section, although you, the boss, are responsible for creating the wounds, it is your people *who suffer the primary pains and agony stemming from them. You will suffer also, of course, from the attitudes of your people toward you, and from the impairment of their effectiveness caused by you. Eventually, like the Ancient Mariner, you will find that in their torment, one way or another, they will hang an albatross around your neck as an overt symbol of your guilt for their suffering.*

You not only tell a subordinate exactly what to do—but exactly how to do it. You are a *HOW-TO-DO-IT BOSS.* 146

You don't care who does the job as long as it gets done. You are a *BOSS WHO ALLOCATES WORK UNFAIRLY.* 149

You think looking busy is being busy; you think being busy is looking busy. You are a *DON'T-LET-ME-CATCH-YOU-THINKING BOSS.* 153

You think that "pinning the blame" on someone will prevent future mistakes by your subordinates. You are a *WITCH-HUNTER BOSS.* 156

You use memos to give orders because you feel it achieves more than face-to-face discussion. You are a *ONE-WAY-COMMUNICA-TION BOSS.* 159

You make up for your small physical stature by belittling others. You are a *RUNT-COMPLEX BOSS.* 162

You are intent on proving that every man has a *breaking point.* You are a *HUMAN-EROSION BOSS.* 166

You are reluctant to promote a man on the grounds that he's not ready for the job. You are a *BOSS WHO NEGLECTS THE DE-VELOPMENT OF HIS SUBORDINATES.* 170

You always use profanity in talking to your employees because you feel it's more effective. You are a *PROFANE-AND-VULGAR BOSS.* 175

You believe that disagreement among your staff is unhealthy business. You are a *BOSS WHO DOES NOT WANT CONFLICT.* 180

Anything that *you* do is right because you're the boss. You are a *BOSS WHO IS DRUNK WITH POWER.* 184

You don't contribute as much effort as you should to your organization. You are a *LAZY BOSS.* 187

You believe the only time anything gets done is when you're around. You are a *BREATHE-DOWN-THEIR-NECKS BOSS.* 191

You believe that threats and fear are the only way to get the job done. You are a *MANAGE-THROUGH-FEAR BOSS.* 196

You view with suspicion the employee who exceeds the established rate of job accomplishment. You are a *BOSS WHO HATES RATE-BUSTERS.* 201

the

TAKE-the-CREDIT BOSS

The Take-the-Credit Boss is the boss who, by personal acts of commission and omission, takes or receives the credit for achievement which rightfully belongs to his subordinates who did the work or performed the tasks. This contemptuous practice and the number of bosses who practice it are growing at an alarming rate, for reasons to be discussed later.

Let's take an actual case in point. One day not long ago a division chief in an administrative office was at his desk when a friend dropped by. The friend asked the division chief about an important special project for which the division chief had the overall responsibility and on which he in turn had assigned action to one of his branch chiefs. The division chief answered his friend by stating that the project was moving along nicely and added that his subordinate branch chief at that very moment was in the office of the chief executive of the organization, briefing him on the project. Upon hearing this the visitor looked startled and asked, "I'm surprised that you are letting your subordinate brief the chief executive. If you do that, how can you be sure that you [the division chief] will get the credit for accomplishing the project?" The division chief's answer was that he felt he could rely on the chief executive to give credit where credit was due and that, as far as he was concerned, he wanted his subordinate, who had worked so hard on the project, to receive proper credit with the chief executive for his efforts. He added that the chief executive knew that he (the division chief) was responsible for the overall accomplishment of the project.

The friend was not satisfied with the answer the division chief gave and he left with the remark that, in his opinion, it was risky business to permit subordinates to get the credit for accomplishments performed under another's supervision. After he left, the division chief, who had high respect for the opinions and judgment of his friend, wondered whether he or his friend had the correct atti-

110

tude on this subject. In this particular case, the division chief continued the practice he had described to his friend.

In a comparable situation, an important project was carried out by a branch chief over a period of time whereby he served under two successive division chiefs during the life of the project. The action on the project was carried out by the branch chief in a highly decentralized manner, with only general and infrequent supervision from the two division chiefs, each of whom left the organization before the branch chief did.

Upon departure, each of the two division chiefs received high written commendation and recognition for his service as division chief based on the work on the project carried out by the branch chief, although the branch chief was not mentioned in the commendations. *In fact, with the two division chiefs gone, the branch chief who had carried out the project never did receive credit or recognition for the outstanding service he had performed!*

I have no doubt that you read the first case with pleasure and the second with anger, but before your emotions subside I suggest that you ask yourself which case reflects your personal behavior as a boss, and which case is typical of what is going on in the overall organization of which you are the head? And after you ask *yourself,* please do additional research to check the validity of your answers!

There will probably be general agreement that the number of Take-the-Credit Bosses is increasing rapidly, although there may be some difference of opinion as to the reason for this trend. In explanation rather than in defense of those bosses, there is beyond a doubt a great deal of pressure on today's boss to somehow or other take, get, or receive the credit for the performance of his organization in order for it to be "on the record" and then considered when promotions or selections for higher key positions are carried out. Merely to do the job in a routine, highly effective job as a team member or director is somehow not enough. For some reason the boss must be shown as the primary reason for everything good that happened. There is not enough confidence in the routine personnel management procedures for it to happen otherwise, or so will argue the Take-the-Credit Boss. He rationalizes this attitude and the behavior which stems from it by stating he cannot afford to outwardly believe in the concept that group-minded individual attitudes result first in greater *group* effective-ness, from which naturally flows increased *individual* effective-ness.

I say again that I am not defending the Take-the-Credit Boss, only trying to explain some of his behavior. If he continues this attitude he will soon have a reputation which follows him wherever he goes, and which will eventually be his downfall. His façade of insincerity will become increasingly transparent, until it can best be described by Casey Stengel's facetious remark to a group of sports writers when the Yankees won another pennant: "I couldn't a-done it without the players!"

If you are a boss who feels he must take the credit from his subordinates, or if you are callously doing it as a routine course, you would do well to heed the advice of an Oriental philosopher of long ago, Lao-Tze, who wrote:

A GOOD LEADER

A leader is best
When people barely know that he exists,
Not so good when people obey and acclaim him.
Worst when they despise him.
'Fail to honor people
They fail to honor you;'
But of a good leader, who talks little,
When his work is done, his aim fulfilled,
They will all say, "We did this ourselves."

SELF-ANALYSIS

Reflect upon the past few weeks and months, and recall those times when something had been done well in your organization—those accomplishments to which both your subordinates *and* you have contributed. In discussing or reporting on those accomplish-ments, have you given the credit to your subordinates and, at the same time or different times, refrained from taking the credit your-self? If the answer to either of those questions is in the negative, you are a Take-the-Credit Boss.

HEAL THE WOUND

Start giving the credit where credit is due and in the doubtful areas resolve the differences in favor of your subordinates. And, stop worrying about whether you will get any of the credit you deserve. You will, if not this month, then next month, or the month after that. Add one bit of therapy: many a night, in organizational life when you must go to bed with the realization that only your Creator and yourself really know what you contributed that day, let that knowledge itself be your reward. If you adopt this view, you can then adopt the philosophy that any credit you *do* receive will be a bonus, a bit of frosting on the cake. You will find organization life a lot easier to cope with, I assure you.

the

NEGATIVE-REPRIMAND BOSS

The next self-inflicted wound I call *the negative reprimand*. I think
you know what I mean. I'm talking about the boss who gives the
reprimand that does more harm than good. Its net effect is negative rather than positive.

A case in point. A paper mill once produced an entire carload
of expensive bank note paper which was returned by the customer
as unsatisfactory. And it *was* unsatisfactory. It was a "goof," and
analysis showed that most of the departments of the mill had contributed in one way or another to the "goof." I know the man who
was manager of the mill at the time. He is now executive vice president of the corporation. He said all personnel at the mill, from
himself on down, were stunned and ashamed. Every man at the
mill, including the manager, came to the mill voluntarily the next
Saturday in a non-pay status, and together they worked out a system of controls which would have positively prevented a recurrence
of such an incident. They went home that night feeling they had
learned a costly lesson, resolving to do better in the future.

Several days later the company president, whose office was a
hundred miles away, made a special trip to the mill, called a mass
meeting, and gave a great tongue-lashing to one and all, the manager included! I will not insult your intelligence by describing the
reactions of the mill personnel! Suffice it to say the company president's parentage was questioned by everyone there, and he was
persona non grata at that mill from that day forward!

Another case in point. A very conscientious military officer,
with high personal and professional standards, made an error in
judgment in preparing for an inspection by higher headquarters. It
placed his unit in a bad light when the inspection took place.
Members of his organization, his peers and subordinates who respected him highly, and he himself became immediately aware of
the error in judgment. This awareness was more of a reprimand
than could possibly be administered by a superior. However, weeks

after the incident, a written reprimand came through the mail to the officer and copies were put in his personnel file! He was furious, and justifiably so. And so were his peers and subordinates. The superior who signed the reprimand, and the officer's immediate superior who recommended it, felt good about it. They had taught *him* a lesson. But had they, really? All they accomplished was to lose the respect and loyalty of a fine officer, his peers and subordinates. Pretty stupid, weren't they? By the way, would you please analyze the last five reprimands *you* passed out? Did they benefit the recipients *and* the organization? How do you know?

One company commander was hated and detested by his peers and his subordinates because of this system: He had a white spot painted on the floor in front of his desk. As he went through the day searching for "offenders" he would identify them and bark, "I'll see you on the spot at (time)!" When the man would report to his office, the company commander would require him to stand at attention on the "spot" while he berated and degraded him. After several minutes of demonstrating his "leadership," he would then dismiss the man. He completely fooled his superiors, who felt he was running a tight outfit! It was a common prediction among subordinates and peers that, if combat came, he would stand a good chance of coming into contact with a "friendly" bullet.

Where do you stand in the *reprimand* department these days?

SELF-ANALYSIS

Recall the last several reprimands you have administered. Did they result in a benefit to: (1) the organization (2) the subordinate offender and (3) his boss (you)? If the answers to these questions are in any way negative, you are guilty of incurring this self-inflicted wound.

HEAL THE WOUND

This formula consists of advance use of the above diagnosis. When you consider administering a reprimand when something has gone wrong, ask yourself the questions: Has the individual already reprimanded himself because he knows that the incident itself is *below* the standards that he sets for himself, and below the standards which I have set for the organization as a whole? Will the reprimand that I am planning benefit the organization, the offender, and me as his boss? If the answer to the first question is *Yes,* and/or the answer to the second question is *No,* you are better off *not* to administer the reprimand.

the

QUICK-to-CRITICIZE–
SLOW-to-PRAISE BOSS

We now come to the Quick-to-Criticize—Slow-to-Praise Boss. A few paragraphs will expose this fellow, plus several measures of well-earned contempt. He almost never gives out a compliment, and he strikes like a rattlesnake when he thinks anything is done poorly.

Some of these bosses base their attitudes on some fallacious notion, dreamed up long ago and propagated by ignorance, that a good subordinate neither deserves nor expects praise when he does a good job. Whoever thinks that, is disagreeing with some very basic psychology, and he is very wrong. A human being (and that's what a subordinate is, believe it or not) has basic needs, and among these is the need to feel that his boss approves of his work.

I'm not even saying you must speak or write words of commendation to your people. All I am saying is that you must *communicate* to them, in the way you *send* best and the way they *receive* best, your approval or disapproval of what they are doing. There are few feelings in life worse than that uncertain, insecure, and anxious feeling of not knowing whether your on-the-job performance meets with your boss's approval or not. Or have you forgotten that feeling? If you have, I am sure that your subordinates have not!

An ancient Indian proverb states: "Work without hope draws nectar in a sieve, and hope without an object cannot live." One of the ablest civilian executives I know is involved in making plans to retire and leave an organization he loves—one to which he has devoted twenty years of fine service—because his immediate superior for three years has not given him one slight indication of approval or appreciation of his efforts.

To make it even worse, the subordinate has virtually carried his superior during that time. The boss has never taken an official action, gone to an important conference, or signed an important paper without first draining the knowledge and judgment—"picking the brains"—of his subordinate. He has relied on him in every way possible, including calling him in on weekends and refusing to let him take vacations. I tried to convince him to stay on, that his loyalty should be to his organization and not to his stumble-bum of a boss (who, by the way, was a graduate of a famous executive development course). My counsel fell on deaf ears, ears controlled by the brain of a sad and disappointed man.

You say this is a rare case. I say it is not. Of the hundreds and hundreds of bosses and subordinates I have interviewed, this situation has come up over and over and over again. And this type of stupidity on the part of the boss does not seem to correlate in any way with his other strong or weak points. Incredible as it may seem, one of the bosses who is guilty of this sin is a Ph.D. and ex-professor of personnel administration at a leading university, now a "successful executive" by conventional standards. This offender once asked his office manager to design a layout for their immediate group's new offices. The office manager welcomed the task, spent the entire weekend in making a detailed plan, and came to the office optimistically on Monday morning, enthusiastic and eager to show his plan to his boss. He walked in to his office with his layout sketches in his hand and announced to his boss that he was all set and ready to go. His boss remarked, "Oh, you can forget about that. I laid out my own design over the weekend. Here it is. Put it into effect immediately."

The subordinate boss told me about the incident the same day. He was completely and thoroughly depressed and dejected. He ended by saying, "Chuck, what's the use of even trying?" I tried to convince him that many brilliant men had stupid ways and stupid days. This was hardly helpful, for it did nothing to satisfy his basic needs.

In each of these true stories, the boss was not only slow to praise, but he was also quick to criticize his subordinates whenever anything went wrong. They saw their service with him as primarily consisting of opportunities for reprimand, rather than as opportunities for accomplishment. The result was that they did as little as possible, not wanting to risk the possibility of getting the reprimands.

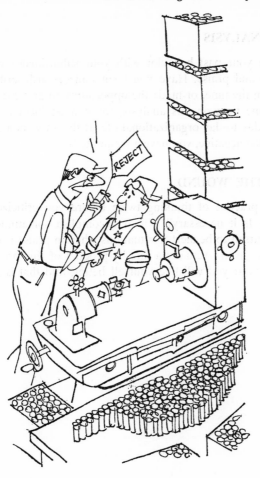

I hope these true stories have jolted you, not only into sympathizing with the subordinates involved, for you may have been treated similarly on occasion, but also into wondering how *you* are doing in this department of executive behavior. Now, I did *not* say you should go around patting everyone on the back. I stated that there are few feelings in life worse than the uncertain, insecure, and anxious feelings of not knowing whether or not your on-the-job performance meets with your boss's approval.

SELF-ANALYSIS

Examine your past behavior with your subordinates in terms of criticism and praise. Have you been unnecessarily critical? Have you taken the time, or made the opportunity to give earned praise? Take some time on this analysis, for it must involve many incidents in day-to-day organizational life. If the answers are even partially in the negative, you have a wound to heal.

HEAL THE WOUND

Make a practice of thinking twice before you criticize, and ask yourself: Is it necessary? Will it accomplish something positive? Train yourself to be alert to situations wherein praise is earned and should be given. Actually a fine by-product of this procedure will come to you: you will like yourself better, and that is a bonus in itself!

the

BOSS WHO LEANS
on the CRUTCH of AUTHORITY

This wound needs very little explanation, for it depicts the
"leader" who uses his military rank or civilian authority as a substitute for personal leadership. He really doesn't need to be a
leader. He can fire or courtmartial people if they don't obey him,
so why should he bother to demonstrate any genuine leadership?
This man may even often complain: "I don't have enough authority to get the job done." Actually, he has all the authority he needs.
He has enough authority to keep his people anxious and insecure,
to exploit them or burn them out, then take the credit and go on
his way. His authority to mistreat subordinates is unlimited, and if
he is clever his own boss will never find it out. You have worked
many times for this boss who leans so heavily on his *crutch of authority*. Do your subordinates think your prosthetic attachment is
in danger of wearing out?

On many occasions at the U.S. Army Management School, I
heard General Lucian Truscott, the late famed World War II
leader, reflect on observed leadership throughout his long years of
Army service. In his talks he stated that one of the two most common failings of leaders of all ranks was the use of the threat of
punishment as a substitute for true leadership. I agree with him,
and warn my non-military readers that they, as civilian and industrial bosses, have just as much power to punish as military bosses
do. Research indicates they misuse it as much as or more than
their military counterparts do! (For the second most prevalent
leadership failure observed by General Truscott, see page 191, The
Breathe-Down-their-Necks Boss.)

SELF-ANALYSIS

In this diagnosis you must determine the degree to which you are
using *authority* rather than persuasion and leadership, to get the

job done. This requires you to examine your past and present behavior rather carefully in order to arrive at valid findings and conclusions. It has been said, and I think quite accurately, that the best leaders and executives—that is, the most effective ones—rely very little on their authority to get things done; rather, their subordinates, through their respect for their boss and their organization, respond best to the situation as they see it, and to the requests and suggestions of their boss. Therefore, if you find that you are relying more than *very little* upon your vested authority to get the job done, you are a Boss Who Leans on the Crutch of Authority.

HEAL THE WOUND

Having made your diagnosis and finding yourself wanting in this department, the next step is to reduce your reliance upon authority and to increase your reliance upon persuasion and leadership. You may feel uncertain and insecure as you set your crutch aside, and you may wish to do it gradually in the same manner as the patient recovering from a broken leg learns to walk without his crutch. This is understandable and permissible, as long as you get rid of it eventually. And, in the words of an advertising slogan of some years ago, "If eventually, why not now?"

SUGGESTIONS FOR FURTHER READING

Tead, Ordway, "Personal Power and Authority in Administration," *The Art of Administration.* New York, McGraw-Hill, 1951, Chap. 8, pp. 116–132.

the

BOSS WHO DISAPPROVES
in WRITING

This one will make your blood boil in a hurry. Please think of the last time you sent your boss a carefully prepared written proposal which you had spent many hours or days thinking about and working on. Remember, if you will, when the next thing you saw or heard about it was when you found it in your In-basket with a short, *written* disapproval on it! Conjure, if you can, the emotions you experienced at that moment. You were simultaneously hurt and furious. *Hurt* that your boss was not even courteous enough to call you in and discuss it with you before he made his decision, and *furious* because he took the cowardly way out—he didn't even have the guts to discuss it with you.

Now for the acid test question: When was the last time *you* were the guy without the guts, the boss who penned the written disapproval? And if you felt you couldn't afford to take the time to discuss it with your subordinate—brother, there isn't a psychologist in the country who wouldn't say you couldn't afford *not* to take the time if you valued the future services of that subordinate.

I would like to pass along to you a system to use on *your* boss in case he is prone to misbehave in the same manner. One of the ablest executives I know has used this system most successfully with the succession of bosses he has had over him. He does not submit a proposal in writing until he has attempted to sell his ideas with the *spoken* word. Further, he presents his proposals in such a manner that they neither invite nor risk a disapproving decision in the early discussion stages. In effect, he sells his proposals like a good life insurance salesman sells life insurance—the prospect is sold before the application (or staff study) appears on the client's (boss') desk! I recommend this procedure and add one footnote. By this procedure the subordinate has improved the effectiveness of his boss! How about that?

SELF-ANALYSIS

Reflect on the last several proposals you have received in writing from your subordinates, particularly those which you have disapproved. Did you call your subordinate in and point out the good points of the proposal and then explain carefully why you were *not* adopting the proposal? Or did you disapprove it in writing and return the paper to him without a face-to-face discussion. If the answer to the latter question is in the affirmative, you are a Boss Who Disapproves in Writing.

HEAL THE WOUND

The answer to this one is obvious. You must find the time (and the courage if this has been your problem) to call your subordinates in to explain your non-acceptance of their proposals. And while you are at it you will earn some very fine by-products if you will also call them in and inform them face-to-face when you accept and approve their proposals.

the

HAPPY-BIRTHDAY BOSS

The Happy-Birthday Boss has read or heard somewhere that it is a mark of good leadership to send a birthday greeting to each of his subordinates on their individual birthday anniversaries, and decided to adopt this good leadership procedure. And he *does* adopt it, and install it, and implement it—without one thought to the psychology involved in his own particular situation and his normal relationships with his subordinates. You can be sure he is now unknowingly suffering from this self-inflicted wound. A few actual cases in point will illustrate this much better than theoretical discussion.

One senior executive gets around in his organization a great deal and meets and sees several echelons of subordinates quite frequently, knows them by name, and is quite cordial with them. Some time ago he heard about the happy-birthday letter and decided to adopt and implement the idea. He had, and still has, a very efficient secretary and front office staff. He wrote the first few letters, had them typed, and signed them personally. Then his secretary and office manager got a bright idea. They developed an all-purpose happy-birthday letter which could be neatly multilithed and signed by a rubber-stamp signature which the boss' secretary kept for emergency use in his absence.

The first time they showed him the finished product it was a particularly busy day, and he permitted it to be done only with some reluctance. That was the last such letter he ever saw. His secretary and office manager now have the function completely managed. They maintain the tickler file on birthdates and keep a supply of the stereotyped all-purpose letter on hand; they address them, sign them with the rubber stamp, and turn them out with machine-like precision.

Since then, many an individual employee has met and chatted with the boss on his rounds on or about the same day he had received his written birthday greeting. Has the boss mentioned the anniversary? Of course not. He doesn't even know about the happy day. For a while the subordinates were puzzled about this, but not for long. There are no secrets in the office grapevine, as we see in the chapter about the Boss Who Tries to Starve the Grapevine. The actual system employed was shortly known throughout the organization and is regarded with derision and contempt. His annual greeting received by a subordinate (sent to his office to save postage) is the occasion for much laughter and scorn. The sad part of all this is that it has lowered the boss in the eyes of his subordinates, who respected him highly before he adopted this "good leadership" practice.

Another case in point. The chief executive in a small organization used a happy-birthday letter, which he signed personally and dispatched to his principal subordinate executives. I was visiting one of those executives at his office the day he received his greeting. It made him feel pretty good, for lately he had been having difficulties with his boss, having been treated quite unfairly by him several times.

Shortly after receiving the letter and having been encouraged by it, he met his boss in the hallway. He expected to hear the greeting repeated and, when it was not, started to thank his boss anyway for the letter. Before he could do this, his boss found fault with him in the presence of his own subordinates. When it was over, he returned to his office where I was waiting, jerked the letter from his desk, showed it to me, recounted the hallway incident, and tore the letter into little pieces as he simultaneously gritted his teeth and said, "That son-of-a-bitch!" As this book approaches publication date, I have just been informed of another incident which bears describing here. A senior executive that I know recently received his happy-birthday letter from his boss—*Unsigned!* You can imagine the warmth and joy this brought to his heart, and lest you be mislead by this, the anger and contempt which it actually aroused in him. Since he is also a fine, charitable gentleman, he also had a feeling of sympathy for the poor simpleton of a boss who used the system.

I hasten to state that I am not against happy-birthday letters. I *do* strongly recommend against the blind or inept use of them, for they can do much more harm than good to an organization and to the individuals in it, and to the boss of that organization. Do I intend to give you specifics on when to use them and when not to use them? I do not. You would be insulted if I did. However, I do suggest that you analyze the general idea in terms of the specific situation from the point of view of the recipient of the letter; you should then not have great difficulty in arriving at a calculated attitude on the matter, rather than doing it by default as it is so often

done. I should close with the statement that many executives use the happy-birthday letter quite successfully, but then, they know what they are doing. Where do *you* fit in here?

SELF-ANALYSIS

Do you now use or are you contemplating the use of happy-birth-day letters to your subordinates? If so, have you taken every possible precaution to prevent the type of situations described in this chapter? If not, you are a Happy-Birthday Boss.

HEAL THE WOUND

The best example that I have ever seen of the happy-birthday letter system was used by a boss who insisted that each letter cross his desk for signature and with it, some current information about the addressee. The boss then, in a matter of seconds, added something to the letter in his own longhand and carried with him either a mental or written list of the current letters so that he could comment in person on the subject if he had occasion (or better yet, made the occasion) to see that employee in the near future. I commend this system to your consideration.

the

BRAINWASHER BOSS

How many times have you been present at a meeting of subordinates, chairmanned by their immediate superior, called for the purpose of solving a problem and/or selecting the best of several alternative solutions, at which the chairman made his views known at the start of, or early in the meeting? I know you'll agree that what happened afterward and the product of the meeting was more damaging than useful. You've been present at several meetings like this. *How often were you the chairman?*

How many times has this happened to you? After careful and thorough analysis and research you gave your boss the benefits of it, along with your comments and recommendations. He did not choose the alternative you recommended but decided to adopt another. This was his privilege and duty as a boss. Then he explained his reasoning to you, which was also good boss procedure. Then he did something every subordinate despises: he tried to force you to agree with him that he had made the right decision—and that you had made the wrong recommendation. And you not only resented this tactic bitterly, but you had the strongest urge to answer his question, "Don't you agree with me?" with the answer, "Hell, no, I don't agree with you. If I did, I would have recommended that alternative in the first place! I still think I am right and you are wrong." You've been caught in this trap many times; I know. How many times were you the trapper?

The first instance, I like to call *The Structured Conference;* the chairman-boss (either by calculation or default—probably the latter) by his actions had a tremendous impact upon the conference and its products. But letting his own views be known on how the problem should be solved, he divided his subordinates into three groups: (1) the *yes men,* who exist in any organization, not merely in Hollywood (2) the *half-honest men,* who will vote either way, depending upon the pressure, when it comes time to stand up and be counted (3) the *honest men,* who place a high value upon

131

their intellectual integrity. Having made this division, the boss then does not have a conference of *individuals,* he has a battle of *factions,* the outcome of which is never very much in doubt. After some backing and filling, the *half-honest men* side with the *yes men* who sided with the boss in the first place, and the conference is adjourned by the boss with the following line-up: the *honest men* clearly in his disfavor, with the *yes men* approving of their own actions by rationalization, and with the *half-honest men* alter-

nately approving and detesting themselves for their actions. Every time you are chairman at such a conference, you incur a very ugly self-inflicted wound.

In the second conference, the handcuffed subordinate walked out of his boss' office a bitter and resentful man. He should have been told that he had done a good job on the study, that his efforts were appreciated, but that his boss was taking an action different from that recommended *because he was assigning differing values to the critical elements of the problem, and explaining why.* This would have been an honest statement of fact, and it would have met the needs of the situation. Instead, the boss chose to try to deprive his subordinate of his intellectual integrity, and the conference had a negative impact on both individuals. If you have conducted such a conference, you have inflicted a serious wound upon your subordinate.

Another important managerial factor is involved here, and that is the question of how to get the most from your subordinates (and from yourself) in the conduct of a problem-solving conference. Many researchers feel, and I have seen this happen time after time, that the conference chairman should spend *all* his time getting the most from the conferees, rather than making his own views known (and trying to sell them) for a solution to the problem. It is a rare executive who can do both, for to do both demands a skill which is rarely found, both from a personal capability and because of the negative effects described in the preceding third paragraph. You may find this difficult to accept, but why not give it a chance?

SELF-ANALYSIS

Apply the yardsticks described in this chapter to your day-to-day activities, by reflecting upon several recent problem-solving conferences you chaired, and upon several instances in which you did not adopt the recommendations of your subordinates? Did you behave as did the bosses described in the two instances? Did you spend your time making input to the problem-solving rather than devoting your time to getting the most from your subordinates? If the answer to any of these questions is in the affirmative, you are a Brainwasher Boss.

HEAL THE WOUND

This will be difficult, for you must not only change your behavior, you must convince your subordinates that you are sincere in doing so. This will cause consternation among your *yes men;* the *half-honest men* will secretly feel better but worry about past guilt; and your *honest men,* having been wounded by you many times, will be very skeptical and will withhold judgment until you have convinced them. During the first few days and weeks of your changed behavior, you must be constantly on the alert and guard against an unwitting reversion to your former type. However, many executives before you have seen the light, taken this action, and been successful. Why not join the ever-growing crowd?

the

SECRET-PERFORMANCE-
APPRAISAL BOSS

How did you feel the last time your superior(s) prepared an efficiency, performance or merit rating on you and sent it on without discussing it with you? You felt that he was a mental coward who didn't have the guts to face you with an unfair rating, didn't you? Of course you did, and you were justified in feeling that way, whether or not the rating was in fact unfair. But how many times have *you* been the man without the guts? That's a little different, isn't it? You were too busy to show the rating to the man (it would have probably taken all of ten minutes). Besides, you gave the man as good a rating as you got last time—you couldn't give him a higher rating than you had received—you're his superior! If these answers are in your mouth, swallow them! Besides, you don't really believe them, do you?

The above words were written in the original *wounds* article in 1959, and were also included in the lecture developed at that time. From the start, the response from my readers/listeners was at the emotional level, for it was a subject on which all had *gut-level* feelings. I know of no act of the superior-subordinate relationship which is more important, more difficult, and more fraught with human emotion on the part of each than the preparation of a written evaluation of the subordinate by his boss. This is true because the task in itself is a function of a highly inexact science when performed at its best, and at its worst it is an invitation for the inadequate and ineffective superior to consciously or unconsciously compensate for his shortcomings by finding fault with his subordinates, or, more precisely, attributing the impact of his shortcomings to those subordinates.

Thorough treatment of this one subject alone would require more space than is devoted to this entire book, and such is not attempted here. The development and administration of performance appraisal programs is extremely difficult. (By performance appraisals I mean all individual written evaluations of subordinates by superiors, from military efficiency ratings to merit or performance ratings in business and industry.) The most disturbing aspect of this problem is that even though the psychology of the situation is generally agreed upon, different large organizations take differing views of that psychology, and adopt exactly opposite policies. Some require or encourage the superior to show the written performance appraisal to the subordinate, and to discuss it with him, while other large organizations either prevent the superior from showing the appraisal to the subordinate or do not encourage the act. And on this matter, it is no defense to say that the policy, whichever it is, is better for any particular organization because of its uniqueness. This just can not be true, for the human factors and reactions involved are the same in *any* organization.

For many years it was considered a hallmark of fine leadership for the superior to show the performance appraisal to the subordinate to whom it meant so much, and to discuss it with him. The reaction to the superior who did not show the rating to his subordinate differed, however there was a common pattern; a belief that he did not have the guts to face the subordinate with the rating. It was as simple as that. This view prevailed as long as it was optional on the part of the superior whether or not he showed the rating to his subordinate. When a boss discontinued this practice, or a new boss declined to do it, there was the inevitable dilution of the superior-subordinate relationship which occurred in the situation wherein one man played God in secret with another man's career, with the latter being helpless to do anything about it. And this dilution occurred even in those cases where it was later revealed that the written rating was in fact complimentary to the subordinate; it was caused by the basic psychology of the situation.

Some time ago I had occasion to conduct a study of the performance rating practices in business and industry. My study indicated that here also was a highly inexact science and a not-well-developed state of the art, with wide variations in forms, frequency, and purpose. One company, for example, used two ratings; one open for salary administration and one secret for career management. The executive who explained it to me made quite a point of stating that they didn't mind ratings which treated the truth loosely for salary administration, but that the only way they could hope for an unvarnished rating for career management, including the selection of executives at all levels, was to have these ratings prepared secretly and kept that way. The stark truth of what he was saying is that it is too much to ask *any* executive or superior to prepare a truthful and factual evaluation of a subordinate with the knowledge that he himself must show the rating to the subordinate and be prepared to discuss it with him, defending it and changing it if the discussion makes such action advisable! If this is true, it is a sad commentary on today's executive, and is further proof of his relative shortcomings, compared with his counterpart of several decades ago.

I would be remiss if I did not pay tribute to a significant number of unsung heroes who have made a practice of showing their ratings to the subordinates concerned, both in the military and in business and industry. They and their subordinates, and their organizations, have been the direct beneficiaries of this courageous practice.

There is much written on this subject in the form of chapters in books on personnel management and numerous articles in personnel magazines. Rather than referring to or quoting from them I suggest that you be guided by the obvious psychology of the subject, and let your conscience, sense of fair play, and good common sense be your guide. Further, I suggest that you seriously consider the use of "peer" ratings and also give considerable thought to the benefits from a system that includes the preparation of ratings by subordinates of their bosses! Subordinates evaluate and rate their bosses every day of their lives. Why not capitalize on this most valuable research data? If you do, you may very likely create the finest executive development and selection system in history. If you do so, I recommend using the rating scale outlined in the Preface to this book.

Whatever you do, I can assure you that you will never be a full-fledged executive, boss, leader, commander or manager unless you communicate, in one way or another, quite clearly to your subordinates your evaluation of their performance and of them as individuals with a future. You must also insure that *your written appraisals coincide with those communications*. I know of no more important facet of the superior-subordinate relationship than the appraisal process. When done well, it is a process which is of tremendous value to the individual, the superior, and the organization. When it is done poorly, all three suffer immeasurably.

How do *you* score on this measurement of leadership? (Don't trust your opinion only on this, check with your peers and subordinates in a way you can depend on for validity.)

SELF-ANALYSIS

Reflect upon the two types of performance appraisals you typically render on your subordinates: the periodic evaluation and your day-to-day communications, written and otherwise, which express your evaluation of the performance of your subordinates. If it is not expressly prohibited by organization regulation, have you made it a practice to show the performance appraisal to your subordinates? In your day-to-day activities, are your actions such that they clearly communicate to your subordinates how you are appraising their efforts? If the answer to either of these questions is in the negative, you are a Secret-Performance-Appraisal Boss.

HEAL THE WOUND

Your prescription is more easily stated than applied. However, many executives are using it successfully. When you have completed your written performance appraisals, show them to your subordinates in a calm and relaxed atmosphere, sincerely inviting discussion of the contents of the document. The opposite of this is to fling it at them and to dare them to talk you out of any of it. And this has happened many times. You must also make it clear that the document is in draft form as far as you are concerned, and can be changed. On the second type of appraisal, that is your day-to-day communication, make sure that you actually do communicate your evaluations of your subordinate's performance, both positive and negative. In this way, your subordinates would seldom be in doubt about their impression of your evaluation of their performance.

the

MANIPULATOR BOSS

The Manipulator Boss is the man who feels he can accomplish more by motivating his subordinates through the use of various insincere and dishonest methods and techniques, all operated behind a façade of apparent sincerity. These methods and techniques range all the way from compliments he does not really mean, moods or attitudes which he feigns instead of feeling, such as anger and disappointment to outright lies and dishonest acts. Somewhere along the line he has acquired a smattering of psychology, and then he becomes a perfect example of the old saying that a little knowledge is a dangerous thing. He sees himself and his people as a "manager and marionette" combination, with himself pulling the strings and his subordinates dancing on the end of them. The more he practices these tactics, the more he believes he is doing it very effectively and very subtly, when actually his frequent use of manipulative techniques makes it crystal clear to all concerned just what he is doing, or trying to do.

I am the proud father of a fourteen-year-old daughter. One of the things I noticed about her well before she was three years old was her intuitive awareness of those of our visitors who were being nice to her because they liked children, and of those who were making conventional gestures toward her just to be polite. There was no doubt whatsoever in her mind as to who was sincere and who was not. I have never forgotten this. I am also the owner of a loveable little dachshund, eight years old. While by definition she may be a "dumb animal" (her owners think she is anything but that), she has always been able to separate dog-lovers from the dog-dislikers when they have come to our home, even though their outward behavior has been very similar. Her behavior at times in this regard is so indicative that she has made positive diagnoses that were almost embarrassing.

I am sure that you have been on the receiving end of manipulative actions of one or more bosses along the way, and that you became furious when you realized what was going on. I am also sure that many of you have succumbed to the desire to try your hand at the same techniques and even now think you have had some success at it. My question is, if you can't fool a dog, and you can't fool a child, what in the world makes you think you can fool grown-up people?

Several years ago, one of the required courses in the first year of the Master in Business Administration (MBA) program at the Harvard Graduate School of Business Administration was called "Administrative Practices." Its general purpose, as stated in the school catalogue, was "to provide each student with an opportunity to develop useful and responsible ways of thinking about the human and social realities in business organizations." It was a splendid course which provided a foundation for many students upon which to build future knowledge and awareness of human factors in organizational situations. It had a great hazard, however, which I observed over and over again when I took the course at an age fifteen years older than the average student's. The hard-working and astute professors, in trying to bring about an awareness of the benefits of participation in many aspects of job activities, were often rewarded on examination papers with, "Make your subordinates think *your* idea was *their* idea, and then everything will be swell and they will really try to make it work." This was a complete misunderstanding on the part of the student; who would eventually become the Manipulator Boss.

A well-known businessman turned researcher, lecturer and author, Mr. Cameron Hawley, has expressed himself most forcibly on this same point, and has depicted an excellent example to prove his point in his article, "The Quality of Leadership," when he states:

I suggest that a lot of our top-level executives are kidding themselves about how cleverly they're handling the younger men under them. At a conference of corporation presidents I attended not too long ago, one of them held forth at considerable length on how he never openly proposed any idea of his own but always worked things around so that one of his younger men thought that it was *his* idea. Later that day, leaving the very building where we'd had our meeting, I picked up a young man who had been attending another conference there. By coincidence, he happened to be a junior executive in that same corporation. Later, we stopped to have a drink, and in the course of chatting about his company, I brought up the subject of his president. He chuckled and said, "Well, right now I think he's a wonderful fellow. You see, I've won three pools on him lately." I said, "What do you mean—a pool on him?" And he said, "Well, every time we have a meeting we always make a pool on which one of us he's picked that day to have *his* idea." Good young men don't want that kind of manipulated monkey business—they want *leadership*.[1]

I agree with Mr. Hawley. However, lest his speaker give the wrong impression, he didn't think his boss was a wonderful fellow. Actually he thought he was stupid. And you can be sure that your subordinates think nothing nicer than that of you if you are practicing the fine art of manipulation. I suggest that you choose some other methods, preferably some with the word "sincerity" related to them.

[1] *Personnel,* American Management Association (May–June 1960), p. 15.

SELF-ANALYSIS

This one requires highly effective introspection on your part in which you must ask yourself to examine your past activities to determine whether your dealings with your subordinates have been completely sincere, or whether you have been guilty of manipulating your subordinates. I have no mechanical aid for you on this, but if you will combine your efforts to look backward with a very objective analysis of your intent during the instance involved, you should be able to answer this question.

HEAL THE WOUND

This will be a little easier than the diagnosis. What it requires is a frame of mind and an alertness as you plan your day-to-day activities and conferences to assure that you are frank and straightforward with your subordinates and that your actions are devoid of insincerity. If you have actually been in the habit of manipulating your subordinates, you must then develop a pattern of action which will meet the needs of the situation without insincerity. You can do it, and you will be glad that you did.

the

NO-POPULARITY-CONTEST BOSS

This boss will get short treatment here, for that is all he deserves. I am talking about the boss who goes around explaining his behavior by the oft-repeated remark, "I'm not running a popularity contest." Ostensibly he is communicating that he has been given a job to do, and he intends to get it done, even if he must antagonize some people—particularly subordinates—in the process of getting that job done. He also purports to indicate that the lot of a boss is a lonely one, and that popularity and effectiveness are two incompatible attributes.

If all this were true, we could tolerate this man. Certainly, there are no doubt some rare cases where the situation justifies the statement. However, I fear the vast majority of cases would not stand the test of thorough research. Instead, the research is more likely to reveal (unmask might be a better word) the inadequate executive who is outwardly regretting that he cannot run a popularity contest while he is inwardly sweeping his deficient leadership under a figurative rug.

A case in point. A new boss took over an organization. He brought with him many strong feelings, along with a large number of biases and prejudices, as to how the organization should operate. (He did not *own* the organization—he merely worked for it, like all the other members of it.) He immediately started announcing *decision* after decision, which were not decisions at all, but changes which he wanted made to get the organization to resemble the image of his last organization. Each time he did announce a change, he followed his announcement with a statement to the effect that he expected the change to be unpopular, but that he was a man who had to get a job done, and that "I'm not running a popularity contest." This was intended to explain and justify everything. All it accomplished, however, was to antagonize the other members of the organization. They saw no merit in his changes, but identified them accurately as his biased and prejudiced efforts to re-mold his new organization into the image of the last organization he had bossed. One thing was certain. He certainly was *not* running a popularity contest. In fact, he became very unpopular, but not for the reasons he espoused.

The executive who uses this expression would do well to in-

dulge in some careful soul-searching to evaluate his own situation. For those of you who honestly feel you can and should make the remark about not running a popularity contest, I suggest you choose some other way of describing your situation, lest you be tarred with the same brush that perceptive subordinates and peers use in distinguishing the type of boss we are criticizing here.

SELF-ANALYSIS

Try to recall the last several decisions which you made on controversial subjects, the very nature of which meant that some of your subordinates would be pleased to hear of your decision; others would be disappointed because it meant it had gone against their recommendations and/or their interests. Recall, if you will, whether in the course of announcing your decision or explaining it afterward you used the expression, "I'm not running a popularity contest." And even if you did not use this expression, did you communicate something of the sort? If you did, you are probably a No-Popularity-Contest Boss.

HEAL THE WOUND

Recognize that this type of a remark and attitude is a liability rather than an asset to you and omit it from your explanations of your decisions. Stick to the merits of those decisions and the rationale behind them.

the

HOW-TO-DO-IT BOSS

We can handle this man in a hurry. You and I sin often on this one. We have known and believed for years that "you tell a man what to do but you don't tell him how to do it." And then you and I tell him *how* to do it! We should! We're smarter than he is. We have higher rank or position. We must be smarter. Perhaps we are, but not at the actual performance of our subordinate's work.

This sin can extend to entire elements of the various echelons of command and/or administration which many large organizations have today. I know of a major higher echelon of a large corporation which has actually *directed* the types of organizations which their subordinate establishments will use. In fact, they have furnished them with standard organizational and functional charts to use! In effect, the higher office has told the lower office, "Don't use brains. Don't use organizational science. Don't use local know-how. Don't consider the uniqueness of your local situation (although any student of business administration would flunk an exam in which he did not!). Don't use anything—*use our chart!*

I'd better stop on this one before I become too emotional or too sarcastic. My research question to you is, "When was the last time you told a subordinate *how* to do something?"

Please don't misunderstand me on this one. I am *not* talking about situations where a prescribed method is part of the job, such as Frederick W. Taylor's "science of shovelling" and pig-iron handling, or the scientific bricklaying methods developed by Gilbreth wherein detailed and exhaustive study developed the one best way to perform specific functions. Even here, I'm sure these two great men would have welcomed suggestions for further improvement in methods on the functions performed.

What I *am* talking about is what seems to be a basic need on the part of human beings for latitude of decision on their part as to exactly *how* they will carry out the desires and orders of their bosses. I will leave to others the task of defining this need psycho-

146

logically, but any parent knows it begins at the young age of two or three when an infant takes pride in announcing, "I did it all by myself!"; or upon being told to do something, accepts the task, and then states emphatically that, "I want to do it all by myself!" It is my belief that the desire never leaves the infant and that it grows

in intensity as he grows older and later becomes an adult with a boss.

On the subjective side of yourself, the boss who wants things done efficiently, you can rest assured that the end result will be a better one if the subordinate is permitted latitude in the choice of method of accomplishing tasks or missions, whether they be physical or administrative in nature. If this is so, both the boss and the bossed will be happy. Why not give it a try?

SELF-ANALYSIS

Reflect upon your recent discussions with your subordinates. The question is simple. In telling them *what* to do have you also told them, or suggested to them, how to do it? If so, you have incurred your self-inflicted wound.

HEAL THE WOUND

Make a conscious effort from this day forward to refrain from telling your subordinates *how* they should accomplish the things that you tell them to do. At the very most, and you must handle this very carefully, you may suggest that they *consider* one or more alternative methods, but you must make it very clear, with complete sincerity, that they are in no way obligated to adopt those methods. If you do this you will soon become the happy beneficiary of ingenuity and creativity that you never dreamed existed in your organization.

the

BOSS WHO ALLOCATES
WORK UNFAIRLY

This boss is the executive whose allocation of work * to his subordinates results in an unfair distribution of the workload of the organization. He makes this unbalanced distribution either by calculation or default—usually the latter. He is often blissfully unaware that the imbalance exists.

There are few things that will keep team members in a constant, smouldering turmoil more than the knowledge that the work of the team or organization is not being shared evenly by its members. And if it is in fact true, the situation usually tends to divide the individuals into three groups, insofar as their attitudes toward the situation are concerned:

1. The members who have *more* than their fair share of the work to do.
2. The members who have *less* than their fair share of the work.
3. The members who have a fair share of the work.

The actions of these three groups tend to propagate the situation, once the boss brings it into being. The "overworked" members resent the situation, particularly the boss whose fault it is, and further resent the other two groups who do nothing to alleviate the situation. The "underworked" members, instead of asking for more work, actively or passively try to give the impression that they are *not* underworked, rather that they have been given a fair share of the work. The third group, which has a fair allocation of the work, is aware of the situation, but is primarily concerned with insuring their own status quo, often making conscious efforts to avoid receiving work that would result in an increase in their workload.

These reactions in this unfortunate situation make the role of

* My use of the word "work" here includes all the measurements of work which employees use to assess the work distribution situation, such as quantity, degree of difficulty of the work, and relative importance.

the boss a very critical one. In fact, he is the *critical variable,* the only one who can change the situation by his own behavior. Unless he acts, the bad situation will stay bad, or even get worse. It certainly will not improve.

Situations involving the unfair allocation of work are very prevalent, particularly in administrative organizations where measurement of workloads is not as precise as in piecework situations. In the minds of the people involved, however, the work is measured rather precisely, and all the peers involved have measured it to the extent necessary to cause the division into the three subgroups described.

The prevalence of these situations is so great that I have no doubt that it exists in well over half of all administrative work situations, and it is harmful to everyone. It is somewhat like parochialism, discussed in the chapter on the Parochial Boss, which is built into *all* organizations and can only be reduced by continuing combat waged by the boss. Any boss can be reasonably sure he is guilty unless he can state honestly that he is consciously making a competent effort to allocate the work fairly among his subordinates. My research question is, how do *you* rate in this department of executive behavior?

SELF-ANALYSIS

If you are going to avoid this self-inflicted wound, or heal it if you already bear it, you must stop and take an inventory of all the unfinished work which is now in the hands of your subordinates. This inventory must include not only what work is unfinished, but an accurate estimate of the amount of time it will take a specified number of people to complete it. Having figured this out, you must relate the work on hand to the manpower resources available to accomplish this work. This will enable you to see whether the work, as it stands at that point in time, has been unfairly allocated. If it is, you are a Boss Who Allocates Work Unfairly.

HEAL THE WOUND

Having performed your diagnosis, you can then adjust the situation by either re-allocating existing work to be accomplished, or by

keeping the situation in mind as you allocate work for the immediate future, assigning extra portions of work to the presently underworked group and refraining from assigning work to the presently
overworked group. As you begin this process I urge you with all the
sincerity at my command to make future assignments of work *in
the presence of* all the members of your management team, commenting on your reasons for doing it in terms of the existing work
loads they bear. Encourage responses to your actions before assigning the work at these conferences. You should describe the

work and give your subordinates the opportunity to volunteer for it.

SUGGESTIONS FOR FURTHER READING

Jaques, Elliott, *Measurement of Responsibility*. Cambridge, Massachusetts, Harvard University Press, 1956.

the

DON'T-LET-ME-
CATCH-YOU-THINKING BOSS

If this chapter could start off with the results of a survey of subordinates to determine what percent would place their bosses in this category, those statistics alone would satisfy the needs of this chapter. Unfortunately, as in so many areas of executive behavior, there are no statistics on the number of subordinates who feel with good reason that their bosses disapprove when they observe them spending time thinking. Here again, perceptions are involved. It seems to be a common practice for a supervisor at any level to assume that a subordinate who is motionless therefore is not doing his job; that if he is not shuffling papers, rushing from one office to another, or otherwise outwardly evidencing productivity, then he is at worst loafing on the job, and at best he is not being as productive as he might be if he were more active—that is, if he were making more motions.

In most organizations, an employee does not feel free to sit and think at his desk, or even to read a professional or scientific journal for the purpose of improving his on-the-job abilities. He does not feel free to do this because when he does so, his boss lets him know, directly or indirectly, that he disapproves of behavior that he considers to be loafing, malingering or "soldiering," as Taylor referred to it.[1] I will not ascribe any profound facets to this executive deficiency. Rather, I will state flatly that this boss has not acquired the degree of finesse in supervision which enables him to evaluate the overall performance of his subordinates, and to observe and to evaluate their individual behavior and actions within the context of that overall performance. In this instance, lack of finesse is a nice way of calling him stupid. This boss is easily fooled by the low-performance subordinate who has a high-performance ratio of paper-shuffling and the ability to look and act busy.

[1] Frederick W. Taylor, *Scientific Management.* (New York, Harper and Brothers, 1947), pp. 30–42.

153

This executive or supervisory deficiency is quickly detected by the subordinates, with results that you would expect. After those who can't stand him have transferred, those who can't stand him but can't arrange a transfer will adjust to the normal behavior

and begin the "systematic soldiering" that Taylor referred to. They do this, *not* because of any basic deficiencies of their own, but because of the shortcomings of their boss.

My research question here is; in what category do *your* subordinates fall, and what behavior of yours has caused them to fall into that category?

SELF-ANALYSIS

This diagnosis is a little easier than most. Answer this question: Do you get excited and disturbed when you see one of your subordinates motionless and in deep thought? Have you reprimanded your subordinates for being motionless lately? Or, worse still, have you marked them down on their performance appraisals for what you *thought* was loafing, without calling it to their attention so they could explain what they were doing? If you answer "yes" to any of these, you bear this wound.

HEAL THE WOUND

Let your employees know that you are aware that a significant portion of their work requires deep thought and analysis. Concurrently with this, of course, STOP reprimanding them for thinking in a motionless position!

the

WITCH-HUNTER BOSS

Some of the best-known wrong kinds of bosses are the quickest and most easily described. The Witch-Hunter Boss is one of these. When anything goes wrong, his first act is to try to pin the fault or blame on some subordinate, punish him, and publicize it. He just has to have a fall guy or whipping boy, and he often has them selected in advance of the event, or so it seems in the writhing, unhappy organization he heads.

There are several reasons for his behavior, most of which are psychological and stem in one way or another from basic personality defects. One additional reason, which does not fall into this category, is his belief or hope that by his act of offering up a sacrifice in the form of one of his subordinates, that he himself will be absolved of any blame by *his own* boss. In this man's organization, people walk in fear of making a mistake or error, and in so doing they either make more than the normal amount of each, or they take such detailed precautions to avoid them that very little work is accomplished. One thing is certain, the unwritten motto, "Don't stick your neck out" is omnipresent in their minds, and is their primary motivation, satisfying as it does the basic need of survival.

This boss has never read, or doesn't believe, that people do their best when they can operate in a climate or atmosphere of approval. Or he may have read it, believed it until the next crisis developed, and then quickly reverted to type and ruthlessly went through the process of selecting and offering up a subordinate in sacrifice, much in the same manner of the ancient tribal rites. With this man, the state of the art of leadership has not progressed beyond the tribal days.

A good example of this which illustrates the point in a military setting, but which has its thousands of business and industrial counterparts, was described in a movie about World War I entitled, *Paths of Glory*. With its setting in trench warfare, an impossible attack had been ordered by the commanding general, derived

156

from a general staff directive, on a heavily fortified objective known as the Beehive. The attack failed, as all but the general who ordered it felt that it would. When the commanding general was called to account for the failure by the senior officer of the general staff, the commanding general's solution was to order the regimental commander (Kirk Douglas in the movie) to order three company commanders to each select one scapegoat, to be courtmartialed for the failure of the regiment. This was done, and though they were intelligently and courageously defended by the regimental commander as defense counsel, the three were found guilty and executed, thereby expunging the "disgrace" of the attack that failed.

I am sure you have recoiled at the callous and cruel stupidity of the senior executives involved, and I am sure that you would like to think that nothing like this could happen in *your* organization. On the other hand, if you will reflect a bit, you will probably easily remember some very similar counterparts in your organizational life. In fact, you are a very lucky peson if you have not been the sacrificial lamb on at least a few occasions. My question is, when did *you* as a boss offer up *your* last sacrifice?

SELF-ANALYSIS

Reflect upon the last several times that something went wrong within your organization. Did you assume that someone made an honest error of judgment, and then go on to help him correct that error and look to the future? Or, did you first fix or pin the blame upon someone and scourge him publicly, and then order him to correct his error without any help from you? If your answer to the first question is in the negative, and/or the answer to the second is in the affirmative, then you are a Witch-Hunter Boss.

HEAL THE WOUND

Stop your ruthless sacrificial actions when something goes wrong —but, wait—that is not enough. If this is all you do, your people will merely think you have missed something. You will not have truly healed the wound until you have established an atmosphere of approval within your organization—one in which individuals go

about their daily efforts with the feeling that their efforts are generally appreciated and that honest mistakes will be regarded as

such. Only then will you be giving up your modern version of the
witch hunters of Salem of long ago.

SUGGESTIONS FOR FURTHER READING

McGregor, Douglas, *The Human Side of Enterprise*. New York, Mc-
Graw-Hill, 1960.

the

ONE-WAY-COMMUNICATION BOSS

The One-Way-Communication Boss believes, and acts accordingly, that there should be only a one-way street of communication between himself and his subordinates, and the traffic flow on that street should be from him to them, never the reverse. This is true whatever the method of communication, whether it be with the spoken or written word. With the spoken word, he calls in a subordinate, tells him what he wants done, and then tells him to go do it. If the subordinate tries to discuss the problem in order to do it better (or not do it at all, which may be desirable), the boss silences him with a glance or a gesture, and sends him on his way, often admonishing him to listen better or to adopt a "can-do" attitude.

This type of boss often avoids face-to-face discussion with his subordinates by writing them a multitude of memoranda containing directives which are annoying and frustrating to receive. The glaring weakness in all of this is that any problem or task benefits from discussion between the boss and the bossed for several reasons: (1) better understanding (2) the subordinate may already have solved the problem, or he may have a better approach to its solution (3) there may be valid reasons for not taking the action which the boss is directing, and last but probably even more important than the rest (4) the *acceptance* of the directive is enhanced by the discussion.

The last item often gets an angry response from the bosses —and there are thousands of them—who feel that acceptance of directives is full and automatic merely because of the *authority* of the boss; and that it is foolish and useless to consider this factor in exercising the functions of direction and supervision. This is another of the many false assumptions upon which conventional leadership has been based so long. By acceptance I do not mean that by the lack of it the subordinate will refuse to perform the tasks or comply with directives. He will do so, after a fashion, but

159

if he has not accepted the task in his heart and mind, he will not perform it nearly as well when the reverse is true. He will more likely do it in a minimum adequate fashion, just well enough to get it past the boss, for he would prefer to not perform it at all.

The intriguing aspect of the One-Way-Communication Boss is that he himself resents and resists the same type of treatment

when he is on the receiving end. You have no difficulty believing this, for you have so reacted. If this is so, why then do you feel *your own* subordinates have different feelings when *you* give them the one-way communication treatment?

SELF-ANALYSIS

Study your past written and spoken communications to your subordinates. Have any required or resulted in action by those subordinates without prior discussion with or comments from them? If the answer is yes, you most certainly have this self-inflicted wound. If you rationalize this and tell yourself it is merely because you give such good directions that they need no discussion, you are fooling no one but yourself—you are certainly not fooling your subordinates. If you wish to verify this finding, you can perhaps ask one of your peer bosses to research your subordinates on this subject, in a confidential manner. Your own direct research would be rather worthless since, if you *are* a One-Way-Communication Boss, your subordinates will not feel free to tell you.

HEAL THE WOUND

On your *written* communications, automatically add the note, "Let's discuss this before you act on it." Then, when your subordinate comes to see you about it, make it absolutely clear that you want his reactions and comments on the subject before he carries it out. With your *spoken* communications, begin with, "I'm about to give you a task, but I want your honest and frank reactions to the idea before you get to work on it." This definitive action is necessary therapy for this wound, for it is a deep one which has been festering a long time, and it will not respond to superficial medication.

the

RUNT-COMPLEX BOSS

The boss of relatively small physical stature who acquires or acquiesces to a "runt complex" has a serious wound which he may never discover, for he often appears to be rather unaware that he bears this complex. Here the physically small boss tries to compensate for his physical size by cutting others, particularly subordinates, down to his size by extreme methods directed at belittling them, humiliating them or at best casting them in an unfavorable light.

There are deep psychological bases for this behavior which need not be discussed here. Suffice it to say that it is not compulsion which causes the small-statured man to behave badly—it is rather a weakness to which many give in, but which others control quite adequately. The bad behavior has several common patterns. It is usually directed at individuals who are of significantly larger physical stature than the Runt-Complex Boss. In fact, the cruelty of his methods seems to vary in direct proportion to the margin of size difference which the other fellow enjoys. (Here the word "enjoy" is strictly a figure of speech.)

I have observed first-hand, and been on the receiving end of the behavior, of one runty superior who would never *stand* face-to-face with his larger subordinates. His customary procedure was to call his subordinates into his office where he sat like an autocratic pygmy behind a massive, oversize desk and issued his orders or dished out his cruel, degrading behavior. His authority, his seated position while his subordinates stood, and the massive desk seemed to compensate in his twisted mind for his lack of physical size, which he secretly regarded as a great weakness.

Take another Runt-Complex Boss as a case in point. Not only did he behave toward his *subordinates* in the manner just described, but the feeling was so strong within him that when his own boss approached him, he would maneuver himself never to be closer than six feet to him; they kept constantly in motion, some-

162

thing like a slow waltz. This same man often watched for his boss to turn his head as an opportunity to walk away from him, which he frequently did. Time after time his superiors discovered after minutes of talking while looking the other way, that the runt-complex subordinate was many yards away. In this way he not only got himself out of the physical comparison situation, but he was able to show his contempt for his larger boss in a way for which he

could never be punished; he could always state that he had thought that the conference had ended.

Those who are not of small physical stature stand a good chance of being on the receiving end of the runt-complex behavior, so these few lines can also serve a useful purpose for them, to help them guard against it, and to provide copy for reproducing and placing in the boss' in-basket. I do not guarantee this type of therapy. A man with a well-established runt complex has a wound that perhaps only psychotherapy can heal. But the in-basket shock treatment may help. If you use it, I need not suggest that you remain very anonymous. If you do not, you will find yourself being sought in the same manner as the infamous "strawberry hunt" in

The Caine Mutiny,[1] and you will find yourself being drawn and quartered in a manner that will make the Spanish Inquisition look like a parlor game.

The other side of this coin must be turned, or I shall be guilty of one-sided reporting. There are thousands of bosses of small physical stature who cope very well with the situation and are admired by their peers and their subordinates. Because of this they should be even more admired, for they have overcome some rather powerful stimulants toward bad executive behavior. This chapter is intended to point the finger at those who have not exercised that control, and it is further intended to help the guilty ones experience a moment of truth in the privacy of their own minds, and to do something about it. Remember, contrary to some rather widespread beliefs, it is never too late to change one's behavior, for behavior stems from attitudes, and attitudes *can* be changed, if one knows how to go about inducing that change.

One final thought. As you are well aware, there are intellectual runts as well as physical runts, and their behavior toward subordinates is often quite similar to that of their physical counterparts. If your subordinates are working for such a boss, you will find that a moment of truth will benefit yourself, your subordinates, and your organization. And remember, you can have that moment of truth in complete privacy.

SELF-ANALYSIS

One way to tackle this is to pray that if you *are* guilty of this self-inflicted wound, one of your subordinates will so inform you as he hands or speaks his resignation to you. You will be indeed fortunate if this happens, and if you then take his action to heart. Another way is to somehow find a "moment of truth" during which you carry on an intensely frank self-analysis to determine if you are guilty of this type of behavior. Another way is to ask your closest friend for his opinion on this subject, *after* he has interviewed your subordinates, after pledging to them in an oath signed in blood that he will not divulge their confidences.

[1] Herman Wouk, *The Caine Mutiny.* (Garden City, New York, Doubleday & Company, Inc., 1952), Chap. 26.

HEAL THE WOUND

Try to realize, and then accept, that there is absolutely nothing wrong with small physical stature—that such is the way your Creator made you and there is nothing whatsoever to be ashamed or sensitive about. Think, if you will, of the many fine athletes with small physical stature who have become champions in their own right (e.g., Metzger of Notre Dame, the 155-pound guard of years ago, and "Cotton" Warburton of USC of about the same period, a diminutive backfield star). Start relying on your own personal executive and boss-abilities to get the job done, and drop, one by one the sadistic methods you have acquired through the years. You will receive some instant feedback, which will make you feel very, very good. Further, it will make your organizational life, and that of your subordinates, much more livable.

the

HUMAN-EROSION BOSS

The Human-Erosion Boss grinds one or more of his subordinates under his authoritarian heel, through a carefully considered and calculated process carried out on a daily basis, gradually depriving him of his self-respect until he reaches the breaking point. Once he reaches it, any number of things may happen, including mental or physical breakdown, alcoholism, ulcers, mistreatment of loved ones, and, yes, even suicide.

Detestable and despised as he is, this boss is all too prevalent, although there are of course no statistics on this subject, which makes people uncomfortable even to discuss it. The motives for his actions are also cloudy and not easily defined, although there are usually firm opinions on this among his unhappy and unlucky subordinates while he is indulging in the erosion process. In addition, he seems to have as a basic premise the belief that every man has a breaking point, and he does not intend to stop until he proves it.

The best fictional description of this process is contained in Rod Serling's play *Patterns,* in which the extremely autocratic and authoritarian corporation president employs the human-erosion process with fiendish finesse to destroy the senior vice president who had helped create the firm. He drives him to alcoholism, deprives him of his self-respect in the presence of his peers, and finally forces him to suffer a fatal heart attack. His reasons for doing this, as diagnosed by a character in the play, were that he perceived the vice president as his conscience, with which he was carrying on a continuing battle and which he finally won with the death of the vice president.

Another actual case in point took place in the military which in its own way, followed the patterns of the corporation vice president. A senior officer, who apparently through no fault of his own did not see combat in World War II, found himself a decade after that war ended with a subordinate, one grade his junior, with an outstanding combat record, for which he had received some of the country's highest decorations. The subordinate was highly respected by his peers, both as an individual, a family man and as a professional career officer. Both of the officers were "academy" graduates. Their official relationships had hardly begun when the superior officer initiated his human-erosion tactics, including unreasonable and impossible demands and unearned reprimands on a daily basis. It was a small organization in which most of the events and actions were observable by the peers of the mistreated subordinate, who simultaneously felt very uncomfortable, sorry for the mistreated officer and, at the same time secretly glad that someone other than himself was on the receiving end of the human-erosion tactics.

The process continued toward its inevitable climax with a crescendo which reached its height when the persecuted officer reviewed his annual efficiency report in the Pentagon (this superior had not had the courage to show it to him before sending it there) and found, on this life and death evaluation of officers which the military uses for development and promotion, that he had received a very low rating. The crowning blow was an extremely low markdown in the category of the exercise of command, which this officer had demonstrated so often in combat and on which as a professional military man he prided himself and considered the most important hallmark in his life. Coming as it did from a man unfit to shine the shoes of the man he had rated, the expected happened. He collapsed in his home one evening, and was taken to the hospital for observation and treatment, whereupon his cruel superior ordered each of the peers *not* to visit him in the hospital, making it clear he would punish anyone who violated this order. Only one of the peers had the courage—or whatever it took—to visit him in the hospital, which the superior immediately learned through his surveillance system, and for which he was instantly punished. No more details of this story are necessary. Suffice it to say the performance ratings (efficiency reports) received by this officer during this period prevented his promotion and forced his early retirement from the service, a permanently wounded and embittered man.

There are many more examples, but it should not be necessary to cite or describe them. Much as we would like to think that the Human-Erosion Boss does not exist, it is a plain fact that he *does* exist and, furthermore, he is all too prevalent. Perhaps most of them are less dramatic and somewhat less destructive than those I have described, but the results vary only by degree. *Your* problem is to determine whether you are guilty in this department, and if so, to do something about it.

In this regard, each boss has a definite and infrequently dis-

charged responsibility for controlling the subordinate bosses under him. This is usually quite difficult to do for most human-erosion bosses seem to have an uncanny skill at fooling their own bosses and concealing their terrible behavior from them. If you do not know whether your subordinate bosses are practicing human erosion, then you are a deficient boss yourself and must share the guilt for what is going on.

SELF-ANALYSIS

Be careful on this diagnosis. You have probably already decided that you are not like the horrible examples of bosses described under this title. However, you may be guilty in a far less dramatic way, and with results which have about the same negative type of impact on your people. There are thousands of bosses who use a "whipping boy" in their day-to-day activities; that is, they punish a particular subordinate each time they, the boss, does something wrong or makes an error in judgment. Another version is to always punish one particular subordinate for the mistakes of his peers. Consider your own situation. Are you punishing the same man all the time for *your* mistakes and the mistakes of his peer subordinates? Do you seem to be finding more fault with one of your subordinates than the others? Do you keep him tense and anxious all the time, so that he never seems to be able to relax around you? Have you answered yes to any one of these questions? Then you are probably some sort of Human-Erosion Boss.

HEAL THE WOUND

Having done some honest soul-searching and found you have this wound in greater or less degree, the most difficult part of the therapy is accomplished, for you could not have located the wound without a very sincere self-analysis. Your problem is now to *stop this practice,* and the best time is *Now.* It is still easier said than done. You will have to develop and practice a constant awareness and alertness in your day-to-day activities to avoid committing this sin, but you can do it. While you're at it, you could collect a lot of votes from your subordinates (and yourself when you look in the mirror) if you would make amends for the wrongs you have done to your whipping boys of the past.

the

BOSS WHO NEGLECTS
the DEVELOPMENT
of HIS SUBORDINATES

The Boss Who Neglects the Development of His Subordinates wounds his people, and in turn he himself is the unfortunate beneficiary of those wounds. It would probably be impossible to find a boss, leader, commander, manager, executive, staff officer or any responsible person of any importance who would not agree that the development of subordinates is a necessary and important function of anyone in a supervisory position. Strangely enough, it is also true that the vast majority of those bosses, in their moments of truth, will admit that this is the executive function which they neglect the most.

There are many differing lists of personal functions of the executive. After much argument and research, the original faculty of the United States Army's executive development school (formerly the Command Management School, now the United States Army Management School) came up with the following list of those functions:

> Establishing Objectives
> Motivating
> Development of Subordinates
> Communicating
> Innovating
> Decision-Making
> Maintaining a Co-operative System

For several years now, before dozens of audiences of many hundreds of executives, I have flashed a chart containing this list of functions on a screen, and then asked the individuals in the audience to indicate which *one* of these functions was typically the

170

most neglected. Well over ninety percent have indicated the most neglected function to be the development of subordinates. I would guess that there would be a similar high rate of agreement with this opinion among the readers of this book. However, I would expect some disagreement as to the basic reasons behind this neglect, although the most popular reason given would be that the boss is too busy getting his job done to devote any time to the development of his subordinates. This reason, of course, does not hold water for, in the final analysis, you can not afford *not* to devote time to this function.

From my own observation, there are probably two more fundamental reasons for a boss to neglect the development of his subordinates. One is short-sighted. He is not able to spare the subordinate from on-the-job time for attendance at schools, courses, seminars, study, professional meetings, and the like, with the additional reluctance to spend organization funds to finance that attendance. I must quickly state that this view is not shared by the more enlightened managements, with several pressing hard on such developmental activities.

The second reason for a boss' neglect of this function is even more fundamental and is so widespread that it exists to some degree in *all* organizations. This boss is wounded by the self-inflicted and usually completely false assumption that subordinates are incapable of, or more accurately stated, *not yet* capable of assuming and discharging greater responsibility. This assumption has been invalidated time and time again, in all types of organizations, by one particular type of event: the situation whereby an individual regarded as not adequately qualified for a job is placed in that job for lack of an individual regarded as qualified. Although his performance should be predictable, to everyone's surprise he does the job well and perhaps outperforms his predecessor, who in the light of conventional wisdom had been far better qualified.

This phenomenon, which is no phenomenon at all but is so regarded—actually it is routine—occurs often in the military and government service, where personnel turnover is high and vacancies are often filled by moving up some available subordinate. It also occurs frequently in industry. Mr. Fred J. Borch, General Electric's able president and chief executive attested to this in newspaper interviews which followed the announcement of his ap-

pointment. The man who started with a low-paying job with the company thirty-two years before stated that his biggest breaks were the bosses who kept pushing him into increasingly demanding jobs he never was quite ready for. His belief: "If a superior waits until a man feels he's ready before nudging him up, the boat will have sailed."

I would add to this the statement that many boats are sailing in a nearly becalmed manner because bosses who have authority to do so are not giving added responsibilities to men who could discharge them well, only because the bosses feel that the subordinates are not yet ready to assume and discharge those responsibilities. These bosses will even fly in the face of research studies which indicate these subordinates want more responsibilities, and feel frustrated because of the lack of them.

How well have *you* been discharging the function of development of subordinates? Do you think those subordinates share your view? How will you find out?

SELF-ANALYSIS

In this diagnosis you must check yourself to determine if you are failing in either of two ways to develop your subordinates: (1) Do you have a mutually agreed upon plan, including on-duty and off-duty educational courses, whereby each of your subordinates, with your help and guidance, is developing himself? (2) In your day-to-day activities, do you use things that are done poorly—and things that are done well—as discussion items with the goal of subordinate development? If the answer to either of these questions is in the negative, you have this self-inflicted wound.

HEAL THE WOUND

If your answer was no to the first question, the therapy is evident from the question itself; you should have such a plan, and it is not difficult to arrange it. An assist to this, and used in many organizations, is to draw up a job description of the next higher pay scale, discuss it with your subordinate, and explain what he now lacks to qualify for such a position. On the second question, I offer you my own system, which I have found to be quite successful. For nine months on a foreign assignment, my "management team" consisted of two inexperienced lieutenants (one a foreign national) and a captain with limited experience in a few specialized areas. We were in a situation of constant stress, with staggering workloads. My team members made many mistakes (their boss also made his share). Each time a mistake was made, I insisted that we make a quick analysis to see what went wrong and *why* it went wrong. I would lead the discussion in a non-threatening manner, asking questions rather than giving answers, trying to discover Mary Parker Follett's "law of the situation" previously alluded to. Almost without exception, the man who made the mistake would come up with the correct analysis, we would agree upon it, and would go on from there, with no punishment or recriminations. I don't consider it boasting that, years later, these able men give me a lot of credit for helping them along the way. Try it. You can't lose. And, really, it doesn't cost much in time. In fact, it saves you time in the later *avoided* mistakes.

the

PROFANE-and-VULGAR BOSS

The Profane-and-Vulgar Boss is an ugly blotch on the escutcheon of the supervisory scene, and he is far more prevalent than anyone cares to admit. He is the boss who uses vulgarity and profanity as an "aid" to supervision, both directly and indirectly, and in so doing he wounds his people, his organization and himself.

The impact of profane and vulgar behavior on the part of the boss is far easier to observe and understand than are the fundamental causes of such behavior. It affects the attitudes and behavior of his subordinates in three general ways: (1) the subordinates who are otherwise inclined to profanity and vulgarity will increase this practice (2) the subordinates who are rarely profane and vulgar, or not at all, increase or begin the foul mouthed practice (3) those subordinates who do *not* use profanity and vulgarity feel, but resist, a pressure to do so, and are criticized and often ostracized by the foul-mouthed ones. This three-way impact, of course, has many by-products in addition to their overall sum of degradation of the organization.

I have never read or heard a learned dissertation on the *prevalence, cause, effect,* and *cure* of profanity and vulgarity, and I don't know anyone who has; however, this chapter would be somewhat irresponsible if it did not examine into those four aspects of the practice.

As to the incidence and prevalence of profanity and vulgarity, I am inclined to agree with the consensus of a group of two hundred fifty clergymen with whom I conducted a discussion on character guidance three years ago. It was an active, spirited discussion, with emotions running high. There was much agreement (with some dissent) that there was no correlation between the practice of profanity and vulgarity and education. Further, when I asked if there was any correlation between executive position and character, a crescendo of "no!" roared up from the audience.

From my personal observation, this practice is indulged in

without distinction by vice presidents, general and flag officers and Ph.D.'s alike. In fact, many people in high positions are best known by this "executive trait," and an appalling number of would-be successful executives are inclined to believe that their climb up the ladder was somehow made easier by their profane and vulgar behavior. Perhaps the only conclusion as to the prevalency of the practice is that it is *not* restricted to groups or categories of people. A theological explanation of this might be that, since it is a form of immorality, no group or category is immune.

The basic causes of executive profanity and vulgarity are not at all clear, and most of the theories on the subject are superficial. One of the most commonly given, and highly stupid, is that it is caused by the practitioner's limited vocabulary!

Another view is that it is a form of inner rebellion, but this analysis loses strength, it seems to me, when the behavior is practiced by a boss for the "benefit" of his subordinates.

One theory that has much validity, I believe, is that it is a manifestation of power and authority. Anyone who has observed a profane and vulgar executive forcing his subordinates to listen to and observe his foul-mouthed behavior cannot help being struck at the obvious pleasure of the practitioner in doing it, with cruelty being clearly indicated. If the observer is a psychiatrist, he is likely to ascribe much of the behavior as an outward manifestation of inner insecurity. You will probably object to this analysis, because we are inclined to correlate security with executive rank and position.

Finally, the profane and vulgar boss may feel compelled to "ape" *his own* boss in a monkey see—monkey do situation, as a method of conformity. Obviously the cause for a boss who uses profanity varies, is obscure, and is rooted deeply. Why are *you* a profane and vulgar boss in the presence of your subordinates? I suggest that you will best discover the reason with the help of a psychiatrist or other professional counselors.

The impact of the profane and vulgar boss is more easily observed and understood than is the cause of it. As indicated in the second paragraph of this chapter, there is a general increase in profane and vulgar behavior throughout the organization, or organizational element, that he heads. In this respect, subordinates of all ages, education and backgrounds play "follow the leader," just as surely as sheep follow a Judas Goat to the slaughter, which in some ways is not an inept analogy. This copying of the executive's behavior is usually regarded as a prerequisite to promotion and other approval and advancement. It is rare for a foul-mouthed executive to promote a clean-mouthed subordinate, although it is sometimes done as a track-covering device to avoid specific criticism.

These effects are bad enough, but the worst aspect of all is that in perverting the behavior of his subordinates, the profane and vulgar boss is exploiting his peoples' greatest weakness, the basic, fundamental need for acceptance which is felt by all human beings. Men and women can stand almost anything except rejection, which is the opposite of acceptance, and in order to gain this acceptance

they will stoop to depths far below any they would otherwise consider. This craving for acceptance will make a strong man weak.

In an actual case a very senior executive who regularly had lunch in the executive dining room with his principal subordinates was given to foul-mouthed remarks at the table, with frequent use of four-letter words and allusions to sex. It was appalling to observe his subordinates, senior executives in their own right, not only respond in kind, but even vie with each other for his favor with vile remarks. He would not even permit the saying of grace or offering of thanks at the meal. The few attempts to bring this about brought on quick punishment. In summary, the effect of executive profanity and vulgarity is predictably destructive, and varies only by degree.

The cure for executive profanity and vulgarity, if there is one, seldom comes from within the man himself unless, like Saul on the road to Damascus, he suddenly sees the light. In this regard, it is hoped that these paragraphs may provide some assistance in helping the guilty boss identify himself and initiate the corrective action. Perhaps the most effective method however, is for the profane and vulgar boss' own boss to seek him out and castigate such behavior, *in the presence of his subordinates*. This will put pressure on the profane and vulgar boss to behave. This will also encourage subordinates of the profane and vulgar boss to secretly inform his superior of his bad behavior.

SELF-ANALYSIS

This diagnosis requires you to answer two questions: (1) Do you use profanity and/or vulgarity in *your* day-to-day organizational activities? (2) Do your subordinates use profanity and/or vulgarity in *their* day-to-day organizational activities? It's as simple as that. The first question requires considerable sincerity, but you can muster it. The second question requires some research on your part, but you are defaulting and guilty if you do not do it.

HEAL THE WOUND

If *you* are guilty, there is only one answer: STOP IT! Watch out for self-alibis, and for alibis furnished by others. There is a follow-up therapy which is absolutely necessary: Find the guts (or intestinal fortitude if you prefer the term) to tell your subordinates that *you* are turning over a new leaf in the profanity and vulgarity department. You must also make it clear that such action on their part will not only go *unrewarded* in the future, but that it will also be punished. Make it clear that what they do off the job is also your concern in this department, and that you don't want any foulmouthed ambassadors of yours moving in the social circles in your community. Finally, make it clear that people have difficulty changing overnight, and that there may be reversions during the therapy period, which will be overlooked for the immediate present, but not tolerated over a period of time. You'll find that the new policy will catch on, perhaps after some resentment and ridicule, but there will soon be a new, self-propagating way of life in your organization, and everyone will benefit from it.

the

BOSS WHO DOES NOT
WANT CONFLICT

The Boss Who Does Not Want Conflict in his organization is the man who has come to believe, consciously or subconsciously, that conflict is bad and that it should be stamped out if it exists currently, and should be prevented in the future. By this wound he is depriving himself, his people, and his organization of an asset so vital that it is the life-blood of a healthy organization, without which it can not long exist.

It is not as easy to generalize on the *cause* of this executive's erroneous belief as it is to identify his attitude and behavior. Certainly one of its bases is ignorance, another no doubt is insecurity with a generous mixture of indecision or lack of desire to make decisions. He becomes quite upset and angry when he receives conflicting opinions and recommendations from his staff or subordinates, and he lets them know about it in no uncertain terms with remarks such as, "Why can't you people get together and agree on the solution to these problems? Why can't you solve your differences by yourselves?" He is extremely happy and pleased when he receives a unanimously agreed upon proposal from his subordinates, and he approves it with a flourish, or even goes so far as to disapprove it, but he feels good that his subordinates "finally" agreed about something. What the poor soul doesn't realize is that he should be very suspicious of any solution to a problem which has been the subject of unanimous opinion by his subordinates, for it is probably not the best solution. In this day and age of complex problems, things just don't happen that way.

By striving to eliminate conflict, this boss is actually eliminating diversity; without it no organization can long survive. As Mary Parker Follett stated:

What people often mean by getting rid of conflict is getting rid of diversity, and it is of the utmost importance that these should not be

180

considered the same. We may wish to abolish conflict, but we cannot get rid of diversity. We must face life as it is and understand that diversity is its most essential feature. . . . Fear of difference is dread of life itself. It is possible to conceive conflict as not necessarily a wasteful outbreak of incompatibilities, but a *normal* process by which socially valuable differences register themselves for the enrichment of all concerned.[1]

Some executives will not even consider a paper from their staffs which contains differing opinions. They even go so far as to have it understood that "no paper with a disagreement in it will hit my desk without the statement that the chiefs of the disagreeing divisions have *personally* tried unsuccessfully to resolve the disagreement." The obvious purpose of this procedure has merit, but if the executive who uses it isn't very, very careful, he will have a system which becomes a breeding and spawning ground for watered-down compromises which are easily "approved" by him —or since everyone "agrees," they are implemented and executed without him even knowing about them! If this executive isn't careful, his decision-making days are over, because he never gets a chance to make one!

The regrettable effect of this executive's "anti-conflict" attitude is its effect upon his subordinates. It causes them to regard disagreement as a dirty word and an undesirable thing. If one attacks the *opinion* of another, the latter regards it instead as an attack upon *himself,* with the expected destructive results to the command or management team.

You, the executive who reads this, have no doubt had a boss who did not want conflict in his organization, and you probably shudder to remember the experience. This part of the analysis is easy, but answering the following question may make you rather uncomfortable: *Are your subordinates now working for a boss who doesn't want conflict in his organization?*

SELF-ANALYSIS

You must examine both your basic philosophy on this subject and your day-to-day actions and organizational climate to determine whether they are consistent. These questions may help. Do you

[1] Follett, Mary Parker, "Constructive Conflict," in Henry C. Metcalf and L. Urwick. eds., *Dynamic Administration* (New York, Harper and Brothers, 1940), p. 31.

welcome conflict in your organization? Do you accept it as an inevitable aspect of organization life and have you trained yourself to manage this conflict so that it becomes a constructive element of that life? Do you welcome your subordinates to bring you opposing recommendations for solving problems, or do you bring overt or covert pressure upon them to reach agreement before they bring the problem to you for decision? Only by answering questions like these can you determine whether you have inflicted this wound upon your people.

HEAL THE WOUND

Orient yourself to the point where you can only give the correct answers to the questions in the above diagnosis. However, if you have trained yourself in the past to avoid conflict, you will find that you must undertake a significant attitude and behavioral change to bring this about. You will also have to communicate this to your subordinates who have learned throughout the years that you believed conflict to be a dirty word and an undesirable aspect of organization life. However, it can be done and you can do it.

SUGGESTIONS FOR FURTHER READING

Thompson, Victor A., "Conflict," *Modern Organization*. New York, Alfred A. Knopf, 1961, Chap. 5, pp. 81–133.

the

BOSS WHO IS DRUNK WITH POWER

The Boss Who Is Drunk With Power is far more prevalent than we care to admit. He is the man whose basic human nature is such that the possession of power in the form of authority is more than he can cope with in a positive, humane way, and he demonstrates this by abusing that power and authority in many ways.

While it is not necessary to attempt an analysis of the reasons for it in this chapter, it is an age-old fact that the nature of power is such that many men succumb to its intoxicating effects and, as many a social drinker evolves into an alcoholic, many men upon whom power and authority are bestowed not only become drunk with it, but acquire a self-generated insatiable desire to increase and abuse it. Lord Acton, the English clergyman and historian who was an influential advisor to Gladstone, is quoted as saying "Power corrupts. Absolute power corrupts absolutely." Nothing could be more true. The Devil works overtime where Power is concerned.

It is a rare organization which does not contain at least one boss, supervisor or executive who is not intoxicated with his authority or drunk with his power. They vary from the well-known corporation president who frequently demonstrated his power by getting down on his hands and knees and eating grass from the lawn, and then forcing his top management team to do the same thing (and they did); the gang politician who sent a nondescript ward heeler politician to the national senate for the sole reason, as he put it, to prove that "you can put a yellow dog in the senate if you have a good political machine"; to the foreman who forces his men to provide him free drinks at the neighborhood bar after work; to the military commander who forced his staff chaplain to drink against his will; to the executive who at social occasions indulges in off-color remarks or actions with his subordinates' wives; to any supervisor who dispenses the organizational benefits, tangible and intangible in an unfair manner. The examples are unending.

H. G. Wells stated that "It is a universal weakness of mankind that what we are given to administer, we presently imagine that we own." [1] There are few who serve in organizational life who would disagree with him, and then the difference of opinion would vary only in degree. A very common manifestation is the newly arrived or newly promoted executive who announces that, "Anything can be improved. I intend to improve this organization." And then like

a bull in a china shop he sets out on his "improvement" program with more energy than brains, as is soon indicated by results. What he is blissfully unaware of is the fact that the power to improve is also the power to destroy, and with his inept handling of authority and power he is more likely to do the latter than he is to do the former.

Unless you are unusually fortunate, you have had bosses who were drunk with power. My question, what is *your* level of intoxication at the moment?

SELF-ANALYSIS

This wound is among the most difficult to diagnose for it requires the utmost sincerity from yourself. The American slang expression

[1] L. Urwick, *The Elements of Administration* (New York, Harper and Brothers, 1943), p. 81.

"throwing your weight around" may be quite helpful here because it is actually referring to the improper use of power. Another way to analyze this is to examine your day-to-day activities to determine whether you are using influence, authority, or power to get the job done. A third method is to determine whether you are using power to require things to be done which really are not necessary to organizational accomplishment. A word of caution here. You are probably not guilty of the specific examples cited in the third paragraph, but you still may be either drunk or slightly intoxicated with power. Only a thorough, sincere analysis will help you find out for sure.

HEAL THE WOUND

The therapy on this wound is predicted by the methods of diagnosis outlined above. However, it is not quite as simple as this. If you are guilty you may have some needs for power which have psychological bases. My only suggestion here is to ignore, or not satisfy, those needs in the same manner that you attempt to avoid other actions, equally immoral, but not conventionally defined as such. You may find it somewhat like a drinking or smoking habit, which while difficult to dispense with, pales in its attractiveness as the period of abstention grows.

the

LAZY BOSS

The Lazy Boss is not as easily described as one might imagine from his title. I am *not* talking about the executive who, through careful and clever management of his time, is able to get his job done between nine and five (except for the mental effort he makes on it during normal off-duty periods). I *am* pointing the finger at the boss who, by his action and inaction, is regarded as lazy by his peers and his subordinates. (I do not mention his superiors, for he is usually able to fool *them*.) The impression of laziness is gained through the plain, simple, and obvious fact that he just does not apply the necessary amount of time and energy to his job, with the result that not only his own output suffers, but so do his subordinates and peers through being forced to make up for the deficiencies caused by the laziness of the boss. As they do this, they form a monumental contempt and resentment for the individual whom they are figuratively carrying on their backs because he is too lazy to walk.

I shall leave it to psychiatrists and psychologists to ferret out the whys and wherefores of this despised and resented type of executive behavior, but an effort should be made to describe some of the forms it takes, in order to assist the reader-executive in identifying himself if he is one of the guilty.

One which is spotted instantly is the boss who orders or directs the working of overtime by his subordinates without he himself performing overtime work during all or some of those periods. Many subordinates have worked long, fatiguing nights and weekends without ever seeing the boss who directed that the overtime be worked. The fact that the subordinates did or did not get paid for working overtime is not particularly material to the situation, although the guilty boss probably thinks it is.

A second form of behavior of the lazy boss is the fact, soon known by his peers and his subordinates, that he does not apply himself when he *is* on the job. This man is usually guilty of wasting

187

his time and/or that of his subordinates or peers, the latter act compounding his sin. A final indication of guilt is his failure to do his executive share of individual tasks, projects, and programs, leaving it to subordinates or peers to perform. He usually tries to hide his sin by outwardly declaring that he has "delegated" this function, whereas he has in fact abdicated or sloughed off his rightful work onto his subordinates, or left it to be performed by peers

whose loyalty to the organization causes them to perform the work, rather than let the organization suffer because of the laziness of one defaulting executive.

This chapter will be read by some executives, bosses, and leaders who are currently troubled when they find themselves working longer hours than they think they should be working. They are often plagued by the uncomfortable feeling that they are suffering from some executive deficiency which is causing them to work longer hours than they understand other comparable executives are working. This may be partially true, for it is not easy to manage one's time well; however, it is probably even more true that these executives should be giving themselves a pat on the back for seeing the job needed to be done and doing it, without watching the clock. The world we live in is complex and difficult, and the ratio of executives who cannot get their jobs done between nine and five to those who can, has been increasing geometrically in recent years. Accordingly, they are faced with the choice of devoting enough time to their jobs or defaulting in the form of the laziness which I have described.

Obviously, the conscientious and honorable ones give of themselves to get the job done, at the same time being exacting and demanding of, but not abdicating to, their subordinates.

It is to this category of bosses, executives, and leaders that this chapter is intended to give encouragement, thus performing the dual purpose of castigating the lazy boss and concurrently commending the boss who does his job as he sees it, without watching the clock. In addition to his own questioning of his management of his time, the latter often finds his wife and children also questioning it, so that he finds himself in frequent conflict, which requires careful effort to solve. For him and his family, the following lines may be helpful. They were written long ago, and some will say that they are no longer applicable. On the contrary, they are even more applicable today than when they first appeared in print. A copy of it where it is often noticed by the overworked executive and his family is almost certain to serve a useful purpose.

> Heights by great men reached and kept
> Were not attained by sudden flight;
> For they, while their companions slept
> Were toiling upward in the night.[1]

SELF-ANALYSIS

This diagnosis will be aided if you or your organization have constructed a detailed description of your job, including the levels of responsibility involved. This list, for example, may show where your responsibility for *action* leaves off and the responsibility of your subordinates begins. The question then should be asked: "Am I discharging these responsibilities?" Another aid in this

---

[1] Longfellow, "Ladder of St. Augustine."

diagnosis is the rather simple question: "Am I keeping busy on the job?" In this analysis be sure to allow the proper amount of time for thinking. Finally, either through surreptitious research or frank and effective questioning, try to get the opinions of your subordinates and peer bosses on this subject for they are the best informed in your organization on this subject. Since this is not the easiest type of questioning, you may wish to obtain this information through a third person.

HEAL THE WOUND

If your diagnosis is successful and you have determined that you are a lazy boss, you are probably already well on the road to recovery. However, if your laziness stems from lack of energy, I am not saying that you can conjure up a supply of energy overnight. I think you will find, however, that energetic activity tends to breed more energetic activity, and that having forced yourself to a greater level of activity over a brief period of time, you will find less and less forcing to be necessary.

the

BREATHE-DOWN-THEIR-NECKS BOSS

This boss is so well known, so universally resented, and the cases describing his behavior are so myriad, that my biggest problem with this chapter is to determine how to hold it to normal length. The title words, from the mouths of those being supervised, describe the boss who practices *excessive supervision*. His subordinates view him as constantly breathing down their necks as they carry out their work, and this behavior makes them absolutely furious.

Regardless of the human or psychological bases, it is a truth that there is something in the nature of the human animal that causes him to dislike and resent close supervision as he performs tasks. It manifests itself in early childhood and remains with us throughout our lives. No one would quarrel with this truth if he were discussing *his own* reactions to close supervision; however, he seems to forget or ignore this entirely when acting in his role as a boss. The theoretical reason for this is not clear, so let's get down to cases.

A well-known senior executive had a favorite saying which went essentially as follows, "Only what the boss checks will be done well." As he went through his career, he required that this statement be put on signs and posted conspicuously in every element, large or small, of the total organization he headed. He and his palace guard set up an inspection system throughout his organization to insure that the signs were omnipresent. As time went on, detailed specifications for the size and appearance of the signs were disseminated. It was not uncommon for a visitor from his headquarters, when making an inspection trip to a field element, to take out a ruler and measure the signs he observed, becoming highly critical when he found minute variations in size or shape. The signs were widely detested by many, for they regarded it as insulting, implying baldly that they could not be trusted to do their job unless their bosses checked their every action. The expense of

191

preparing the thousands of signs was never even considered, except in guarded discussions among subordinates.

On one occasion, when this particular senior executive left his high position to take over a more important job with a larger organization, word was flashed by the man who took his place, a few minutes after assuming the position, to "get rid of those damned signs!" Not only did they disappear in a matter of minutes, but many of them had already been discarded a few minutes after the senior executive left the organization, reflecting the hope of the personnel that the new senior executive would not underwrite the signs.

Hardly anyone ever wondered how the senior executive had come up with the slogan (they were too busy measuring and polishing the signs). Toward the end of his career, in a talk to a group of executives attending an executive development course, he described the birth of the slogan. During his first job as a supervisor at the tender age of twenty-one, he had attended a miscellaneous lecture by a miscellaneous lecturer in business administration. During his remarks, the lecturer was asked the question: Can you give us a good principle of leadership? His response was "only what the boss checks will be done well." The senior executive stated that he had accepted this statement as the gospel, and had propagated it throughout his career. Thus endeth that sad tale.

The human reaction to what subordinates regard as execessive supervision is well described in two cases set forth by Mary Parker Follett:

In a case in Scotland arising under the Minimum Wage Act, the overman was called in to testify whether or not a certain workman did his work properly. The examination was as follows:

MAGISTRATE: But isn't it your duty under the Mines Act to visit each working place twice a day?
OVERMAN: Yes.
MAGISTRATE: Don't you do it?
OVERMAN: Yes.
MAGISTRATE: Then why didn't you ever see him work?
OVERMAN: They always stop work when they see an overman coming and sit down and wait till he's gone—even take out their pipes, if it's a mine free from gas. They won't let anyone watch them.

An equally extreme standard was enforced for a part of the war period at a Clyde engineering works. The chairman of shop stewards was told one morning that there was a grievance at the smithy. He found one of the blacksmiths in a rage because the managing director in his ordinary morning's walk through the works had stopped for five minutes or so and watched this man's fire. After a shop meeting the chairman took up a deputation to the director and secured the promise that this should not happen again. At the next works meeting the chairman reported the incident to the body of workers, with the result that a similar demand was made throughout the works and practically acceded to, so that the director hardly dared to stop at all in his morning's walk.[1]

Before you respond with a comment to the effect that I have chosen stories of reactions in settings in another country many years ago, my response is that these stories were chosen to demonstrate the typical *reaction* to close supervision, both mentally and as manifested by physical behavior. My contention is that the reaction still exists today, and it varies only with the behavior of the boss and the climate he has established within his organization. This contention is based upon the assumption that the problem was not the supervisory behavior (visiting the work area), but rather *the manner in which the visit was perceived by the workers.*

I have a friend who is a first-line supervisor in a large post office in a city which shall remain anonymous. He has several peer supervisors in the work setting. My friend visits his several subordinates on an average of twice a day, stopping and chatting with them about non-work matters, such as family matters, sports, and the like. His peer supervisors visit each of their workers several times a day, chatting very little, primarily about the work and how there is a need for more of it to be performed. My friend's work group has the highest performance records in the total organization. His peer supervisors are constantly struggling to get the work out, and even suspect that their subordinates are practicing slow-down tactics, which they (the supervisors) are making every effort to counteract with close supervision.

The generality of this type of situation is described by Dr. Rensis Likert in his book, *New Patterns of Management* (New York, McGraw-Hill, 1961), in a study which was described as validated by other studies. In research of an organization it was found that 90 percent of all high-producing sections had supervisors who practiced only *general* supervision, while 67 percent of

---

[1] "The Giving of Orders" in Henry C. Metcalf and L. Urwick, eds., *Dynamic Administration* (New York, Harper and Brothers, 1940), p. 66, 67.

all low-producing sections had supervisors who practiced *close* supervision.

I know another man, now a senior executive, who fondly recalls the advice he received on his first job, from his first boss, to the effect, "Young man, you should spend three percent of your time *giving* orders, and the other 97 percent of your time checking to see that those orders are carried out." Like the "what the boss checks" executive referred to earlier, he has repeated this advice to all his subordinates along the way. I will leave it to you to conjecture the results of such beliefs.

This chapter could go on and on, but if the point has not been made by now it never will be. *You* don't like a boss who breathes down your neck, and you don't like him for good and sufficient reason. Why do you think *your* subordinates feel differently as they feel your hot breath on *their* necks?

SELF-ANALYSIS

Examine your actions of the past week or two. What kind of supervision did you give to your subordinates? Was it in great detail? Or did you limit it to periodic requests for progress reports which the subordinates could not have interpreted as "breathing down their necks." Also, what was the frequency of your checking, and finally, what was the reaction of your subordinates to your inquiries? The answers to these questions will help you determine whether you bear this self-inflicted wound.

HEAL THE WOUND

The simplest answer here is to adopt the procedure and behavior that you have found yourself lacking in. That is, less frequent checking on your subordinates and less detailed inquiry when you do check up on them. Finally, develop your sensitivity to the point where you are accurately "reading" their reactions to your supervisory behavior. On this last point, if you are performing this function properly, they will regard your actions as help rather than as annoyances. Finally, if *your* breathing down your subordinates necks has been caused to some extent by similar behavior on the part of your boss, you must somehow or other influence him to diminish this type of behavior. One way to do this is to be prepared to give him progress reports which communicate very clearly the status of the situation and further communicate your confidence as to the adequacy of the level of detail in which you are reporting.

the

MANAGE-THROUGH-FEAR BOSS

"I got to where I am today through the use of fear as my primary leadership tool, and I have no intention of changing my methods. Furthermore, I have good reason to believe I will continue up the ladder of executive success." These were the words of a senior executive in a group of similarly senior executives who had met in an executive development course and were discussing various forms of leadership behavior.

Your immediate reaction is probably that the speaker's words elicited immediate critical responses from the others, with perhaps ostracism from the group. They did not. There was a murmur of dissent, but there were also several comments, mostly in low asides to seat partners to the effect that "fear is a pretty effective form of leadership." Then, in response to the moderator who insisted they discuss the subject, there followed considerable difference of opinion. Those in favor of fear as a primary leadership style, cited example after example of individuals who had risen to the heights of their various professions through heavy reliance on fear. Others cited examples of several men, well known in their professions, who had *neared* the heights through the use of leadership techniques which had as their central theme the belief in human beings as human beings but who, when final selections for promotion were made, had lost out to the men who had used fear to rise to the heights. The discussion ended with much frustration within the group because they had failed, in their opinion, to answer the study question, "What leadership practices are most desirable?" Their moderator ended the discussion by suggesting that their frustration probably stemmed from the inability of the group to answer the *unassigned* question within the group, "How do I become a successful executive?"

This chapter will make no attempt to examine the psychological bases for the widespread use of fear as a leadership technique. It existed long before the galley slaves of old were locked into their seats and then motivated by the whip of the slave master. It existed long before the infamous Captain Bligh of the Bounty decided upon keel-hauling and the cat-of-nine-tails as his baton of leadership. Most people on the receiving end of fear tactics today would say that the galley slaves and the Bounty seamen had it easy—they were subjected to *physical* fear only, the fear of brutal physical treatment. They would say that today's fear tactics have much more finesse, are much more ravaging and far more destructive of the individual, for they employ the fear of mental rather than physical punishment.

A case in point. An executive who managed through fear had the sadistic "hobby" of tongue-lashing a selected number of his subordinates on a regular basis. Nothing they could do was right. In this case, two junior executives were on the receiving end of his tactics. Both of the junior executives suffered nervous breakdowns, and one of them committed suicide a few years afterward. The senior executive who had brought this about continued to rise in his profession, using exactly the same tactics. Was this man rare? I do not think so, except by degree, but I will not be the judge. You can judge best if you will confine your analysis to those you have observed along the way, before you analyze your own behavior as a boss, and the degree to which you use fear as a style of leadership.

This book attempts at times to point the way out of some of the dilemmas into which it leads its readers. Perhaps some such effort is in order here. The subject we are discussing, of course, is *motivation* and, more specifically, the motivation of individuals in organizational settings. The central question to be explored is obvious: Why do people work? Several years ago the late Douglas McGregor set forth the now famous "Theory X and Theory Y" [1] approach to analyzing this question. Pointing out that assumptions about human nature and human behavior lie behind every managerial action or decision, he described the two theories, here shown in outline, as follows:

THEORY X: THE TRADITIONAL VIEW OF DIRECTION AND CONTROL

1. The average human being has an inherent dislike of work and will avoid it if he can.

2. Because of this human characteristic of dislike of work, most people must be coerced, controlled, directed, threatened with punishment to get them to put forth adequate effort toward the achievement of organizational objectives.

3. The average human being prefers to be directed, wishes to avoid responsibility, has relatively little ambition, wants security above all.

THEORY Y: THE INTEGRATION OF INDIVIDUAL AND ORGANIZATIONAL GOALS

1. The expenditure of physical and mental effort in work is as natural as play or rest.

2. External control and the threat of punishment are not the only means for bringing about effort toward organizational objectives. Man will exercise self-direction and self-control in the service of objectives to which he is committed.

[1] Now contained in his book, *The Human Side of Enterprise*. (New York, McGraw-Hill, 1960).

3. Commitment to objectives is a function of (depends upon) the rewards associated with their achievement.

4. The average human being learns, under proper conditions, not only to accept but to seek responsibility.

5. The capacity to exercise a relatively high degree of imagination, ingenuity, and creativity in the solution of organizational problems is widely, not narrowly, distributed in the population.

6. Under the conditions of modern industrial life, the intellectual potentialities of the average human being are only partially utilized.

If your analysis of the subject of this chapter accomplishes nothing more than inducing you to ask yourself the questions, "Which theory do I believe in?" "Which theory do I *practice?*" (The answers are often different) "What *are* my beliefs and assumptions about human nature and human behavior?"—a good portion of the chapter's purpose will have been accomplished. If you wish to take the analysis a step further, you might struggle with this question; "In a country which prides itself as being a *democracy,* why are its organizations (e.g., business, industry, government, military) set up on an *autocratic* basis?"

Finally, to end with a focus on the central theme of the chapter: You have had bosses who managed through fear and you detested them. Are you a fear manager yourself?

SELF-ANALYSIS

You will probably need help on this one. It has been said that individuals who are *managed* through fear can be detected by checking the palms of their hands for sweat. I am not suggesting that you go through your organization looking for sweaty palms, although there would probably be some benefit to such research. I once visited an organization which had been described to me by the statement that every man in it walked around with sweaty palms. It soon was clear to me that fear was the primary and destructive motivation in that organization. Two types of inquiry are all I have to offer you here: (1) To the extent you are capable of doing so in the privacy of your own mind, ask yourself the question: "Do I use fear in my day to day organizational activities" and (2) find out, if necessary through a third person, how your subordinates and peer bosses would answer this question. If the answer to either of these questions is in the affirmative, you are a Manage-Through-Fear Boss.

HEAL THE WOUND

Examine your basic assumptions about people. The best means I know for this examination are Theory X and Theory Y. Having done so, identify those actions or behavior patterns of yours through which you generate fear among your subordinates. Make a conscious effort to discontinue those activities, communicating instead that your subordinates have self respect and do not need to be motivated through fear. You will soon find that this is a self-propagating type of behavior on your part and the benefits you will accrue will exceed your most extravagant estimates.

the

BOSS WHO HATES RATEBUSTERS

This boss has a self-inflicted attitude and behavior pattern which is truly a wound in every sense of the word, and the wound is inflicted upon himself, his organization, and his subordinates. The word "hate" might be better stated as "resents" or "dislikes." The result is the same. He is not much talked about, nor written about (I have no writings on this subject to refer you to), partly because his problem is usually not clearly defined; the primary sufferers are a non-organized minority, and, I suspect, the bosses who like to write about executive behavior dislike to admit that they were not able to come to grips with the problem, and the theorists have not been able to offer any acceptable solutions.

While the term "ratebuster" is well-known and understood in American industrial life, a definition for readers outside that environment and in other countries may be in order. Plainly and simply, I am talking about the *individual in a peer group who excels the other members of his peer group in quantity and quality of performance.* There are other more complicated definitions, but this should be the least misunderstood. Without further elaboration, let's look at the problems of the ratebuster, through his eyes, and *study the behavior of his bosses,* for that is the focus of our analysis. The following description was given by the executive vice-president of a large corporation (who shall remain anonymous) in discussing the major problems of his career with a group of executives attending an executive development course at a well-known university:

My first big problem occurred during my first job in industry, and was repeated two organizations later when I was a junior executive. In my first job I was one of a group of workers serving under a foreman in a factory, and I can assure you that I was not able to see the problem as clearly then as I now describe it to you. I had been taught by my very fine parents that hard work was a virtue and laziness was a sin, and that as I went through life I could expect the former to be rewarded and the latter to be punished. With this as a basic belief, I entered into my first job with gusto and was pleasantly surprised to find without actually counting that I was not only holding my own with the older and more experienced workers, but that I was clearly exceeding their output. This gave me the same feeling I had enjoyed in athletics in high school and college, where I had been somewhat of a star performer. I had been admired and cheered on by my teammates and praised by my coaches and managers. I soon found in the factory, however, that my efforts brought out quite different reactions from my new associates. Although they had welcomed me cordially, they cooled off quickly and I was soon puzzled by what was clearly their resentment toward me. I was also puzzled by the foreman's actions toward me. In our initial conference, he had made it clear that he expected a lot of work from me, and I had promised to meet his expectations. He had complimented me the first few days, but shortly thereafter treated me very cooly, for reasons I did not understand, but which I somehow related to the behavior of my fellow workers toward me.

I am sure that you gentlemen are saying to yourselves that I was a "rate-buster," and that I should have recognized it and done something about it. You may also be saying that it would only have happened among hourly employees. If so, you are mistaken, particularly on the latter point. A few years later I found myself in the same predicament as a junior executive. Without going into detail, I was one of seven junior executives who were responsible for directing and supervising departments which were performing the same types of functions. These functions were administrative in nature—that is, they were not manufacturing—and their output was susceptible to work measurement. We seven executives were responsible to the same boss, a rather senior executive in the organization. When I had joined the organization, he had made it clear that he expected a lot of me, and that he would be aware of my performance in terms of the output of my division, which would be measured and compared with the six other divisions. My six peer executives had welcomed me cordially, and I had felt initially that I was all set for a good experience. By this time I had learned something about individual and group motivation and felt that I could hold my own when it came to directing the activities of an administrative organization. My confidence was soon confirmed, for my division soon rose from sixth to first in production. I was not only able to hold first place, but did so by a wide margin. There was not much difference in the production of the other six divisions, even though they were individually ranked. It was not long before I experienced the same feelings of resentment from my six peer division chiefs as I had received from members of the factory working group just described. Further, the superintendent over us seven division chiefs changed his behavior toward me. His initial cordiality, followed by outright commendation when I brought the division up from near-cellar to first place, now changed to downright coolness, until I had the feeling he wished I had never joined the organization.

I wouldn't say that I was an overly sensitive person, at either of the times in my life just described, but I can assure you I became most unhappy. I was proud of my output as a worker. I was proud of my accomplishments as a division chief in the second situation. And I was depressed and hurt by the treatment I received from my two peer groups and from my two bosses. I seriously questioned the values I had learned from my parents, my athletic coaches and my fellow athletes. In each case I considered every alternative from resigning to lowering my standards and changing my basic beliefs. I can assure you, gentlemen, I had lost a lot of sleep before I made my decisions on these two problems.

The executive did not tell the group what his decisions were, for the purpose of the educational effort was to cause the individuals in the audience to discuss first, what each would have done if he had been the ratebuster in the case, and second, to cause each of them to discuss what he would have done if he had been the

boss of the ratebuster in each case. In other words, what did the boss have in the ratebuster: (1) a thorn in his side? (2) a tiger by the tail? (3) a golden nugget? (4) a diamond in the rough? (5) what?

Before your adrenalin subsides from the involvement with the two cases just described, will you please do the same thing? If *you* had been the ratebuster in each case described, what would have been your decision? If *you* had been the boss of the ratebuster, what would you have done?

SELF-ANALYSIS

How do you sincerely regard the one or two subordinates who clearly are exceeding the norms of your team for individual output either in quality or quantity, or both? Do you see them as assets who may inspire their peers to greater effort, or do you see them as annoying liabilities who cause resentment of their peers, requiring from you a higher quality of leadership? These two questions are not entirely all-embracing, however they should help you determine whether you bear this self-inflicted wound.

HEAL THE WOUND

Take a page from the book of the athletic team manager who capitalizes on his star performers by developing them into concurrent individual stars *and* team members who will not hesitate to place team goals ahead of individual goals. In order to achieve this you must sell the concept and prove by your day-to-day actions that team effort and individual effort are not only not incompatible, but they are part of an integrated whole: an effective team. If you want to cite an example from the world of sport you can describe the year that Joe Dimaggio was in the process of setting a new record for consecutive games in which he hit safely at least once. Those of you who know the sport of baseball are well aware that trying to hit a long ball carries with it the concurrent risk of striking out. It has been said of Joe that he never hesitated to carry out his manager's orders to swing for the long ball even though in so doing he risked striking out and breaking his hitting streak.

On
Wounding Your Organization

In this section, the wounds discussed are inflicted by you, but the primary sufferer is your organization. You will find the wrong kind of management that hurts you as well as your people, but the nature of these wounds is such that it is the organization itself which writhes in agony and convulsions, with a multiplier impact that reaches every facet of corporate life. In a total sense, the results add to up organizational ineffectiveness. At best, you have a weak and ailing organization. In any event, considerable therapy is in order.

As long as the parts come to a 100% standard, you don't bother to look at each part. You are a *100-PERCENT BOSS*.   209

Every project that you give out has equal importance at any given time. You are a *HORIZONTAL-PRIORITY-LIST BOSS*.   213

You know how to do the work but you don't know how to get it done. You are a *BOSS WHO DOESN'T KNOW HOW TO GET COMPLETED STAFF WORK*.   216

You insist on an employee taking a stand on a proposal without benefit of discussion with others. You are a *SEQUENTIAL–CO-ORDINATION BOSS*.   219

You believe that as long as you get rid of a symptom, the illness will disappear with it. You are a *BOSS WHO TREATS THE SYMPTOM AND IGNORES THE ILLNESS*.   222

Your employees know that whatever proposal they offer, it will be watered down by everyone else's proposal. You are a *BOSS WHO MANAGES BY COMPROMISE*.   225

When you are on a business trip, you always have the same person to take over for you. You are a *BOSS WHO USES ACTING CORPORALS*.   229

The loneliest man in your organization is the man with the new idea. You are a *BOSS WHO STIFLES CREATIVITY*.   232

You feel that all problems can be solved according to standard policies you've set up. You are a *POLICY MANAGER*.   238

You believe that, if you take care of the smallest details, the whole will take care of itself. You are a *BOSS WHO STRAINS OUT GNATS BUT SWALLOWS CAMELS.*   241

You believe that recognitions and awards are hardly important in a corporate system. You are a *BOSS WHO MISUSES RECOGNITIONS AND AWARDS.*   244

You demand flattery and deference from your employees—even in a social situation. You are a *BOSS WHOSE BOOTS MUST BE LICKED.*   247

There is no doubt that you can solve any problem before anyone can say "think." You are a *SOLVE-THE-WRONG-PROBLEM BOSS.*   252

You know that your decisions are often retractable because you often make decisions just to pacify one subordinate. You are a *YO-YO-PROCESS BOSS.*   255

There is no such thing as an honest mistake in your organization. You are a *NO-FREEDOM-TO-FAIL BOSS.*   263

You want all your people to act and think alike. You are a *BOSS WHO CRAVES CONFORMITY.*   267

All you are interested in is results; you don't care what methods your subordinate bosses use to get them. You are a *GET-ME-RESULTS—I-DON'T-CARE-HOW BOSS.*   271

You believe that it is better to make a wrong decision than no decision at all. You are an *OFTEN-IN-ERROR-BUT-NEVER-IN-DOUBT BOSS.*   276

You surround yourself with assistants and have no thought of its effect on the organization. You are a *HIGH-OVERHEAD BOSS.* 279

Supervision is an absolute; it cannot vary in kind with different organizations. You are a *BOSS WHO WORSHIPS THE UNITY OF COMMAND CONCEPT.*   283

You believe that preventing information from reaching the grapevine will eliminate it altogether. You are a *STARVE-THE-GRAPEVINE BOSS.*   288

You try to solve your problems by reshaping your organization. You are a *REORGANIZER BOSS.*   291

You're the first one to say that informal personnel relationships have no bearing on the job you are doing. You are a *BOSS WHO IGNORES THE INFORMAL ORGANIZATION*.   296

What your organization does is its problem—you declare yourself innocent of any action by "higher-ups." You are a *BOSS WHO DOES NOT CARRY THE CONSCIENCE OF HIS ORGANIZATION*.   300

You believe that civil rights are all well and good, but it just wouldn't work in your organization. You are a *CIVIL-WRONGS BOSS*.   306

the

100-PERCENT BOSS

Then there is the top executive who saw a statistical report on his organization which indicated some elements were *less* than 100 percent effective, and that other elements were *more* than 100 percent effective. (A common situation when standards are used.) He then gave a peremptory order that, "from now on this will be a 100 percent organization." Sure enough, every report he received thereafter showed that every element was 100 percent effective, and he was very pleased. What he was blissfully unaware of was the countless hours spent changing figures to make everything come out to 100 percent, making the system of comparison worse than useless! You think he was pretty stupid, but wait a minute! How do *you* discharge the managerial function of quality control?

And I am not talking about control of the quality of razor blades or ball bearings. I'm talking about the evaluation of the relative effectiveness of the organizational elements under your control, direction or command. If you feel inadequate in this function, you should not feel lonely, however. The state of this art is not well advanced, but some bosses do it better than others, and I can assure you that those who do it best combine brains, knowledge, personal observation, and intuition before they give any indication as to the relative ranking of their subordinate organizational elements.

I shall never forget the company commander, detested by his six peer company commanders and despised by his subordinates, whose company scored highest in the battle group in the basic combat proficiency test (a test at the end of basic training for each individual soldier to demonstrate how well he has learned the individual skills and knowledge covered in basic training).

During the weeks leading up to the completion of basic training and the test, the company commander's behavior had been so bad that the deputy battle group commander had taken him to task many times, and at one time in reprimanding him stated the opinion that if the unit were in battle instead of in mere training, the company commander would be in great danger of harm from his own men. Notwithstanding all I have stated, the battle group commander felt incapable of handling the situation in any other way but to honor the company commander whose company had scored highest in the basic combat proficiency test.

In the final analysis, the battle group commander had failed to develop an overall rating system which would "grind in" or consider the intangible elements which are the critical variables which truly make one organization better than another. And I can assure you that *any* system of evaluation which ignores the opinions of peers and subordinates of the bosses involved will never be an effective system.

Cameron Hawley has stated that "the quality of leadership is the determining factor in every institution that makes up our soci-

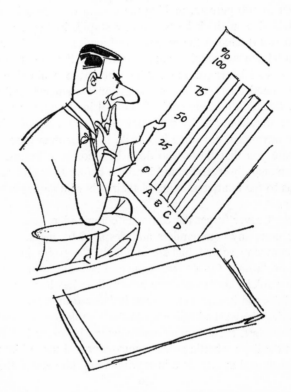

ety." [1] No one could quarrel seriously with that statement. But it is the *evaluation* of leaders and of the organizations they head that is the stumbling block of many a higher-level manager, commander or leader. And all too often they take the easy way out by giving the accolade (and the promotions) to those who have achieved *apparent* results in the *statistical* competition, without going through the difficult but necessary process of comprehensive evaluation and measurement.

I assure you that this process is not being done well today in business, industry or the military. To you I fling the gauntlet. And to those of you who feel in your hearts that you do it well, more power to you. If your subordinates *also* feel in their hearts and minds that you do it well, you are a rare and fortunate man.

SELF-ANALYSIS

Consider the factors you are currently using to measure the performance of your subordinates *and* those which you are using as a basis for promotion or non-promotion. Make a list of those factors. Examine them to see if they are primarily quantitative rather than qualitative. For example, are you giving a lot of attention and weight to measured output and little or no attention to the leadership qualities (or lack of them) which your subordinates demonstrate in their day-to-day activities? If your organizational performance appraisal form is limited in this regard, are you allowing it to limit you or are you adding, with additional remarks, your comments on the more intangible but important aspects of executive and individual behavior. If you are not doing the things implied by these questions, your organization bears this self-inflicted wound.

HEAL THE WOUND

Amend your personnel performance appraisal system to include the intangible but important factors just discussed, thereby putting into proper perspective the "quantifiable" aspects of your subordinates' performance. Having done this, make clear to all concerned how performance is measured by you. Also make it clear to your

[1] "The Quality of Leadership," *Personnel*, American Management Association. (May–June 1960), p. 14.

subordinates that they will not be stacked from top to bottom in your ratings; but that they will be competing against an "organizational par" which any one of them has the opportunity of achieving, not just a few. The benefits which you will accrue from this will be tremendous and the destructive competition among the members of your management team will be reduced or eliminated.

the

HORIZONTAL-PRIORITY-LIST BOSS

Among the most prevalent of self-inflicted wounds is the use of a *horizontal priority list.* This is probably self-defining, but I'm speaking of the executive who attaches and communicates the same degree of importance on every project he assigns to his subordinates. These subordinates are thereby prevented from doing first things first and from devoting varying time and effort in proportion to the importance of the projects. The result is that instead of having a vertical priority list, starting with first, second, and third, priorities, the list is a horizontal one, with every item bearing the number "one." You have worked for bosses who had horizontal priority lists. What is the angle of *yours* these days? (Now, don't trust *your own* answer—ask your subordinates to answer that question for you).

When I served in Korea in February of 1963, I had four principal subordinates: a lieutenant colonel, a major, a captain, and a second lieutenant. Each of the four had more than he and his subordinates could accomplish in one week, or two, or three. I was under pressure to get things done, and I was forced to pass on the pressure. Each week we had a brief discussion of workloads. Each of my subordinates had a list of the programs, projects, and tasks which had to be done. And their boss, your author, had identical lists. My two bosses, the Chief of Staff and the Commanding General, had similar lists, less detailed and partly written, partly mental. (They were also quite busy in adding to *my* list, which I in turn partially passed along to my four subordinates.)

During my weekly conferences with my subordinates, we went over these programs, projects, and tasks, trying to keep the priority list vertical. We applied Don Schoeller's "principle of calculated neglect." * Actually, it worked quite well. When we disagreed on relative priorities, I tried to get us to apply Mary Parker Follett's "Law of the Situation," [1] and that also worked quite well.

---

* See chapter entitled, "The Boss Who Does Not Practice the Principle of Calculated Neglect."
[1] Mary Parker Follett, *The Giving of Orders,* 1925. Published in Henry C. Metcalf and L. Urwick, eds., *Dynamic Administration, The Collected Papers of Mary Parker Follett,* (New York, Harper and Brothers, 1940), pp. 50-70.

When we were still in disagreement, I set the priorities by decree, trying to carry out the classical general-staff concept of my being an extension of the commander's mind as I did so, attempting to set the same priorities that he (my commander) would have set if he had been setting them personally. I think it was a pretty good system. It worked for us. How about trying it?

SELF-ANALYSIS

To achieve this diagnosis you must first check the angle of your priority list. This is easier said than done. As I indicated earlier you are not the best source of information on this. Rather, your subordinates can tell you what they understand to be your relative priorities. That being the case, periodically you should take inventory of your priorities with your subordinates. When you have done so and set them on a scale, if you find that all or most of them have essentially the same priority, you are a Horizontal-Priority-List Boss.

HEAL THE WOUND

Having taken your inventory, set a relative priority on each project you have previously given to your subordinates. This is not difficult to do if you will arrange them in a vertical list of relative priority. If you find that two items require the same priority, you can also communicate this. Having taken this action, as you assign tasks in the future you should integrate them into the existing priority list so that your subordinates will understand the relative importance you attach to them. Your self-inflicted wound will not heal until you have achieved this process.

the

BOSS WHO DOESN'T KNOW HOW
TO GET COMPLETED STAFF WORK

In lectures to thousands of executives on the general subject of this book I have included the following question in each lecture: "How many of you have read and are familiar with a small pamphlet entitled 'Completed Staff Work—How To Do It?' " The response to this question from each audience is a large number of raised hands. The next question I asked them is "How many of you have read and understand the small pamphlet entitled 'Completed Staff Work—How To Get It?' " In audience after audience either no hands have gone up or at the most, one or two. This research has been followed by my reprimanding the audience for being workers and not executives; they know how to *do* completed staff work, but they do not know how to get completed staff work, which is an executive function. I must now ask you the question: Into which category do you fall? I will now predict that you are like the vast majority of individuals in my lecture audiences and that your organization bears this self-inflicted wound.

COMPLETED STAFF WORK—THE COMMANDER'S PART

Everyone who has been in the Army for any length of time is familiar with the chart entitled "Completed Staff Work" which hangs conspicuously in many head-quarters offices. It tells the staff officer the steps he must follow to turn out completed staff work—how he should work out all details completely; consult other staff officers; study, write, restudy, re-write; present a single co-ordinated proposed action; avoid long memoranda or explanations; advise the chief what to do. But that is only half the story. Completed staff work is a two-way relationship between superior and subordinate. The subordinate does the work, but it is the superior who assigns the work to him. And it is the part played by the superior—his manner and method of assigning work —that can make completed staff work simple and useful or complex and wasteful.

Practically all of us are, during the course of a day, both superiors and subordinates. We assign jobs to our subordinates and we, ourselves, are given tasks by our superiors. It is necessary, therefore, to see both sides of the coin at all times. Heads—you assign a job and expect completed staff work; tails—you are given a job and are expected to produce completed staff work.

Since there already exists a fine set of principles to guide us in the role of subordinate, we need only the companion set of principles to guide us when we are cast in the role of superior.

That is the purpose of this article—to outline those steps which you, as a superior assigning a task, must follow if you expect to receive from your subordinates completed staff work. There are six basic steps to follow:

1. Know the problem. Obvious? Of course; but how many times are you, as the superior officer, not too sure of just what you are looking for? It is as simple as this —if you do not know, how can your subordinate? Perhaps the basic problem may be merely to find out whether or not there is a problem. Then why not be frank and say so? You may really have two problems. The first is to find out whether there is a problem. When that question is answered, you can decide whether or not you need to go further.

2. Make one individual responsible for the solution. During World War II a high ranking officer asked me to participate in one of his staff meetings. For almost an hour he discussed a most serious personnel problem that badly needed a suitable remedy. Walking back to my office after the meeting, I heard one of his staff officers ask, "Who has the ball on this one?" Apparently everyone—and that meant, of course, that no one individual felt in any way responsible for doing the job of research and investigation required before a sound and workable solution could be reached. Completed staff work, in this case, was less than a pious hope. Fixing individual responsibility is an essential and primary step.

3. State the problem clearly, precisely; explain reasons, background; limit the area to be studied. Having followed steps one and two, you are ready to explain the job to be done. Of especial importance is the "why" of the problem. If you know what is behind the problem, tell your subordinate. If you do not know why there is a problem, you had better find out or you are likely to get a piece of work which is itself a shot in the dark because, actually, there is no target. And while you are at it, limit the field of study as much as you can. Delving too far into a problem can be an endless and useless task; it is always possible to dig a little deeper and a little wider. So suggest a few areas to avoid. "Don't look into this or that" can sometimes be as good advice as positive suggestions.

4. Give from your knowledge and experience in the problem. You have learned a lot about your work. Pass it on to your subordinate. Save him the time and effort of pioneering along a road you have already travelled. He will not only appreciate your paternal display of competence, experience and knowledge, but you will make the development of his final solution easier and better for both of you.

5. Set a time limit; or request the assignee to estimate a completion date. Here is another "must." Give your subordinate the time he needs to do an adequate job. "If you want it bad, you get it bad," is a frequently heard caution. On the other hand, you must make certain that your subordinate realizes that you need the completed answer by a certain date. Assigning a task without a deadline for completion is like being asked by a friend "to come over to dinner sometime." Its very indefiniteness provokes a feeling of insincerity and unimportance.

6. Assure your subordinate that you are available for discussion as work progresses. This step provides the flexibility that any good plan needs to be workable. Despite all your efforts to explain the problem, its whys, wherefores and limitations, you can be sure that questions which only you can answer will arise in your subordinate's mind as the study progresses. The English language is deceiving and confusing. What you said and what he understood it to mean may be along two very different lines. Being available for discussion does not mean that you are going to do your subordinate's thinking for him. But you should make him feel that if he gets stuck, you are still his guiding star. That's why you're the boss.

Follow these six basic steps and you will have every reason to expect completed staff work. Test it the next time you receive an assignment or you are ready to give a job to one of your staff.

Remember that the caliber of the completed staff work you receive is in direct ratio to the guidance you give to obtain it. It is a two-way proposition—any way you look at it.

COMPLETED STAFF WORK

How To Do It

Study of a problem and presentation of its solution in such form that only approval or disapproval of the completed action is required.

1. Work out all details completely.
2. Consult other staff officers.
3. Study, write, restudy, rewrite.
4. Present a single, co-ordinated proposed action. Do not equivocate.
5. Do not present long memoranda or explanations. Correct solutions are usually recognizable.
6. Advise the Chief what to do. Do not ask him.

If you were the Chief, would You sign the paper you have prepared and thus stake your professional reputation on its being right? If not, take it back and work it over; it is not yet completed staff work.

How To Get It

Assignment of a problem and a request for a solution in such a way that completed staff work is readily possible.

1. Know the problem.
2. Make one individual responsible to you for the solution.
3. State the problem to him clearly, precisely; explain reasons, background; limit the area to be studied.
4. Give the individual the advantage of your knowledge and experience in this problem.
5. Set a time-limit; or request assignee to estimate a completion date.
6. Assure him that you are available for discussion as work progresses.

If you were the subordinate, would You consider the guidance, given at the time the assignment is made and as the directed work progresses, to be adequate for readily completed staff work? Adequate guidance eliminates wasted effort, makes for completed staff work.[1]

[1] H. A. Damminger, Colonel E. A. Waddell, "Completed Staff Work—The Commander's Part," *Army Information Digest*, January 1953.

the

SEQUENTIAL–CO-ORDINATION BOSS

This boss insists on written co-ordination which consists of addressing a paper to several different addressees, in turn. By the time the paper gets back to the office of origin, each addressee without the benefit of conversation or discussion with the other addressees, has taken a firm *concrete* stand on the subject in writing, and I do mean *concrete*. To change his written opinion later is impossible, for it would mean losing face, which is just as important in the Western World as in the Orient—at least it's just as big a barrier to progress. A corporation recently analyzed ten years of decisions which history (a fairly good judge) had shown to be classified as "good" or "wise." They looked for a common pattern among these decisions. The one I remember hearing the corporation vice president * describe in a talk at the American Management Association was the fact that the good and wise decisions had been the result of *simultaneous co-ordination* rather than *sequential co-ordination*. By simultaneous co-ordination they meant that the problems and other aspects of the decision-making process had been discussed around a table by the *action* people involved, where each could have the benefit of the other's opinions and ideas and where each could take positions and then retreat from them without losing face like he would if he had to retract a written "concrete" paper. I believe you understand and probably agree with my point. My question is: what sort of co-ordination processes do you require *your* subordinates to go through these days?

I know of no more discerning writing on this subject than that of the great Mary Parker Follett who in 1932 stated four fundamental principles of organization, all of which began with the word co-ordination:

1. Co-ordination by direct contact of the responsible people concerned.

* Charles W. L. Foreman, AMA Fellow and Vice-President, United Parcel Service, Inc., New York, N.Y.

2. Co-ordination in the early stages.
3. Co-ordination as the reciprocal relating of all the factors in a situation.
4. Co-ordination as a continuing process.[1]

Her chapter entitled "Individualism in a Planned Society," is a "must" for anyone truly wishing to understand the psychology of co-ordination. However, I must warn the reader that others before him have been reading it for thirty years and failing to demonstrate in practice that they have benfited from it!

SELF-ANALYSIS

Reflect upon the problem-solving processes which have been used in your organization in the past weeks and months. Have they relied primarily upon *simultaneous co-ordination* or *sequential co-*

[1] Published in Henry C. Metcalf and L. Urwick, eds., *Dynamic Administration, The Collected Papers of Mary Parker Follett* (New York, Harper and Brothers, 1940).

ordination? If your answer is *simultaneous* you are in good shape. If your answer is *sequential* your organization has a self-inflicted wound.

HEAL THE WOUND

Therapy for this wound is predicted by the diagnosis, but it requires elaboration. In fact, it may run contrary to your feelings about conferences and meetings, because they are the most common form of *simultaneous co-ordination*. You may have acquired prejudice or bias along the way with the belief that meetings or conferences are for the most part unproductive. I would argue that this was because the meetings were ineffectively conducted, rather than because of the meetings themselves. The best research I know on this subject is contained in Dr. Rensis Likert's book *New Patterns of Management* (New York, McGraw-Hill, 1961) in Chapter 3, pp. 27 and 28. The research findings showed a direct correlation among the frequency of the supervisors' use of work group meetings, his use of ideas which emerged from the meetings, and management's evaluation of the supervisor. Perhaps this will help you dispel your previous notions about work-group meetings. I promise you many benefits from this procedure.

the

BOSS WHO TREATS the SYMPTOM and IGNORES the ILLNESS

An undesirable custom so prevalent today is one I call *treating the symptom and ignoring the illness.*

An example in military management happened in the winter of 1957–58 at a military post during the extreme financial "austerity" period. The motor officer learned gasoline was being used unnecessarily during cold weather by men running the engines of parked trucks with the heaters turned on, trying to keep warm. The officer solved the problem by having the heaters removed, whereupon there occurred a series of driving accidents caused by faulty vision, caused in turn by clouded windshields, caused by lack of heaters. You think this was stupid, don't you? But stop a minute! How many symptoms have *you* treated the past year?

Of course, making the distinction between symptom and illness is not easy. But then, nothing is easy in this complex world which demands so much of commanders, managers, and leaders. A humorous example is the story of the smoking man who had read so much about smoking and lung cancer that he became very worried and anxious and finally decided to stop. Did he stop *smoking?* No. He stopped reading!

Here is a rule of thumb for you. I recommend that you remember it every time you tackle a new problem, or an old one, for that matter:

> Whatever you think the problem is,
> You can be sure that's not the problem.

The overall managerial subject we are discussing here is how to get at the roots of a problem in order to deal with it properly, rather than treating it in the shallow, superficial manner demonstrated in the preceding samples. As we have seen in the chapter on the Boss Who Solves the Wrong Problem, there is a tendency to start solving problems before they have been clearly diagnosed as to cause and effect. This is caused in part by the rapid tempo of today's organizational life, but somehow it must be resisted by you because in the long run treating the symptom and ignoring the illness is even more costly and time consuming.

SELF-ANALYSIS

Examine the last several problem solving events in your organization, particularly those which were "solved" long enough ago for you to determine whether you treated the symptom or the illness. In other words, if you treated the symptom only, the illness will have caused another misleading symptom to bubble to the top after a period of time. If this has happened in more than a small percentage of the cases, your organization bears this self-inflicted wound.

HEAL THE WOUND

Increase the depth of your analysis of each problem prior to adopting solutions. Don't examine cause and effect, but identify them positively before you act. If you will do this effectively, your solved problems will stay in the grave once you put them there, rather than returning to haunt you in a manner befitting a first-class horror story. If you are not successful in this process, you will find yourself chasing vampires (problems) on a full time basis with a stake in one hand and a hammer in the other.

the

BOSS WHO MANAGES
BY COMPROMISE

I'm sure the Boss Who Manages By Compromise is not a stranger to you, but my particular breed requires some description. I'm not talking about the kind of compromise which often is a necessity in democratic government.

The boss I refer to gives his subordinates a problem to solve, one which can only be solved by a "black" or "white" decision, as indicated by the opposing alternative courses of action which an honest staff eventually comes up with. Then the boss, instead of making a black or white decision, comes up with a "gray" decision which is nothing more than a partial sop to each of the disagreeing groups, satisfying neither and ending up with a solution that is unsatisfactory, or at best less than the best.

This boss probably thinks he has solved the problem. He has not. He has merely traded one self-inflicted wound for another just as painful and just as serious. While there are different ways of analyzing this problem, I have a personal view on this which has been quite helpful to myself and to others. It has to do with *attitudes* of the boss and his subordinates as to what is expected from subordinates, and what is rewarded when it is produced. In other words, does the boss reward agreement among his staff before they come to him with proposed solutions to problems, or does he reward healthy argument and honest disagreement? Does he receive watered-down compromises for rubber-stamp decisions, or well-developed and analyzed opposing alternatives which require only the exercise of executive judgment (which is what he is being paid for) to result in a good decision?

Returning to attitudes and to the decision-making climate, a boss will get objective staff work if in his decision-making he can avoid the aura of status-gaining and status-losing on the part of his subordinates when he adopts one recommendation and rejects another. Perhaps worded in a better way, he accepts the recommendation of one over the recommendation of the other as being, in his opinion, the better of two good proposals. Then, if he rewards *both* subordinates for having turned in good honest staff work, he will have avoided the winner-loser attitudes and all the undesirable by-products.

Lest the reader regard this approach as unrealistic rationalization, may I suggest that, in the final analysis, the decision which chooses one alternative course of action over another is made because the decision-maker—the boss—assigns *values* to the incremental factors which are weighed on the decision scale, and those values, when summed up, determine the choice. Nor should the boss be disturbed because he finds a subordinate assigning different values than he to the same factors involved in the problem-solving and decision-making. This merely means, on the part of the honest subordinate, that he has done his best in assigning those values and has furnished his boss with his best analyses and recommendations. If, in applying his final, conceptual analysis to the problem, his boss changes those values and comes up with a decision different from that which he has recommended, the subordinate should be made aware of those differing values, but also should be made aware that he turned in good, honest, and skillful work, rather than made to feel that he turned in something with which his boss disagreed.

In proceeding along this line of action, after he has made the decision and chosen a recommendation of one subordinate and not chosen the recommendation of another subordinate—and explained his decision to both—the boss has avoided an unsatisfactory compromise, he has insured objective analysis and recommendations in the future, and he has made the best possible decision.

It has become fashionable in recent years for self-appointed critics of committee action to refer to the camel as "an animal put together by a committee." The subject of committees is dealt with in other chapters, such as "The Unaware-of-Groups Boss," but here and now I wish to state that I consider it far more likely that the "ship of the desert" was the product of a boss who managed by compromise. I hope I have proven my point.

My final comment is: what is the color of your decisions these days—black, white or gray?

SELF-ANALYSIS

Reflect upon the last several times two or more of your subordinates have come to you with opposing recommendations for solving the same problem. In other words, one was recommending a black solution and the other was recommending a white solution. How did you resolve this situation? Did you end up with a black or white decision? Or did you end up with a gray one that was actually a hybrid of the two problems? If a significant number of your solutions have been gray, your organization probably bears this self-inflicted wound.

HEAL THE WOUND

Try to convince yourself and your subordinates that there is absolutely nothing wrong when one subordinate's recommendation is not adopted and another's is. Convince them that you believe that the process of seeking solutions to problems requires the type of independent thinking that produces multiple proposals for solution, including some that are diametrically opposed to each other. Further, develop within yourself the ability to recognize the valuable elements of opposing recommendations so that it will not be uncommon for you to come up with a solution of your own which incorporates the best elements of other proposed solutions. In this way you will not be guilty of *management* by *compromise,* rather you will be guilty of using the brain the dear Lord gave you.

SUGGESTIONS FOR FURTHER READING

Barnard, Chester I., "The Environment of Decision." *The Functions of the Executive,* Cambridge, Mass., Harvard University Press, 1953. Chap. XIII, pp. 185–189.

the

BOSS WHO USES ACTING CORPORALS

Many a self-inflicted wound is inherited by managers by the very fact that they are in an "old" organization, such as the military ones, wherein practices once adopted are seldom questioned. One of these I call the *acting corporal* with the same healthy contempt that the term connotes when used by soldiers. It is the idea or belief that "someone has to be in charge when the boss is gone" and that someone *must* be the *senior* person in military or civilian rank, regardless of the capabilities of the individual involved or the demands or unique aspects of the *situation*. This practice is rarely required by the regulation (except where true *command* in its military sense is involved) but it is done by default, only because it has always been the custom to do so. This practice does much harm and almost *no* good. It creates the "crown prince" or "heir apparent" situation, causing discouragement and resentment among the individuals who are the day-to-day peers of the Acting Corporal. They resent both him and the boss who gave him the title, and rightly so.

I have just received detailed information on a typical example of an Acting Corporal and the harm he is doing to the organization. I should say, the harm he and his boss who uses him as such are doing to the organization. The boss is often absent for one to ten days at a time, at which times he places the senior branch chief under him (in point of rank and service), in charge of the division headed by the absent boss. Each time this happens, the Acting Corporal earns the complete contempt of all concerned by "throwing his weight around" in a most nauseating fashion. He treats the other branch chiefs—who are his peers when the boss is not absent—in the most arrogant and officious manner imaginable. He uses the word "I" repeatedly, with statements like "I want this done" or "When I give an order I want it followed. . . ." Recently he held a meeting of the branch chiefs and their principal assistants, and abused and degraded them unmercifully for no ap-

229

parent reason—then he took the day off without anyone's permission. He is held in contempt by all who know him, except for his immediate boss and the boss above him, who seem blissfully unaware of the wound they are inflicting on their organization every time they set him up as an Acting Corporal.

The manager who uses this practice when it is not dictated by command regulations is a defaulter—he has acquired liabilities when he could have acquired assets. I know a large corporation which requires *every* organizational element to have an "acting chief" whenever the boss is gone for a day or more. But is it the Acting Corporal (the senior subordinate)? It is not! The peer subordinates (five division chiefs in a department) *take turns* acting as chief on a rotating basis. This corporation has thereby created a built-in executive development program which is worth its weight in gold, and the effectiveness of the unit could not be higher, devoid as it is of the tensions, jealousies, and other human problems generated by the Acting Corporal situation.

You have been involved in an Acting Corporal situation many times and disliked it heartily (except when you were the corporal!). Then, why are you using it in *your own* organization right now?

SELF-ANALYSIS

This one is easy to test yourself on. You are either guilty or not guilty. When you are absent, do you put an Acting Corporal in charge? If the answer is yes, and it is the same person all the time, you have a self-inflicted wound.

HEAL THE WOUND

Call your management team together—after first telling your Acting Corporal what you're about to do—and explain that, in the future during your absences, when it is clearly necessary that you appoint someone to be in charge temporarily, you are going to do it on a roster basis, with each member of your team taking his turn at being the temporary boss. They will be delighted with the news, and you will be delighted with the results. And the man who has been your Acting Corporal in the past will get to like it also, unless

he is not man enough to adjust to it and compete with his peers. If he can not take it, it is well to know it now, and perhaps he may offer his services elsewhere.

SUGGESTIONS FOR FURTHER READING

Christensen, C. Roland, *Management Succession in Small and Growing Enterprises.* Boston, Division of Research, Graduate School of Business Administration, Harvard University, 1953.

Zaleznik, A., *Worker Satisfaction and Development, A Case Study of Work and Social Behavior in a Factory Group.* Boston, Harvard University Division of Research Graduate School of Business Administration, 1956.

the

BOSS WHO STIFLES CREATIVITY

The loneliest man in your organization is the man with a new idea.
This is another sad fact you must face if you hope to purge yourself of self-inflicted wounds. Some time ago I managed to "screw
my courage to the sticking point" and wrote an article entitled,
"The Loneliest Man in the Military is the Man with a New Idea."
As publication date neared, I prepared to beat a hasty retreat and,
if necessary, to go south for my health. Publication day arrived,
however, and so did several telephone calls. In the days, weeks,
and months that followed, the editor and the author were swamped
with letters of approbation, most of which asked for permission to
republish or reproduce the article. In addition to being reproduced
and republished widely throughout the Army, Navy, Air Force,
and Marine Corps, the National Association of Suggestion Systems
reproduced and distributed it to the approximately twelve-hundred
business, industrial, and governmental organizations which form
its membership.

My original plan for this book was to rewrite the article for
the purpose of demilitarizing and heterogenizing it, but I have
changed my mind because of the response to the original article
from all types of organizations. For fear of disturbing whatever it
contains that struck such a responsive chord among the many who
read it, it is quoted verbatim in the following paragraphs. My only
request of you is that you "internalize" its contents into *your* organization, which no doubt contains many, many very lonely men.

THE LONELIEST MAN IN THE MILITARY IS THE MAN WITH A NEW IDEA

If we examine this statement objectively, there is ample reason to believe that it is
all too true.

We talk of management tools today. The most neglected and improperly used
management tool, in my opinion, is the suggestion program.

It is a fact of life that the best ideas don't reach fruition through command
channels. The very nature of our military relationship actively works against radically
new ideas, believe it or not. A case in point: Tomorrow morning your immediate sub-

ordinate may come to you with a new idea—a radically new idea. If you are typical (and you are, whether you want to be or not) you will either pour cold water on it or "'damn it with faint praise."

Your subordinate with the new idea has only two alternatives. One, he can take the idea up with you again, and risk your ire by appearing to disagree with your prior "judgment." If he does this you will probably set him straight in no uncertain terms—and that will be the last new idea you ever hear about from him. Two, your subordinate can put his idea on paper, and drop it in the nearest suggestion box. The

suggestion will then be forwarded to you for evaluation, since it pertains to your organization. You are filled with consternation when you realize that your subordinate has by-passed you, and you become even more concerned when you remember that you have already expressed an opinion to him on the idea.

You realize you must reprimand him, for his own good, which you do very earnestly. You may even order him to prepare the endorsement recommending non-adoption of the suggestion. This is real poetic justice, and the second alternative available to your subordinate will have the same result: it will be the last new idea he attempts to sell while he is with your organization, or perhaps with any other.

Another thing which will kill a new idea—and prevent future ones from even being submitted—is inept and subjective suggestion evaluation. It seems to be a fact of life that people resent suggestions for improvement in their own organizations because they regard them as criticisms of existing situations, for which they feel at least in part responsible, or guilty. Let's take a couple of horrible examples.

At one large military post, a suggestion was submitted that employees in post exchanges wear nameplates, enabling customers to perform the common (and very desirable) courtesy of addressing them by name. The suggestion was rejected for the ridiculous reason that such an action "would cause overfamiliarity with employees."

A suggestion that a drinking fountain be installed near a tennis court was rejected because "The suggestion has been given serious consideration and it has been decided that if a drinking fountain were installed a latrine would also have to be installed and a latrine by a tennis court would be undesirable."

The disgusted suggestor was then counselled by his wife to resubmit the suggestion with the obvious solution: That the drinking fountain be installed *without* the latrine, and that a sign be placed over the fountain reading, "For Intake Only!"

Both the nameplate and drinking fountain suggestions went through the complete evaluation process and were rejected by the suggestion committee, as indicated in minutes signed by the chairman!

Fortunately the suggestor of the "nameplate" idea had a temper. He promptly put the same suggestion on a fresh suggestion form and mailed it direct, marked "personal" to Major General H. C. Parks, Director of the Army and Air Force Exchange Service. The suggestion received careful appraisal and was adopted for all exchanges in the Army and Air Force (at the discretion of major commanders). I'm afraid, however, that this is the exception rather than the rule.

HOW TO SAVE IDEAS

What can be done to lower the mortality rate of new ideas in the military? It is a most difficult question, but I may have a partial solution.

One way is to improve the suggestion program, which is easier said than done. I recently interviewed an installation commander who inherited a dead suggestion program and in a short period of time converted it into such a dynamically successful program that it was given department-wide publicity. Based on his experience, my own two years' experience as chairman of an installation incentive awards committee, and interviews with other personnel involved with successful suggestion programs, I have come up with some criteria which may help installation commanders evaluate and improve their own suggestion programs:

1. Put "top management" on the suggestion committee. Since service on the committee is an "additional duty" it is easily sloughed off by missing meetings and/or sending a section representative who is considerably less than inspired by being volunteered for something when he has a full "in" basket. The general staff in the Army (G1, G2, G3, G4, and Comptroller), and comparable individuals in the other services should all be members, by name and not by position.

2. Don't delegate the power to disapprove a suggestion any lower than the power to approve one. There is no more important criterion than this, and probably none that is violated more often. My best example of the observance of this rule is a Major General, chief of staff of a major command, who reserves to himself the right to disapprove, as well as to approve suggestions. I contend that he has insured careful and objective suggestion evaluation, even if he doesn't even read the disapproval he signs.

3. The program must have the commander's personal support, and this doesn't mean lip service. It must be a fact, and it must be common knowledge among all personnel in the command. An action often regarded as lip service is the presentation of awards in the commander's office, rather than in the office of the suggestor and in the presence of his superiors, peers and subordinates. The latter approach is worth dozens of times the value of the former, if it is done sincerely. And it doesn't take any more of the commander's time if it is carefully planned.

4. Suggestions must be processed rapidly. Nothing will discourage an enthusiastic

suggestor sooner than to have to wait months to get results on his suggestion. I know of a post where the suggestion has been sarcastically made that effort be made to process suggestions some time during the present tour of military personnel submitting suggestions.

5. The integrity of the program must be carefully guarded. This sounds obvious, but it is difficult. In fact, it takes a lot of courage to administer a truly objective and honest program. Reversing a subjective initial evaluation by an organizational element requires knowledge and ability. One aid in doing this is to call upon the services of the management assistance group (sometimes called management engineers) usually located in the Comptroller's Office. Another pitfall is the old (and despicable) practice of recommending disapproval of a suggestion, making it stick and then putting the suggestion into effect. This must be watched carefully, for it will give the program a dishonest reputation.

6. When in doubt, adopt. The net result of adopting borderline suggestions will be beneficial. A truism of suggestion programs is that the benefits from the programs vary in direct proportion to the number of suggestions submitted. This, plus the additional fact that a well-administered suggestion program will generate increased participation, makes it incumbent upon the commander that suggestors receive the benefit of any doubt.

There are other criteria for a good suggestion program, but if a commander can insure these six, I feel he can be reasonably sure he has a good suggestion program. The task of measuring his program against these criteria is not easy, and he must do it very carefully, enlisting objective aid when necessary.

I'd like to add this statement of fact: The best ideas in existence at your installation have not been adopted. They probably haven't even been put in writing!

MORE IS NEEDED

I regret to state, however, that a good suggestion program is only a partial solution to the problems described in the first part of this article. What can be done to create a climate in a military organization which encourages offering and support of new ideas (especially *radically* new ideas)?

This question is as difficult as any command, management or leadership problem facing a military commander today. I don't know anyone who has a completely good answer to it. Let's explore it a little.

We are talking about an organizational climate where individuals feel motivated to think creatively, and where they and their superiors feel motivated to actively and vigorously push and sponsor a new idea until it is either adopted or proven to be not useful beyond any reasonable doubt. This would be a wonderful atmosphere —one in which we all would like to serve, but in which few have served. As stated earlier, the very nature of military relationships works against this atmosphere.

The single concept of "You must go through channels," ever-present at all levels in the military, is perhaps the greatest single barrier to effectiveness and efficiency of management that was ever self-inflicted by man. I don't see how we will ever have the desired atmosphere until the concept of that false and artificial barrier is exploded for the myth that it is. I make no attempt to assess the value of "channels" in combat or tactical operations, but I think someone should.

In the meantime, if you would like to have a couple of questions for sampling the atmosphere in your present organization, ask this one of anyone in it. "Do you feel free to propose a new idea, regardless of the subject, to a supervisor two, three or four echelons above you without taking it up first with your immediate and intervening supervisors?"

Ask the next one of higher level supervisors: "Do you encourage lower level

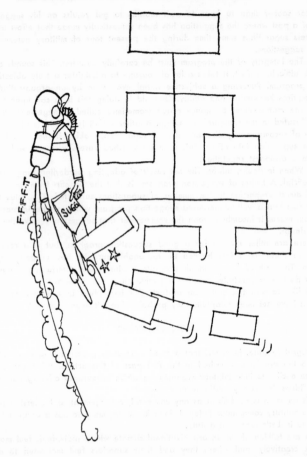

supervisors or employees to communicate new ideas directly to you, by-passing intervening supervisors?"

Obviously, the answer you will get is, "No, of course not, I'm in the military. Haven't you ever heard of military channels?"

Here's another question that will bother you. An eminent university professor after much research has determined that over half of all good ideas that reach fruition are turned down six times before they are adopted. The question that you can't possibly answer with an honest "yes" is: Do the military personnel in your organization feel free to press on with an idea through six successive rejections?

There is a one-in-a-million chance that there is such an organization in the military. If yours is such please let me know. I'd like very much to research it.

I hope you were successful in internalizing this article and that you equated its contents to *your* organization, its "lonely" men, and its boss (you). If you were successful, your plan of action is laid out for you. All you need do is to carry it out. (I believe the Self-Analysis and Heal the Wound sections are adequately covered in this section.)

SUGGESTIONS FOR FURTHER READING

Mason, Joseph G., *How to Be a More Creative Executive*. New York, McGraw-Hill, 1960.

Osborn, Alex F., *Applied Imagination*. New York, Charles Scribner's Sons, 1960.

the

POLICY MANAGER

You know the type—the boss who goes around promulgating policies all over the place. They are both spoken and written, typed and in longhand. He thinks he is insuring good management when he actually is insuring that his subordinates will not be allowed to *Think* in solving his problems. Not long ago the president of a large corporation stated proudly to a group of business men and government students that "no problem can come up to an employee that he cannot find our policy on it in our *Company Policy Book*." I could not refrain from breaking in on the intercom with, "I hope it's a looseleaf book, sir!"

The president did not like my comment. In fact he stiffened up and spent about ten minutes insisting that his organization was quite flexible and made frequent changes in policy. However, I don't think he convinced his audience that such was the case.

A most glaring example is the Pentagon "position" which each organizational element has on controversial subjects. When a new officer joins a staff element, regardless of rank, his "indoctrination" consists of thoroughly implanting "our position" into his brain. He is told what the position is, how to defend it, and how to attack and counterattack to preserve the position. The new officer is not invited to evaluate the position. If he does so voluntarily he'll probably get into trouble. You've probably suffered in such a system and wondered how to keep honest. Are your subordinates working for a Policy Manager now? Stated differently, "Brains or Policy, which are your people using?"

It goes without saying that a certain amount of policies are necessary for organizations to function effectively. If there were no policies whatsoever, employees and executives would be prevented from separating their day-to-day problems into the two general categories of the unique and the routine. Such a situation would tend to prevent the use, for example, of the concept known as *management by exception*. What I am pointing the finger at, however, is the prescription of policies in such detail that they are no longer *guidelines* to action but they prescribe the action itself, thereby preventing individuals from bringing their brainpower to bear upon the problem situations.

SELF-ANALYSIS

Identify and examine the written and unwritten policies which exist in your organization. Don't do this alone, but find out what policies your subordinates believe to exist, whether they are written or unwritten, formal or informal. Consider the detail involved in these policies. If you find that the policies are in such detail that they are forcing your employees to use policies instead of brains, you are a Policy Manager.

HEAL THE WOUND

The prescription for healing this wound is predicted by the diagnosis. Determine and set a proper level of policy for your organization. Avoid excessive detail, permitting your subordinates to utilize their very fine brains, the primary reason for which they were hired. Finally, let your employees participate in this analysis. They will be able to make some very fine input into your policy-decisions as to what policies you should have.

SUGGESTIONS FOR FURTHER READING

Thompson, Stewart, *Management Creeds and Philosophies, Top Management Guides in Our Changing Economy.* American Management Association, Inc., Research Study Number 32, New York, 1958.

the

BOSS WHO STRAINS OUT GNATS
BUT SWALLOWS CAMELS

This one is straight from the Bible. One day Jesus was berating the Scribes and Pharisees. Among other things he said, "These things you ought to have done, while not leaving the others undone. Blind guides, who strain out the gnat but swallow the camel!" (Matt. 23:23–24). The thing He was talking about is done every day, by thousands of executives. Jesus was no doubt visualizing one of the Pharisees carefully removing small insects from their containers of milk, then confidently swallowing the liquid, not noticing the camels which went down with it!

A good present-day example is the budget committee which will argue intensely over a $35-item (with which they feel confident and secure) and then gloss over a $2,000-item with hardly any discussion or evaluation (especially if they think the boss wants the $2,000-item approved).

Another example of this is the "Nitpicker" boss who carefully examines a paper for split infinitives or misspelled words and then doesn't have time to evaluate the "guts" of the document. A typical example of the value of the nitpicker's work is the following suggestion of how a modern-day nitpicker would have assisted Mr. Lincoln on the day before he delivered a certain speech:

Lincoln's Gettysburg Address
(Corrected for rewrite)

SAY "EIGHTY FIVE"   "FOUNDED" WOULD BE BETTER

(Fourscore and seven) years ago our fathers (brought forth)

PUT THE NAME IN!   SOUNDS AWKWARD. SAY "WITH THE IDEA OF FREEDOM"

on this continent a new (nation,) (conceived in liberty) and dedicated

HOW ABOUT WOMEN?

to the proposition that (all men) are created equal.

MAKE THIS THE FIRST PARAGRAPH – WERE TAKING TOO LONG TO GET TO THE STORY!

(Now we are engaged in a great civil war) testing whether

that nation or any nation so conceived and so dedicated can long

ENDURE WHAT? MAKE IT "LAST"   PUT IN NAME OF WAR

(endure.) We are met on a great battlefield of that (war.) We have

come to dedicate a portion of that field as a (final resting-place)

DON'T BEAT ABOUT THE BUSH – SAY "CEMETERY"

for those who here gave their lives that that nation might live.

(This item is not original. By an anonymous author, it has been around the Washington scene for several years.)

SELF-ANALYSIS

Check your executive behavior very carefully on this one. Reflect upon the changes you make in the work presented to you and the requirements you place upon subordinates in this regard. Do you find, for example, that you concentrate more on the form and less on the substance? For example, are you more concerned with having an even margin on the right hand side of the letters you sign than you are with the content of those letters? Are you more concerned with "unsplitting infinitives" than you are with the message of the sentence which contains the infinitive? If so, you are a Boss Who Strains Out Gnats But Swallows Camels.

HEAL THE WOUND

There is more to healing this wound than merely stopping doing the things described in this chapter and in the diagnosis. We have not examined why you behave the way you do in this regard. Unfortunately it is probably because you feel more competent in the *form* department than you do in the *substance* department. And this will be difficult for you to admit, even to yourself in the privacy of your own mind. I can only suggest that if you will take the time you are now spending on the form and devote it to the substance of your job, you will soon become competent in the important aspects of your job and you will not find yourself satisfying your basic needs by checking on margins and unsplitting infinitives. Rather, you will receive your satisfactions from doing your primary job well. Try it. I guarantee this one.

the

BOSS WHO MISUSES RECOGNITIONS and AWARDS

How many times have you received a well-earned commendation or award? How many times have you personally spent time or midnight oil preparing one (or fighting to get one approved—this takes courage and effort) for one of your subordinates. I know of an organization where the number-two man recommended one for the number-three man, and the number-two man spent countless hours on it, finally getting it approved. When this was done, the Chief said to the number-two man, "Now, I want you to receive an award also, but I'm no good at writing them up. If you want one, write it up and I'll sign it." In this case the number-two man refused to do so, and received no award, and will never forget the incident. You couldn't be guilty of anything like this, but these two questions may make you squirm a bit: Is the "recognition and awards" system administered well in your organization? Since you were so quick to answer "Yes," how do you know it is?

This case in point happened in the military, but it has many counterparts in business, industrial, educational, and even clerical activities. While the military systems of recognition and awards are perhaps more formally established, other types of endeavour are expanding their systems, not only for their obvious merit but also for their value to the organizations themselves.

These programs are difficult to administer, but the boss who neglects this function, who delegates and redelegates it, has a serious self-inflicted wound in this day of individual competition between motivated people who are trying to progress up the ladder of accomplishment in organizations.

A prevalent offender in this department of executive leadership is the boss who takes the view that *his* subordinates will not be recommended for overall organizational awards unless they *exceed* the standards set by the overall organization! He does this as a matter of pride, and he stupidly expects his subordinates to share the same feeling as they observe themselves going unrecognized for the same quality of performance which is receiving organization-wide recognition in other departments managed or commanded by the peers of their own boss! His subordinates are proud of their own performance, but they have pure contempt for their boss who

does not go to bat for them when they meet the standards of the overall organization.

If you are this kind of boss, and if you are still not convinced, please do a bit of role-playing by placing yourself in the situation in which your subordinates find themselves, and your research and study of the subject will be completed, I assure you.

SELF-ANALYSIS

How does *your* administration of recognition and awards compare with that of your peer bosses? How do you know? How do the standards which you set for recognition and awards compare with the standards of the larger organization of which yours is a part?

How do you know? In answering these questions the beliefs and perceptions of your subordinates on these subjects must be taken into consideration, even if it develops that they are inaccurate. This is because on a sensitive subject like recognition and awards, the important thing is how the program is perceived by the individuals involved, rather than the actual facts of the case. Of course it is ideal if the facts and perceptions agree. Finally, do you prepare the recommendations for awards during your normal busy working day, or do you prepare them in the calm and quiet of the evening or weekend? If you are able to arrive at valid answers to these questions, you will be able to determine if your organization bears this self-inflicted wound.

HEAL THE WOUND

Having identified your deficiencies and their specific natures, you must set out to correct them in a manner which will be known and publicized throughout your own organization and the larger organization of which yours is a part. I cannot be more specific than this, but if you will apply these two general prescriptions, your wound will begin to heal.

the

BOSS WHOSE BOOTS MUST BE LICKED

Now we come to the boss who communicates in one way or another, by acts of omission and/or commission, that he expects his subordinates to *lick his boots*. This is a subject which is never discussed in the open, but often is discussed in sub rosa fashion, in small subgroups at cocktail or bridge parties, in car pools, and in rest rooms (after carefully looking under doors to make sure that the boss or one of his bootlickers is not there). It is a subject that makes you and me uncomfortable right now, for I do not enjoy writing this and I am sure you do not enjoy reading it, but I'm sure you agree with me that we are discussing a very important subject which is integral to any examination of the organizational environment in which we find ourselves.

The practice of *bootlicking* * is age-old. The Oxford dictionary shows the word "sycophant" first being used in the year 1548, but I'm sure it dates back to the first group of human beings who had any sort of constituted leader, or *boss*. It doesn't take much imagination to visualize the subordinate caveman telling his boss how well he (the boss) swung his club, or even presenting a carefully polished club to him. Nor does it take much observation in this day and age to pinpoint the sycophants and bootlickers hard at work in any business, industry, military, educational, or governmental organization. They are well-known and identified by their peers throughout the organization, and they are regarded with utmost contempt by those peers who do not stoop to licking the boss' boots. The finger of scorn is pointed at them at every opportunity.

The sad, unwelcome, and inescapable truth about all this, which you may be very reluctant to admit, is this: *If bootlicking exists or is allowed to exist in any organization, it is the fault of one man—the boss!* (Plus one woman—the boss' wife.) This will make you squirm a bit, but it is absolutely true! You don't believe me? I'll prove it.

* Other words for it: "brown-noseing", "A-K'ing", "sycophancy" (and other terms too vulgar to mention here; if you don't know them, just ask around.)

247

In the chapter on the Human-Erosion Boss we referred to Rod Serling's television drama *Patterns* which depicts behavior of top management officials (and their wives) in a business organization. The crisis comes when the autocratic president succeeds in riding to death a senior vice president who has had the guts to oppose him at times and to place his loyalty to the organization above his loyalty to the president. At a very dramatic staff meeting, the vice president suffers a fatal heart attack, brought on by the merciless public scourging of the president. In the dramatic moments which follow, the man who had previously been picked to succeed the vice president as soon as the president with his *human erosion* tactics could break or kill him, confronts the president in a showdown situation. He accuses the president of hating the dead vice president because he represented his (the president's) conscience, and makes the statement, "It's a rotten thing to lick a man's boots, but it's a lot worse to be a boss who requires his boots to be licked." If you and I will think of ourselves for awhile as subordinates, rather than as bosses, we will have not the slightest reservation in accepting the stark truth in this statement.

It is also true that bootlicking—like parochialism—will exist to a certain degree in *any* organization unless there is a continuing campaign against it, and the commander-in-chief in this campaign *must* be the boss. To use Mr. Serling's well-chosen word, the "patterns" in the organization are set by the behavior of the top boss in that organization. Human nature, with all its weaknesses, plus the law of averages which allows us to predict human behavior in groups, causes the *initial* practice of bootlicking in any organization. The arrival of each new boss on the scene causes it to rear its ugly head, even if the prior boss had successfully attacked and stamped out the practice. So we can assign the "original sin" to the frailties of human nature, but from that point on, the "sin" cloaks and covers and becomes the sole property of the boss, and the responsibility for what happens after that is his, and his alone.

The most tragic aspect of bootlicking is its vicious, contagious nature. If it is allowed to exist, it becomes the common assumption and belief that the boss likes and desires it, and that it is a necessary (though revolting) thing to do if one is to get along or advance in the organization. It becomes a necessary evil and its erosive nature wears away the otherwise impregnable standard of conduct of many a man.

The man who finds himself in an organization where bootlicking is condoned by the top boss (which almost forces intermediate bosses to condone it) is in a most difficult position of conflict. Even though he despises the practice, he succumbs to it. As psychologists or sociologists put it, he "adjusts to the norm." He is a fly caught in the spider's web. He feels his survival requires bootlicking, and he does it. When night comes he sleeps uncomfortably, but he sleeps.

By now I hope you have refreshed and renewed your contempt for the despicable practice of bootlicking, or sycophancy, if you wish a nice-sounding word. But as we have gone along you and I have thought of ourselves primarily as subordinates—not as bosses. Let us turn that fateful coin and look at the other side by reading the self-analysis questions. If you answer these questions and find you do need to have your boots licked you'd better read how to heal the wound, and do something about it.

SELF-ANALYSIS

"Am I a boss whose boots must be licked?" "Am I a boss whose subordinates feel they must resort to the practice of sycophancy in order to 'get ahead' in my organization?" "How can I distinguish between common courtesy and bootlicking?" "How can I answer these questions?" "Can my wife answer these questions for me, or will she have the same trouble in asking and answering the same questions concerning herself and her relationships with the wives of my subordinates?"

HEAL THE WOUND

Once again there is no single, magic answer. I wish there were. Part of our difficulty lies in the fact that we, ourselves, are human beings. We like to think that our subordinates honor, respect and admire us because of our demonstrated exceptional qualities of professional and human behavior. This is understandable, for we must have *something,* or we wouldn't be bosses. And of course, there is enough fact in this analysis to defend it.

Here is a formula which you may find quite helpful. You have probably read and heard of the practice of "empathy," which the dictionary defines as "the power of projecting one's personality into, and so fully understanding, the object of contemplation." We have already agreed that bootlicking is identified instantly by the peers of the bootlicker. Capitalize, then, on this fact and by prac-

ticing empathy, assume the role of the "typical" subordinate who reports to you, and examine the actions of his peers as they relate to their boss, which is you. Examine the compliments, courtesies, favors, gifts, and other outward evidences of these relationships through the eyes of one of your subordinates and see what you can see. This will not be easy, but to the degree that you can do this effectively, you will be able to separate honest praise from flattery, to distinguish between favors which represent common courtesy and favors which are nothing but sycophancy.

There is also one other method which will prove valuable to you if you are the boss who is "just taking over" his new job. That method is much more direct and, if carefully carried out, can be very effective. It is simply this: when you take over your job, perhaps at your first meeting with your principal subordinates, state in plain and simple American English that you *are not* a boss whose boots must be licked, and that you share their contempt and scorn for the practice of bootlicking. That it is *not* required for promotion or advancement—that instead it will be condemned.

Now, if you do this, be careful or you will acquire the self-inflicted wound, covered elsewhere in this book called "The Unnecessarily Lonely Boss." You must avoid this, but you can do it. And you should speak for your wife also, and she for herself. Tailor your remarks to your audience, for the words you *speak* are not what counts, but the words your listeners *hear* are what counts.

From now on, you're on your own. This is all the help I can give you on this *wound*.

the

SOLVE-the-WRONG-PROBLEM BOSS

The boss who solves the wrong problem can be found everywhere, and the self-inflicted wounds he incurs are myriad. There are two primary causes for this executive deficiency. One, this boss considers himself fully capable of identifying and defining the problem, without consulting with his subordinates. The other is caused by the haste and speed with which the boss demands that the problem be solved. The first boss causes resentment and lack of acceptance on the part of the subordinates who perceive their boss as considering them not competent to help him analyze the symptoms and define the problem. The second boss, in placing the time pressure on his subordinates, deprives them of the time and the initiative they would otherwise utilize to redefine the problem anyway prior to attempting to solve it. They just give up and solve, or try to solve, the problem as their boss fed it to them, with the expected results: a mediocre solution to a problem which was not the real problem at all. In the meantime, the symptoms of the *real* problem are not subjected to competent analysis by the management team, and the *real* problem continues on, begetting more problems in amoeba-like fashion, while the boss is blissfully ignorant of the true situation. And, as usual, the organization suffers from this inept type of executive behavior.

Previously referred to in the chapter on the Sequential-Coordination Boss, one study I know of on this subject is very illuminating. I have heard Mr. Charles Foreman, Vice President of the American Parcel Carrier Company and Fellow of the American Management Association describe at the A.M.A.'s Management Course a study made for his company by a professor of business administration. One of the purposes of the study was to examine and analyze past decisions which history had proven to be *good* decisions, to determine if common patterns existed in the decision-making or problem-solving processes. One of the distinct patterns which emerged from the study of the good decisions was that considerably more time had been spent in discussion of the problems themselves by the team who later solved them.

You may be surprised at the findings of this study. You should not have been. In my opinion the findings of the study could have been predicted, and they would be the same in *any* organization today. The statement, "a problem well stated is half-

solved" is about the most profound formula for problem-solving existent today, if the analysis and statement is a team effort. How does *your* problem-solving process measure up against these criteria?

SELF-ANALYSIS

This analysis is similar to, but somewhat different from, that for the Boss who Treats the Symptom and Ignores the Illness. In this you are trying to determine whether you are actually identifying the problem and defining its nature before you go about solving it. Reflect upon the last several problems you and your management team solved. Has your first step (and an unhurried one) been to analyze and define the nature of the problem, and to re-define it until there is no doubt in anyone's mind as to just what the problem is? If you have not, your organization probably bears this self-inflicted wound.

HEAL THE WOUND

The therapy here is predicted by the diagnosis. Make sure that it is clearly understood by all concerned that time spent on analyzing and defining the problem is time very well spent and that any problem-solving in your organization which does not include this facet will go unrewarded.

the

YO-YO-PROCESS BOSS

This type of boss exists at all levels of supervision, including the highest in the land. He is named for the manner in which he and his team carry out the command and management processes of the organization. The word "bilateral" could be used, but it is not as descriptive. This procedure, *for which the executive himself is completely to blame,* is as follows: A principal staff or operating chief comes to the executive with a proposal for solving a problem, or a new idea for a product or process, or for any of a number of reasons. The executive and his subordinate discuss the proposal, and the former makes a decision on it then and there, without any further discussion of the subject with other staff members or operating officials even though, like most such problems or proposals, the decision will affect various parts of the overall organization.

Word of the decision soon circulates, by a combination of methods of communication, usually with none being entirely accurate. As soon as other staff and operating chiefs hear about the decision and, more importantly, *the method at which it was arrived,* they react, and then act, in a predictable manner, resulting in great harm to the health of the organization.

Here is a typical case. The case description will withhold the nature and details of the actual problems and decisions involved, and discuss the process only. (As a veteran professor of the "case" method of education, I have good reason to believe you would prefer to discuss the *problem* rather than to come to grips with the *process.*)

Early one morning the personnel director of a large organization went to the executive vice president with a proposal for solving a vexing management problem which concerned both staff and operating officials of the overall organization. After some discussion the executive vice president, a veteran of the company with both staff and line experience in the organization, gave clear indi-

255

cation that the proposal for solving the problem seemed good to him, but also gave some indication that he might want to think about it further. The personnel director pressed for a decision, pointing out how the problem had dragged on for some time without solution and that the lack of a solution was impeding organizational progress. The executive then accepted the proposal and told the personnel director to advise other staff members and operating officials of the decision and of his desire that it be implemented without delay.

The personnel director gave the news of the decision to the chief of an operating division, who immediately pointed out serious defects in the proposal to the personnel director. The latter acknowledged that there was perhaps some validity to these comments, but also pointed out that the decision had been made and its immediate implementation was desired by the executive vice president.

The operating division chief did two things in rapid sequence. First, he called another operating division chief who usually shared the same views as he did, and obtained a quick concurrence with his own view that the decision was not a good one. Armed with this, plus his own strong feelings of disapproval, he rushed into the office of the executive vice president, where he quickly stated his views. He gave strong and convincing substantive argument for them, pointing out to his boss that the latter should have no difficulty recognizing the validity of his views, since the executive vice president had actually been head of that particular operating department for a period of time prior to his appointment to the position of second-in-command of the organization. The boss conceded this but, realizing that his earlier decision was probably already common knowledge among his staff and operating officials, was reluctant to change his decision. The operating division chief pressed him, however, casting aspersions on the recommendations of the personnel director, who had had only limited line experience before rising to his present position. He also pointed out his belief that "the staff was supposed to serve the line" and, if the decision were allowed to stand as originally made, the reverse would be the case, confirming a growing suspicion of an evolving pattern of "staff over line" in the organization.

Caught on the horns of a dilemma, the executive vice president made a painful decision. He reversed his decision of ninety minutes earlier, adding a convenient face-saving twist proposed to him by the operating official, and told the operating department chief to inform the personnel director and the other staff and operating department chiefs.

Upon receiving information of two rather opposite policy decisions in less than two hours, the company's chief financial executive became very disturbed, for he found considerable fault with both decisions. One hour earlier, upon hearing of the first decision, he had tried to confer with the executive vice president, only to find that he was in the conference, just described, with the operating division chief.

The financial executive was particularly disturbed over the morning's events, for he felt sure that the company *president* would not have approved of *either* decision, if he had known about them, for financial and legal reasons as well as for philosophical reasons. The company president had come up through the line, and had also served as personnel director and later company comptroller before becoming company president. With this background the company president felt competent in all areas of the company's activities, although it was often remarked among his subordinates that he seemed preoccupied with financial and legal matters and seemed to be losing touch with the line elements. The company was in excellent financial health and was experiencing somewhat faster than average growth in the industry. While the staff was inclined to attribute this financial health to a vigorously pursued "cost effectiveness" program, the line officials attributed the company health to operating efficiency and were irked by the cost effectiveness program. This program had been recommended by the comptroller and approved and initiated by the company president without consultation with other staff and operating chiefs, and with only limited discussion with the executive vice president.

The operating officials and the other staff chiefs had been particularly disturbed over a monthly report which was required by the cost effectiveness program. This report, which went to the president through the comptroller and executive vice president, was intended to show improvements made during the month, particularly in the *cost* of activities. The "buzz" name for the act of arriving at the cost reduction was "value analysis," which had been given wide publicity throughout the company. This had been accomplished through the company house organ and by elaborately and expensively prepared posters which had been placed everywhere. These locations included the company bulletin boards which had been previously placed over urinal stalls after a study on "effective communications" had been conducted by the Organization and Management Chief in the Comptroller's office. (Similar small bulletin boards had been placed in the ladies' rest rooms, although a bitter argument had ensued over whether the location should be on the inside of booth doors or over the mirrors. They were eventually placed on the inside of booth doors when the company psychologist insisted that such would result in more effective communication, taking note of female vanity and female curiosity.)

The now-hated monthly report had in the early days of the program been a source of some satisfaction to the operating officials and staff chiefs as they sought out inefficiencies and made improvements. However, the number of reportable accomplishments soon declined, and negative monthly reports, at first unheard of, were reaching the front office (nicknamed the "head shed") in ever increasing numbers. When the negative reports first started coming in, the executive vice president and president took no direct action, although the comptroller had expressed concern that the organizational elements appeared to be losing interest in the cost effectiveness program. One day however, the president called in the executive vice president and dressed him down in no uncertain terms over the continued submission of negative or nearly-negative reports. He had ended his reprimand with a shouted *"Anything* can be improved. I'll hold you personally responsible for all future negative cost effectiveness and value analysis reports!"

That ultimatum had taken place six months prior to today's *yo-yo* incident. With the receipt of each negative report after the ultimatum, the executive vice president had called in the reporting official, reprimanded him and ordered him to take his report back and redo it to include the reporting of "some improvement, *any* improvement—I don't give a damn what, but don't bring me any more negative reports!" That ended the negative reports, but the grapevine was soon filled with stories of "improvements" which were highly questionable in many ways. It was even suspected that a number of newly devised activities and processes were installed initially in intentionally inefficient manner so that they could be later subjected to value analysis, "improved" and reported in the monthly cost effectiveness report.

This was the backdrop as the company comptroller waited impatiently to talk to the executive vice president about his two decisions of the morning. The "XVP" (as he was often referred to) had made a hasty exit after his second decision, informing his secretary that he would be back in an hour. He had gone to a nearby municipal park which he sometimes frequented to get away from the stress and strain of his job. He sometimes fed the pigeons but more often observed the children at play and the elderly retired personnel at leisure, alternately wishing he could trade places with individual members of either category. This particular morning he had a headache, but he felt he must return to the office, so he stayed in the park only about a half-hour.

When he entered his office, the comptroller was waiting for him, sitting on the highly polished hardwood bench outside his office door. (This bench had several nicknames among those who often sat on it, including "anxious seat" and "mourners bench.") As usual, the comptroller was very confident, efficient and concerned, much in the manner of the comptroller in *Executive Suite*,[1] whose confidence in financial affairs caused insecurity in his non-financial associates. He lost no time in informing the executive of his second-hand knowledge of the two decisions, why *neither* was satisfactory from a financial and legal standpoint, and that he was quite positive that the company president would not go along with either solution for the reasons stated. He pointed out further that he (the comptroller) had been discussing that particular problem with the company president late the prior afternoon, and had obtained tentative approval of a proposal the comptroller had made which met all the financial and legal requirements of the situation. He stated further, and truthfully, that he had tried all morning to give this information to the XVP who had already left for home when yesterday's conference ended and had been unavailable all morning.

[1] Cameron Hawley, *Executive Suite*. (Boston, Houghton Mifflin, 1952).

The comptroller pressed the XVP to cancel his latest decision, and to adopt the proposal that he had discussed with the company president the day before. The XVP was reluctant to do so and resentful of the comptroller's ready access to the president, who often called him into his office direct without the XVP being present or participating. Notwithstanding this reluctance, the comptroller pressed his point, and the XVP grudgingly agreed to cancel his latest decision and to adopt the comptroller's recommendations. He told the comptroller to announce and describe the reasoning behind the decision at the weekly staff and operating officials' conference to be held three days later. This meeting was typically attended by the President, the XVP, staff, and operating division chiefs. While it was "presided" over by the president, it was conducted by the XVP much as would a military chief of staff. As the comptroller and the XVP ended their discussion, the comptroller pointed out that he could more easily explain the financial and legal aspects of the solution with which the XVP occasionally expressed some difficulty in understanding. When the comptroller left his office, the XVP instructed his secretary to call the operating division chief who had caused him to make his second decision of the morning, and whom he had instructed to publicize the decision. He told his secretary to inform the operating official that he had cancelled the decision, that the problem would be discussed at the weekly conference to be held three days later, and that the operating official should so advise everyone he informed of the earlier decision. Before his secretary could make the first call he left for early lunch, and stated he would spend the afternoon visiting some of the organization's "field" activities. Prior to lunch he had three martinis, the first of which he gulped and the next two he sipped, as he reflected upon The Administrative Process.

His latest decision was flashed around before several of the senior staff and operating officials went to lunch. While they sometimes lunched together in the "executive area" of the company's officially democratic cafeteria where "all company personnel lunched together," today they had lunch in sub-groups. The following conversation was typical at the sub-group tables: "I like the XVP, but as a leader or executive he is just a goddamned yo-yo player. What happened this morning has happened over and over again. What in the hell is going to happen to this organization? Personally, I don't intend to stay around to find out!" "Well," remarked another executive, "you had better do some research before you choose your next job, including the company environment and the behavior of the bosses. This is my third company and the XVP is my fourth boss in nine years, and they were all yo-yo players, no better nor worse than our XVP, about whom I share your opinion. I agree that it's the boss' fault, but I think we contribute to his lack of executive ability first by going in to him alone like yo-yo's, and also by not neutralizing his ineffectiveness by our own actions. I'm inclined to at least partly agree with one man's analysis made in the final scene of *The Caine Mutiny* when he expounded the thesis that subordinates should compensate for incompetent bosses for the good of the overall organization. To use the exact words from the book, 'The idea is once you get an incompetent ass as a skipper—and it's a chance of war—there's nothing to do but serve him as though he were the wisest and the best, cover his mistakes, keep the ship going, and bear up.' [2] However, I agree with you that the XVP is a yo-yo player, and in the three days before the meeting, I'm going to do my damndest to find out and sabotage any solution the comptroller sold to the president and XVP, because I'm absolutely sure he has sold them a bill of goods that takes care of the financial and legal aspects of the problem and the rest of the organization can go to hell."

And now for the question-in-the-mirror. You have often been the yo-yo, and have experienced all the feelings and emotions described in this chapter. *Are your subordinates now having the same experience?*

SELF-ANALYSIS

The basic question here really is: Are you dealing with your subordinates as individuals? Or do you deal with them as a team for the purpose of problem-solving, policy-determination, and decision-making? I can assure you that if you are dealing with them as individuals, you are a Yo-Yo-Process Boss. This is axiomatic.

[2] Herman Wouk, *The Caine Mutiny*. (Garden City, New York, Doubleday and Co., 1954).

HEAL THE WOUND

Stop playing with your people as though they were yo-yos and start dealing with them as a team on the things that are important in your organization. If you do this, you will reap a fine harvest of cohesiveness, reduced tensions, and elimination of destructive competition within your management team. Finally, read and re-read Chapter 8 in Dr. Rensis Likert's book *New Patterns of Management* "An Integrating Principle and an Overview" (New York, McGraw-Hill, 1961), pp. 97–118, which is the finest dissertation on this particular subject that I am aware of.

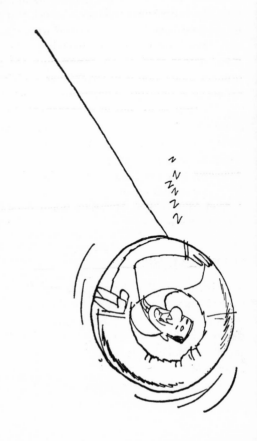

the

NO-FREEDOM-to-FAIL BOSS

The No-Freedom-to-Fail Boss inflicts a wound on his organization, on his people, and on himself of so grievous a nature that it is like a festering cancer which seriously impairs the health of the organization for a long period of time, and then destroys it. This boss has created and fostered, or inherited and propagated, an organizational environment in which executives, supervisors, and workers feel that they cannot afford to make a mistake, for at best they will be reprimanded and at worst they will be discharged. It is an anxious and agonizing climate which stultifies the organization and causes men to regard each day as an opportunity for reprimand rather than as an opportunity for accomplishment. Their primary motivation is to get through the day without making honest mistakes or errors in judgment.

Several years ago in a speech at the United States Army's Command Management School, Mr. John M. "Jack" Fox commented on this aspect of executive behavior and organizational environment in a presentation entitled, "What It Takes to Make a Manager."

I have always liked American Brake Shoe's William Given's term "The Freedom to Fail" as a basic management principle in this matter. Men will not take risks and make decisions if they find mistakes mean dismissal. The climate of a company, set by its top management, must allow for failures in decision-making if there is to be a development of managerial ability within the organization. We learn far more by our errors than our successes, but it takes a courageous executive to encourage this freedom.

Later, I heard him elaborate on this aspect further, somewhat as follows:

I want the mistakes to be made at the lowest levels possible in my organization. If they are not, and they come up to my level in consolidated form, and *I* make the mistake, I've made a million-dollar blooper!

Another personal observation provides an excellent case in point. Not long after my transfer to the Infantry it fell my lot to serve as second-in-command to an outstanding and combat-experienced Army officer named Walter B. Todd. It was our unique task in the Berlin Crisis Summer and Fall of 1961 to create, organize, and train, from a zero-strength beginning, a combat-ready battle group in a telescoped period of time known in the Army as an "Intensified Combat Training Program." Under Colonel Todd's able and perceptive leadership, the job was carried out highly efficiently, with our battle group achieving highest honors of all such newly created organizations in the Division. In doing so we missed by less than a percentage scoring point of excelling the longest constituted battle group in the division.

I have often thought that Colonel Todd was able to accomplish this difficult feat easier by creating his own organization than by taking over an existing battle group from a prior commander, for he was able to establish standards rather than to amend them. We were able to create our own organizational environment as we desired it, rather than to take an inherited organization with its accumulated ills and tensions and to try to reshape it. In those days there were seven companies in the battle group, all commanded by captains with widely varying backgrounds. Early in the life of our unit, Colonel Todd remarked to me as we were discussing the state of affairs as it then existed, "Our company commanders are going to make a lot of mistakes. The sooner they make them, learn from them, and then get them out of their system, the better off we will be." The weeks and months which followed proved that he had not only predicted developments correctly, but had lived up to his own word of regarding the mistakes as learning experiences, from which individual growth would result.

I shall never forget those few months for many reasons, one of which is germane to this discussion. The company commanders made mistakes all right, and one of them, Captain Negris, seemed to get off to a head start in the mistakes department. In fact, he acquired a reputation for mistakes and hard luck in the early weeks, including getting his company lost (location-wise, not casualty-wise) on one occasion. However, he was known for his dogged determination, and he slowly but surely led his company through a painful but rewarding developmental process which found their performance line on the graph finally starting up and not stopping until it had reached the top. In the final weeks of the intensified training period, his company, with the indomitable Captain Rocco Negris at the lead, came out first in all departments of competitive endeavor, from outwitting a cunning aggressor in a maneuver with a surprise attack up a mountainside to coming out

first in the Annual General (IG) Inspection. In Colonel Todd's battle group, *anyone* had the freedom to fail and, contrary to the beliefs of insecure commanders or managers, as time went on the greater the freedom we had to fail, the fewer times we failed, for everyone respected and was proud of their commander and his high quality of personal leadership.

I am sure you will agree with all this, and with the additional statement that bosses whose subordinates have the freedom to fail must also take the blame for the mistakes of their subordinates when they are weighed in the balance by *their own* bosses. The painful question-in-the-mirror here is: *How do you score in this department of boss behavior?*

SELF-ANALYSIS

Do the members of your organization feel that they have the freedom to fail, that is to make mistakes? In answering this question, you must somehow obtain the opinions of the individuals in your organization, including your immediate subordinates, and their subordinates. It is not enough to determine whether mistakes are being made because some mistakes will be made regardless of the type of organization. The important thing here is whether people feel free to risk failure in order to get the job done well. If they do not, you will find fewer mistakes, but only because people are not "sticking their necks out." It will take very careful analysis to determine whether your organization bears this self-inflicted wound.

HEAL THE WOUND

If your diagnosis reveals this wound in your organization, I suggest that you adopt the philosophy of Mr. Fox and Colonel Todd as expressed in this chapter and make it known to all concerned that you know that mistakes will be made, that you want them made at the lowest possible levels of your organization, and that you want the greatest possible learning benefits to be gained from those mistakes. Finally, remember that the man who does not make mistakes now and then is probably not accomplishing very much.

the

BOSS WHO CRAVES CONFORMITY

The Boss Who Craves Conformity in his organization satisfies this craving by insuring that conformity is rewarded and that non-conformity is punished. Some say this boss is a product of the age we live in more than a victim of his own shortcomings in the area of executive behavior. I refuse to accept this thesis for two reasons. First, I find it personally repugnant and find myself subject to self-contempt whenever I even harbor or entertain that rationale. Second, if this is true, we are doomed; all books on leadership might as well be thrown away and leaders, executives, and supervisors of all kinds might as well toss in their cards and call it a day.

When the boss of an organization craves conformity, the plight of the non-conformist in that organization is a sad and lonely one. His rewards for his efforts, instead of being well-earned recognition, are anxiety, ostracism, ridicule, and resentment. While there has been much written and said on this subject, there is general agreement that you should make room for the non-conformist to live, breathe, and contribute, for his ideas may well provide the spark of life which will help you free your organization from the shackles of the past and the present, which is tomorrow's past.

The plight of the non-conformist was strikingly formulated by one of America's most interesting philosophers, Charles S. Peirce, in his article, "The Fixation of Belief," in 1877.

The method of authority will always govern the mass of mankind; and those who wield the various forms of organized force in the state will never be convinced that dangerous reasoning ought not to be suppressed in some way. If liberty of speech is to be untrammelled from the grosser forms of constraint, then uniformity of opinion will be secured by a moral terrorism to which the respectability of society will give its thorough approval. Following the method of authority is the path of peace. Certain non-conformities are permitted; certain others (considered unsafe) are forbidden. These are different in different countries and in different ages; but, wherever you are, let it be known

267

that you seriously hold a tabooed belief, and you may be perfectly sure of being treated with a cruelty less brutal but more refined than hunting you like a wolf. Thus, the greatest intellectual benefactors of mankind have never dared, and dare not now, to utter the whole of their thoughts; and thus a shade of *prima facie* doubt is cast upon every proposition which is considered essential to the security of society. Singularly enough, the persecution does not all come from without; but a man torments himself and is oftentimes most distressed at finding himself believing propositions which he has been brought up to regard with aversion. The peaceful and sympathetic man will, therefore, find it hard to resist the temptation to submit his opinions to authority.[1]

An anonymous author has stated the situation more succinctly, if less scholarly, in the following terms: "Intellectual symmetry is a wicked witch which seduces more people than any other enchantress I know."

One of the best examples of disciplined and enforced organizational conformity I have ever heard of concerned bureaucratic resistance to change. The incident took place in the 1890's. At that time, the headquarters of the United States Navy prevented the improvement of shipboard weapons firing. The system in vogue at the time of the incident was one which allowed the gunner to take his aim and fire only at one point in the ship's roll. This caused the rate of firing to be low and accuracy of firing to be poor. A British admiral named Scott had worked out technical changes which permitted continuous aiming and firing throughout the roll of the ship. A junior American naval officer named Sims learned of the system, saw that it worked splendidly, and wrote up the system and sent it in to Navy headquarters for adoption in the United States Navy. And then he wrote again. And again, and again. He wrote thirteen documented reports in all, but nothing happened. When they took the trouble to answer him at all, they belittled the idea or the men who were attempting to make the present outmoded system work, or both. Fortunately, the young naval officer had guts, and lots of them. He wrote his story to President Theodore Roosevelt. As described by E. E. Morison in *A Case Study of Innovation,*[2] "Only by writing to President Roosevelt himself, was Sims able to accomplish his goal. The President, identified with the superordinate goal of national defense, not in the social groupings in the Navy,

[1] Charles Sanders Peirce, "The Fixation of Belief," in Justus Buchler, ed., *The Philosophy of Peirce* (New York, 1940), p. 20. The article was first published in the *Popular Science Monthly,* 1877.
[2] In W. G. Bennis, K. D. Benne, and R. Chin (eds.), *The Planning of Change* (New York, Holt, Rinehart and Winston, Inc., 1961) pp. 592-605.

and having no pride of authorship to protect, took the action to initiate effective change." (Which is a nice way of saying he shoved the new idea down the throats of the admirals.)

To discuss this subject further would be redundant. The research questions here are these: What is the role of the nonconformist in *your* organization? Is he a hero or a fool, or is he somewhere in between? (Or do you even know enough about him to answer these questions?)

SELF-ANALYSIS

Are you and your people being seduced by that wicked witch known as *intellectual symmetry?* In other words, is your organizational atmosphere such that conformity is rewarded and nonconformity is punished? If so, your organization is suffering from this self-inflicted wound.

HEAL THE WOUND

This therapy is not easy for it requires a change in the climate of your organization and you are the key individual, or the *change agent* to use a behavioral science term. You must use the communication media at your disposal to bring this about, including your organizational intercom, your auditorium, your departmental meetings, your house organ, and your organization's grapevine. The grapevine must be fed generously, for from the day you begin, a continuous test will be conducted to determine whether the stated policy is the actual policy. In other words, whether you mean what you say or whether you are speaking with a forked tongue. This communication campaign must be pursued aggressively for months before you can be confident that you have been successful in changing the climate of your organization.

SUGGESTIONS FOR FURTHER READING

Whyte, William H. Jr., *The Organization Man.* New York, Simon and Schuster, 1956.

Lincoln, Murray D., *Vice President in Charge of Revolution.* New York, McGraw-Hill, 1960.

the source of it? Does your information include opinions of your subordinate bosses' peers? Does your information include opinions and observations of the subordinates of your subordinate bosses? If the answer to either of the last two questions is "no," I can assure you that you do not have adequate bases for your evaluation of your subordinate bosses in the all-important evaluation of their leadership ability, and that you have a self-inflicted wound which, if you ignore it, will bother you considerably when you look in the mirror of executive self-analysis, even though your own boss never criticizes you for this executive defect.

the

GET-ME-RESULTS— I-DON'T-CARE-HOW BOSS

The Get-Me-Results—I-Don't-Care-How Boss demands and gets the desired results from his subordinate bosses, without evaluating or controlling the *methods* by which his subordinate bosses obtain these results. In fact, he couldn't care less *how* his subordinate bosses achieve those results for he is so preoccupied with insuring that they are obtained and reported as accomplishments to *his own* boss. Please do not misunderstand me. I am not saying that the boss higher up should prescribe *methods* used by subordinate bosses. This is covered in the chapter on the How-To-Do-It Boss. What I *am* saying is that every executive is responsible for insuring that the personal-leadership tactics of his subordinate bosses do not violate commonly accepted standards, including the preservation of the dignity and self-respect of those supervised. I am saying that *the higher-up boss is completely responsible for the bad behavior of his subordinate bosses,* even if their conventional production and effectiveness records are satisfactory or even outstanding.

Contrary to classical and idealistic concepts of personal leadership, it is possible for an executive, supervisor or boss to demonstrate the dregs of leadership and still turn in effective, efficient, and even outstanding performances, when measured by conventional standards like profit and loss statements, production records, military training tests, and the like. A boss can exploit and burn out his people, particularly for temporary periods of time, treating them like animals and depriving them of their self-respect, while simultaneously turning in "results" which satisfy or even please the next higher boss. These are undisputed facts and truths of organizational life today.

A significant portion of the fault for all this lies in the state of the art of the function known as performance appraisal, fitness reporting, efficiency reporting, merit ratings, and the various other names for the function of evaluation of subordinate by superior.

While great advances have been made in this area, and many fine rating systems have been developed, it is still rare to find a rating or evaluation system which distinguishes between conventional efficiency and moral leadership. What is needed is obvious, but there has been little reaction to this need. What is needed is a performance appraisal on which a boss can be rated maximum in conventional efficiency and from minimum to maximum in moral leadership. In other words, a system is needed for rating a man on *how* he gets the job done in terms of the moral leadership he practices in getting the job done.

If such a performance-appraisal system were devised, and some progress has been made in this direction, it would still be treating the symptom and more or less ignoring the illness, for this self-inflicted wound has its roots in the attitude of the individual boss that he has no responsibility for evaluating and controlling the human-behavioral tactics employed by his subordinate bosses in getting the conventional results desired by those bosses. The lack of an effective performance-appraisal system contributes to this deficiency in that it does not force or induce the boss to interest himself in this aspect of the executive behavior of his subordinate bosses.

What are the human manifestations of this wound? They are myraid, but they rarely come to light until they are "discovered" in some dramatic way. Or, they are often known to the boss of the offending boss, but they are ignored or covered up by him to avoid criticism of himself as a leader. It is difficult to cite specific cases of this kind and keep them anonymous, but perhaps we can cite a few in a way that illustrates the point.

There was for example, the corporation executive who remarked of a subordinate executive, "I know————is a son-of-a-bitch and I know he treats his people like dogs, but he gets me results, and that's what I'm after. *My* boss evaluates me based on the results I show him, and I'm not about to fire————just because he's a lousy leader. His production record, his quality control, and his cost effectiveness ratings are very high. I know his personnel turnover rates and his grievance rates are also very high, but I can live with those as long as he gets results which keep *me* in good with my own boss. Furthermore, I don't intend to be with this corporation forever. I'm using this job as a stepping-stone to

higher things. Besides, I *inherited*————, I didn't breed him not going to wash my predecessor's dirty linen. I'll let the who follows me in this job try to wash it if he wants to. Right it's results I'm interested in."

Then there is the military commander who was forced by ulations to award the highest unit-award to the unit comman who had the worst record for moral leadership, merely because combat proficiency tests his men took were made *in spite of* own bad leadership instead of because of it.

There is also the boss in all walks of organizational life wh unable to control the moral leadership deficiencies of one or mo subordinates, sweeps them under the rug lest they reflect upon hin the boss of the deficient leaders.

We can't forget the man who practices fine moral leadership but who knows he is not being scored on it or rewarded for it, so he often becomes discouraged and adopts a "what's-the-use?" attitude, and either becomes an embittered individual or he degenerates in his own executive behavior in the moral leadership department. You may ask why? Isn't virtue its own reward? Will a good moral leader continue to practice this fine type of leadership whether or not it is rewarded? I think not, particularly when that type of leader sees others who do *not* practice it being promoted faster than he himself. Such a situation can often shake an executive's basic beliefs and actually cause him to change his behavior in order to get promoted and rise in his profession. In this highly competitive world of organizational life, where such importance is attached to promotion and the status that accompanies it, men's values often become clouded, and what before was black or white can quickly become clouded and gray enough for even good men to compromise their better judgment, when the chips are down and promotions loom in the offing.

We have generalized and talked enough of this problem of executive, boss, leader, and manager behavior. It is time for *you* to stand up and be counted in this measurement of your own behavior as a boss.

SELF-ANALYSIS

Are you well informed on the moral leadership behavior of your subordinate bosses? How accurate is your information? What is

HEAL THE WOUND

Adopt and publicize a performance-appraisal system which includes as an important measurement factor the leadership methods used by all bosses and supervisors as they go about getting the job done in day-to-day organization life. Further make clear that any supervisor who can get the job done but who has to employ deficient leadership practices to do it has a limited future in your organization. Back up this policy and demonstrate that you mean it by identifying the deficient supervisors, giving them an appropriate period of time to correct their deficiencies, and causing those who cannot or do not correct their deficiencies to seek employment elsewhere. Finally, keep the grapevine well fed with information proving that you are administering and enforcing this policy.

the
OFTEN-in-ERROR-
BUT-NEVER-in-DOUBT BOSS

The Often-in-Error-But-Never-in-Doubt Boss has read or heard somewhere that it is better to make a wrong decision or a half-wrong decision than to delay his decision, for at that same lecture or in that same book he also read or heard that an executive must be decisive if he is to be a successful executive.

The net result is that he becomes very decisive and goes around making quick but wrong decisions, half-wrong (synonymous with half-baked) decisions, any kind of decisions just so long as they are quick decisions so he can be a decisive boss. He is decisive, all right. No one will argue that point with him. But neither will anyone tell him that he is decisively stupid. And the people who know this best will not tell him, for the people who are most aware of this are his subordinates, and subordinates do not tell their bosses how stupid they are, even though they are very fine and very able subordinates.

There is only one way that the Often-in-Error-But-Never-in-Doubt Boss will find out how stupid he is, and that is by self-analysis, which is sometimes a painful process. There is a compelling reason for conducting this self-examination, however. If there is one kind of chick that never fails to come home to roost, it is a poor decision. Its return, however, is not always discernible, for the illegitimate manner of its birth causes a basic human reluctance to recognize the full-grown fowl that limps home to be the same little chick that was hatched in such a decisive manner.

I have previously stated in the chapter on the No-Decision Boss that I once heard Professor Howard Baumgartel, Professor of Human Relations at the University of Kansas, while lecturing on decision-making in organizations, make the following comment: "At any point in time an organization is the sum total of the decisions which have been made within it." [1] I know of no more

[1] Lecture at the National Training Laboratory in Group Development at Bethel, Maine.

276

accurate or dramatic truth in the art and science of organizational analysis. And you can be sure that, if it could be depicted as a mural, the organization which is headed by the Often-in-Error-But-Never-in-Doubt Boss would look like a barnyard full of crippled chickens hobbling around in confusion and eventually resorting to cannibalism.

SELF-ANALYSIS

The problem here is not so much to determine whether you are decisive or not. It is rather to make a determination whether you are utilizing the proper amount of time in which to make your decisions. There are many times in organization life, other than in military combat, when quick decisions are necessary. However, it is a rare instance when a quick bad decision is better than no decision at all. The only way that this can be effectively diagnosed is to take a representative number of actual decisions and to analyze them in terms of the circumstances which existed *at the time*. Since we know that behavior stems from attitudes, an additional analysis of value is to ask yourself and your subordinates how you and they truly feel on this subject. These two analyses will help you determine whether your organization bears this self-inflicted wound.

HEAL THE WOUND

Having learned that this wound exists in your organization, probably the best method of healing it is to make it a subject of discussions in staff meetings, conferences, and supervisory-development programs. This should be followed by periodic diagnoses to determine whether the therapy is successful.

the

HIGH-OVERHEAD BOSS

The High-Overhead Boss is the executive who, by default or otherwise, fills his executive suite with far more personnel than is needed and then, as one sin begets another, the executive-suite personnel surround and reinforce the inner fortress with an unnecessarily large layer of "headquarters" personnel. Ninety percent of the executive-suite personnel become a parasitic burden to the operating elements of the organization, simultaneously sucking their blood and drowning them with papers, directives, and reporting requirements.

The results are as you would expect. In all organizations, the result is reduced effectiveness of the operating or line organizations, with reduced effort on mission accomplishment and increased efforts to satisfy the ever-growing requirements of higher headquarters. A concurrent bad effect as Parkinson's Law [1] gets into high gear is that the *necessary* top executives of the organization find themselves spending most of their time "managing" the executive suite and headquarters staff, thereby neglecting the overall direction and control of the operating and line elements. The net effect, then, is reduced effectiveness at increased cost. What could be worse?

In business and industry, the results border on the disastrous as they act to reduce the competitiveness of the organization in its industry, in the nation, and on the international market. This is best demonstrated by Cameron Hawley in his article, "The Quality of Leadership." His brief but revealing description follows:

Here is a case in point. I was fogbound one night in Amsterdam and, as we sat around the airport, I recognized the president of an American company that makes a well-known product in the kitchenware field. He had just concluded, he told me, a manufacturing agreement with a European firm.

"Until I got on the inside," he said, "I thought they had us licked

[1] Cyril Northcote Parkinson, *Parkinson's Law*. (New York, Houghton-Mifflin, 1957).

over here because of wage rates. I know differently now. For every penny they're saving in direct labor costs, they've got us whipped by three cents in general overhead and burden. Inside the plant, it's about a stand-off—but when you get to the office, they make us look like fools."

He went on to give me some interesting figures. His company and this European firm are about the same size in terms of units of production. The American company has about 1,200 hourly workers in its plant, the overseas factory a few more—roughly 1,300. But in terms of salaried employees, it's a different story: 912 in America versus 221 in Europe. There's a clue to the real answer—and it's the answer you find everywhere. Here in the United States we have built up—drifted into or allowed to grow up, however you want to put it—the most expensive approach to industrial management that exists anywhere on earth. This is our basic disadvantage in foreign competition today.

It starts right at the top. In the case I have just mentioned, the American firm has an active chairman of the board, a president, five vice presidents, and an executive-suite staff of 42 people. The European firm is run by a managing director and one key assistant. Counting their two secretaries, the top-management staff totals only nine. The contrast continues right down the line. This American president said, "They could pay our wage rates and we still couldn't compete—our overhead would lick us hands down."

When he said that, I asked, "If you know the answer, why don't you apply it? Why don't you go home with a big axe and chop yourself down to size?" And his reply pretty well defined the problem. He said, "How can I? Even if I were capable of running our company as a one-man show—which is virtually what's happening over here—I'm not at all certain that I could get away with it as far as our organization is concerned. Our second-level executives have all been brought up in a different school. They just haven't been trained to take over in the same way that these European boys have." [2]

Obviously, there are two general categories of the High-Overhead Boss: those who have personally created their own Frankenstein, and those whose monster has been inherited. You may argue that the remedial task of one is more difficult than that of the other, although I would guess that *if* you were one or the other you would feel that the executive which you were *not* would have the less difficult task.

I will offer one approach to a solution, which I call the *druthers* approach, with the word used in the same sense that it is employed in Al Capp's famous comic strip, "Li'l Abner" and the song, "If I Had My Druthers" from the Broadway play of the same name as the strip. The approach would be somewhat as follows: (1) employing the art and science of organization, determine the type and size organization of the executive suite and headquarters that you would have if you were to create such an organization today from a "zero" beginning. This becomes your

druthers organization—you would *druther* have it than the one you have now (2) identify the fundamental and detailed differences in the two organizations (3) determine what facets, components, and personnel of the present organization should be retained for the pure and simple reason that you are *not* starting from zero (4) identify the unique aspects of the present situation which make the *exact* druthers organization not desirable (5) develop an orderly plan for the transition from one organization to the other. The plan for transition, of course, requires the greatest perception and, if not done well, can make you worse off than you were before. The inability to handle this phase well is the reason that most reorganizations do more harm than good.

One general, golden guideline, which is violated as often as is the Golden Rule, is that the reorganization must be *accepted* in every sense of the word if it is to be truly successful. This is true whether the organization be in business, industry, government, education or the military. This has been proven over and over again, but is not accepted because of the authority complex of the executive at the head of the organization. He just cannot believe that the individuals in his organization will not necessarily jump every time he yells "Frog!"

Now comes the inevitable question-in-the-mirror. Are you a High-Overhead Boss? *If the answer is "yes," what do you plan to do about it? If the answer is "no," how do you plan to avoid becoming one?*

the

BOSS WHO WORSHIPS
the UNITY of COMMAND CONCEPT

The Unity-of-Command Boss is the executive who has read or heard of this principle of organization, accepted it as the gospel, and instituted it in its entirety, without examining the literature and history on the subject and without considering whether or not is is applicable to his organization, or whether another approach, such as functional supervision, should be utilized.

The opening sentence is a mouthful, and it is intended to be, for most of the things which happen in an organization are brought about because of the manner in which it is organized. And this particular facet of the study of organization is probably the most controversial and the most highly unresolved. This chapter is not intended to resolve the conflict between *unity of command* on the one hand and *functional supervision* on the other, and it will not contain a lengthy dissertation on the pros and cons of each organizational approach. Rather, it is intended to highlight the problem, and to point the finger of guilt at the executive who applies and supports either concept blindly. This will be accomplished, I hope, by allusions to literature on the subject.

The American and European fathers of scientific management, respectively, Frederick Winslow Taylor and Henri Fayol, each a practicing executive in his own right, had opposing views on this subject, views which were developed independently of each other. Taylor, who brought efficiency to American industry, was very critical of the fact that most of American industry was organized upon what he called *the military plan* on which he commented:

The orders from the general are transmitted through the colonels, majors, captains, lieutenants and noncommissioned officers to the men. In the same way the orders in industrial establishments go from the manager through superintendents, foremen of shops, assistant foremen and gang bosses to the men. In an establishment of this kind the duties of the foremen, gang bosses, etc., are so varied, and call for such a variety of natural ability, that only men of years of special training, can perform them in a satisfactory manner.[1]

He then recommended:

Throughout the whole field of management the military type of organization should be abandoned, and what may be called the "functional type" be substituted in its place. "Functional management" consists in so dividing the work of management that each man from the assistant superintendent down shall have as few functions as possible to perform. . . . Certainly the most marked outward characteristic of functional management lies in the fact that each workman, instead of coming in direct contact with the management at one point only, namely, through his gang boss, receives his daily orders and help directly from *eight different* bosses, each of whom performs his own particular function.[2] (My italics.)

On the other hand, Fayol, who had promulgated *unity of command* as one of his fourteen "General Principles of Management," felt quite strongly on this subject:

For any action whatsoever, an employee should receive orders from one superior only. Such is the rule of unity of command, arising from general and ever-present necessity and wielding an influence on the conduct of affairs, which to my way of thinking, is at least equal to any other principle whatsoever. Should it be violated, authority is undermined, discipline is in jeopardy, order disturbed and stability threatened. This rule seems fundamental to me and so I have given it the rank of principle. As soon as two superiors wield their authority over the same person or department, uneasiness makes itself felt and should the cause persist, the disorder increases, the malady takes on the appearance of an animal organism troubled by a foreign body, and the following consequences are to be observed: either the dual command ends in disappearance or elimination of one of the superiors and organic well-being is restored, or else the organism continues to wither away. In no case is there adaptation of the social organism to dual command.[3]

Clearly, Fayol visualized the largest number of bosses one man could have as two, and he felt that was one too many. When he later read about the Taylor system of scientific management he

---

[1] Frederick Winslow Taylor, *Shop Management.* (New York, Harper & Bros., 1911), pp. 92-93.
[2] *Ibid.,* p. 99.
[3] Henri Fayol, *General and Industrial Management.* (London, Sir Isaac Pitman & Sons, Ltd., 1949), p. 24.

became very disturbed about Taylor's functional foremanship concept in which each man had eight bosses, but Fayol was objective enough to wonder about Taylor's outstanding success while violating this principle. He then conjectured that the latter had somehow been able to reconcile functionalism with the principle of unity of command, but expressed considerable apprehension in part as follows:

I think it dangerous to allow the idea to gain ground that unity of command is unimportant and can be violated with impunity. So, until things change, let us treasure the old type of organization in which unity of command is honoured. It can, after all, be easily reconciled, as recommended by Taylor, with the assistance given to superintendents and foremen.[4]

The United States Army lists *unity of command* as one of its nine "Principles of War" (the other eight: maneuver, mass, objective, economy of force, surprise, security, simplicity, attack), and it is customary in military instruction to cite examples of battles which have been lost by failure to observe this principle. Since the early days of this century, the United States Army has also used the general staff concept which tends to reconcile functionalism with unity of command. Even here, however, there is room for argument, with General MacArthur taking the opposite view during the Korean Conflict as described in the following excerpt from an article based on newly declassified documents, "What Really Happened in Korea—a House Divided."

MacArthur had divided his forces into two commands, the Eighth Army under Lt. Gen. Walton Walker and the Tenth Corps under Maj. Gen. E. M. Almond. The two commanders, not on friendly personal terms anyway, were obliged to communicate with one another through MacArthur's Tokyo headquarters.

This split worried the Joint Chiefs, but MacArthur insisted nothing would be gained by combining the two armies. His message No. C-50332, dated December 3, explained: "Both forces are completely outnumbered, and their juncture would, therefore, not only not produce added strength but actually jeopardize the free flow of movement that arises from two separate logistical lines."

But the Chinese drove a wedge between the two commands, forcing retreats, until MacArthur on December 7, Pearl Harbor Day, drew up

[4] *Ibid.,* pp. 69–70.

plans for evacuating Korea. The plans were okayed by the Joint Chiefs two days later, but never had to be carried out.[5]

Taylor became puzzled, frustrated, and discouraged when American industry failed to adopt his principle of functional foremanship (with the exception of the companies he worked with or advised). Those who did would not admit they were doing it because it was the right principle. Victor A. Thompson in his recent book *Modern Organizations* explains this reluctance as a clinging to the hierarchical concept of organization and all that it entails; ". . . . The hierarchical institution is monocratic. Among the many suggestions which Frederick Taylor made, his suggestion for "functional foremen" for each operator was never taken seriously by management. Such an arrangement would attack the very heart of the institution of hierarchy." [6]

As indicated earlier, this chapter should not be regarded as a treatise on unity of command versus functional foremanship. Instead, it is intended to highlight the problem, and to point the finger of blame at the manager or commander who sets up or continues his organization in blind adherence to one or the other. However, lest you suspect me of unwillingness to stand up and be counted, I must agree with the last quoted author, Thompson, in his contention that functional foremanship has never been seriously considered in this country for the reason he stated. Further, I would challenge you to ponder why, in this Democracy of which we are all so proud, we would never think of setting up an organization along democratic lines. It is a strange phenomenon which is very rarely the subject of a study or discussion. If this chapter accomplishes nothing more than to cause you to indulge in a small amount of study and discussion of the subject, it will have served its purpose.

SELF-ANALYSIS

If this subject is not a problem in your present situation you can analyze it as a student of management and arrive at your own con-

[5] *Parade,* September 22, 1963.
[6] Victor A. Thompson, *Modern Organization.* (New York, Alfred A. Knopf, 1961), p. 104.

clusions. If it is a problem in your present organization, you can use the views of Taylor and Fayol as a backdrop for your analysis. For example, do you have more than one boss? Do your subordinates have more than one boss? Is this happening by calculation or is it happening by default? What is the impact on your organization? By answering these questions and related ones not stated here, you should be able to determine whether your organization is suffering from this self-inflicted wound.

HEAL THE WOUND

Having made your diagnosis, the best therapy I can recommend is to bring your actual situation into agreement with what is intended. For example, if *unity of command* is intended and desired, carry it out that way. If *functional supervision* is desired wherein many men will have several bosses, then see to it that this is understood and take action to prevent any bad effects from resulting. The best example of a negative effect is for two or more functional supervisors to be giving conflicting directives to the same individual. By careful attention to this subject you should be able to heal or avoid this particular wound.

the

STARVE-the-GRAPEVINE BOSS

The Boss Who Starves the Grapevine thinks that he can and should prevent information from reaching and flowing through the organization's grapevine (informal channels of communication). The reasons for his beliefs and actions are varied, and they are not a necessary part of the description of this self-inflicted wound; however, as with so many executive deficiencies, the basic insecurity of the boss is a major contributing factor.

The Boss Who Starves the Grapevine (one British term for it is the "Bush Telegraph") is blissfully ignorant of one well-established fact of organizational life. A grapevine will always have about the same *amount* of information in it. The only significant variable is the *authenticity* of that information. If a grapevine does not have the *facts* of a situation, it supplies its own "facts," garbled or distorted as they may be, and this information is accepted as fact by its recipients, in the absence of the correct information. Therefore this boss feeds inaccurate and perhaps harmful information by withholding the facts or starving the grapevine.

Probably the most prevalent topic of grapevine communication concerns *change* of any kind which may be impending, particularly change which may affect the status or security of individuals in the organization. One of the most common of these is change which brings about layoffs, reductions in force, retraining, changes in status, grade or rank, and the like. Many bosses feel that items like these should be withheld from the grapevine until they have been thoroughly threshed about by top management and decided in detail. They often make the remark that they don't want their people worrying about it any longer than they need to, without realizing that by this very act they are actually generating the worry and anxiety they say they are trying to avoid.

The boss who tries to starve the grapevine soon finds that this effort is a full-time job, and that he is spending all of his time running around trying to plug leaks and punishing the people respon-

sible for the leaks. His primary duties suffer badly as he emulates a
school-boy trying to amputate the tentacles of an octopus with a
dull and rusty pocket knife, further complicated by the amoeba-
like capability of the octopus to immediately grow two tentacles to

replace each one which is amputated. His task is hopeless, and he
is hopelessly unaware of his own hopelessness.

My question to you: Is *your* organization's grapevine enjoying a balanced diet, or are you causing it to suffer from malnutri-
tion?

SELF-ANALYSIS

Do you have an openly stated policy of feeding the grapevine in
your organization? Does this policy consist of putting all possible
information into the grapevine avoiding, of course, classified security information, and any other information which you sincerely
feel would be detrimental if disseminated? Do you have a system
for "tapping the grapevine" to determine whether information is

being communicated accurately or whether it is suffering in the same manner as the parlor game in which identical messages are repeated through whispering and from which horrible garbling results? If the answer to any of these questions is "no," your organization is suffering from this wound.

HEAL THE WOUND

The therapy here is dictated by the diagnosis. Take the actions and verify them frequently; that will result in the answers to all the diagnostic questions to be "yes," and don't forget to tap the grapevine frequently.

the

REORGANIZER BOSS

If there is one chapter title in this book which will strike a quick and responsive chord, it is this one, for no less than ninety percent of its readers, and perhaps more, have suffered under the executive who ascribed all the deficiencies of his organization to the *manner* in which it was organized, and then went about correcting them all in one fell swoop by reorganizing all over the place, with the results you would expect. Those results were, simply stated, that a few were good, but most were bad, with an overall net-negative effect.

I have never read a good analysis of the propensity to reorganize, if we may call it that, but I think we can give it all the analysis we need here. Any good analysis should begin with facts. It is a fact that there is a very prevalent propensity to reorganize among executives, particularly among executives who are either new or newly promoted in the organization. It is also a fact that, in a vast majority of the cases, the reorganization which takes place is regarded as a failure by the individuals involved. It is a further fact that the executives directing the reorganization, by and large, have not studied the art and science of organization, particularly the human factors involved. The logical question follows: Why is this?

I believe most students of executive behavior would agree that the propensity to reorganize stems from one or more, or a combination of, the following reasons. The new or newly promoted executive sees in reorganization an opportunity to make his presence felt, to make his mark on the organization. Another reason may be that the inept executive who is not coping satisfactorily with the problems *not* caused by manner of organization, tries to make up for this inadequacy by either solving them by reorganizing, or at worst he hopes to muddle and confuse the situation so that the existing problems will be buried in the bigger problems caused by the reorganization. That way, when they crop up again as they always do, he can state wearily that, "even reorganization didn't solve these perplexing problems." Finally, in this day

291

and age of transient managers and commanders in all fields of activity, reorganization gives the status-seeking executive a significant item for his terminal report, and in his own boss' performance appraisal of him. In this case, it takes very little intellectual rationalization and compromise for him to credit the accomplishments of the organization while he headed it to the *reorganization* he conceived and put into effect. The thought that the accomplishments were made *in spite of* his reorganization never enters his executive head.

The tragic effect of the amateur reorganizer—and most reorganizers fit this definition—is that they are completely ignorant of the human factors of organization, and they are further unaware of the mental turmoil and anxiety which results from the ineptly conceived and executed reorganization. To illustrate this sad fact, let us look briefly at two actual cases of reorganization, one a complete success and the other a complete failure, the entire difference being caused by the differing manner in which the reorganizing executives regarded the human factors involved.

The two organizations were as similar as it is possible for two large organizations to be, in size, purpose, internal organization, effectiveness, and the like. Each was *reorganized* in the same fashion, insofar as the revised organizational charts were concerned, but that is where the similarity ended. In one case the chief executive, feeling that a significant organizational change was perhaps in order, appointed an ad hoc committee to study the problem. The committee contained key personnel from the organizational elements most likely to be affected if a reorganization resulted from the study. He appointed as chairman of the group an individual *not* a member of those organizational elements, and divorced him from his own element for the duration of the study. The fact and purpose of the study were published to the entire organization, and information flowed freely from the committee members as the study progressed. A primary consideration of the study was the *future* of any individuals who would be affected by any reorganization which might result from the study. The committee completed its study, recommended a major reorganization and published its report, which was later approved by the chief executive. The reorganization was carried out in due time with particular attention being given to the individuals affected by the change. By all measurements it was a complete success.

In the second case, the chief executive decided in the secrecy of his own mind to carry out the exact same reorganization which had resulted in the other organization from the study just described. Still keeping it a secret, he called in a senior subordinate executive, told him of his decision, and directed him to make a "study" which would have as its final paragraph a recommendation that the reorganization he contemplated be made. He further directed that the study be a completely secret one. When the study was completed and the report written, he "approved" it in writing, called a surprise staff meeting, and confronted his staff with the approved study, and announced the forthcoming reorganization. Further, he directed that it be implemented and executed on a "crash" basis, that is, that it be done immediately.

A first-year student of psychology could write *this* paragraph in a purely conjectural manner. The organization, defined as a group of people, suffered a traumatic shock from which it never recovered. The human animals reacted like jungle animals. After recoiling from the initial wound, they fought back with every tooth and claw they could muster. They fought back with a brand of sabotage which would have earned the unadulterated admiration of the European underground fighters of World War II. Years later the then chief of the large organizational element most affected by the reorganization looked out over his people and remarked, "There they are. As they arise each morning, I swear they say to themselves, this is the day it will fall apart and we can go back to the former organization, the way it was before that S.O.B. reorganized it."

Interestingly enough, of the two chief executives who directed the two reorganizations, the director of the one that failed was more respected by his peers and superiors than was the perceptive executive who carried out the successful reorganization, and therefore was repeatedly promoted and assigned to higher positions, while the other went more or less unnoticed and gradually passed from the active scene.

To add a final sad tale to the sorrowful recital that this chapter is, it is well to drive a few final nails in the coffin of the Reorganizer Boss, though he shall never be laid to rest. In 1960, the American Management Association announced a new seminar entitled, "Human Factors in Decision-Making." It was planned by people knowledgeable in organizational science with a view to opening new frontiers in the ages-old process of decision-making,

which had made only inch-worm progress during those ages. Even though the seminar was planned with high hopes, the first seminar was under-subscribed. However, it was considered to be a huge success by those who participated. The second seminar, announced some months later, was completely undersubscribed and was not held. Its puzzled planners did not schedule any further seminars on this vital subject.

Only one conclusion can be drawn, and it is the central thesis of this chapter: the state of the art of appreciation of human factors in organization and decision-making has not emerged from the Neanderthal cave, and it never will unless the Reorganizer Boss learns about organization and the human factors of organization before he takes his meat axe in hand and plys his trade.

SELF-ANALYSIS

Have you caused any reorganization to take place in recent weeks, months or years? What was the reason for the reorganization? Did those reasons have their bases in fact and logic, or were they subjective and emotional? Did your plans for reorganization take into account, and deal with, the human factors involved? Only through answering these questions and others deriving from them can you discover if you have inflicted this wound upon your organization.

HEAL THE WOUND

In the future, make very careful analyses before you decide to reorganize. This matter is so important that you should discuss your proposed decision, before communicating it to anyone, with an expert or consultant before you make your final decision. If you *do* decide to reorganize, take a page from the book of the executive described in this chapter who carried out the successful reorganization, proceeding in the same manner he did on your very important project. And, above all, give very careful consideration and attention to the human factors involved. Only then can you even hope to carry off a successful reorganization.

the

BOSS WHO IGNORES
the INFORMAL ORGANIZATION

This boss lives in a fool's paradise. He has decided, by calculation or default, to ignore or be unaware of the informal groups and the informal personal relationships which make up the informal organization within his formal organization, and has thereby incurred a mortal self-inflicted wound. The vital importance of the informal organization has been well established by experience and research; however, the vast majority of bosses choose to not recognize this social phenomenon.

As described by the late Chester I. Barnard, able manager and author, in his book, *The Functions of the Executive*:

It seems not easily to be recognized without long and close observation that an important and often indispensable part of a formal system of cooperation is informal. In fact, more often than not those with ample experience (officials and executives of all sorts of formal organizations) will deny or neglect the existence of informal organizations within their "own" formal organizations. Whether this is due to excessive concentration on the problems of formal organization, or to reluctance to acknowledge the existence of what is difficult to define or describe, or what lacks in concreteness, it is unnecessary to consider. *But it is undeniable that major executives and even entire executive organizations are often completely unaware of widespread influences, attitudes, and agitations within their organizations.* This is true not only of business organizations but also of political organizations, governments, armies, churches, and universities.[1] (My italics.)

I agree completely with the statement that it is unnecessary to consider the reasons for this executive deficiency, and this book will not attempt to do so. Suffice it to say, as one author has put it, that the most commonly held view is that informal groups are subversive of the purposes of the formal organization. They can be, of course, but it is also true that the informal group is the social unit

[1] Chester I. Barnard, *The Functions of the Executive*. (Cambridge, Mass., Harvard University Press, 1953) p. 120, 121.

within which motivation to get work done is sustained. Whether it is one or the other depends primarily upon the boss and his effectiveness in influencing the goals of the informal groups to parallel or coincide with the formal organization.

While there are many types of problems our particular boss in this chapter may experience through his ignorance and/or unawareness of the informal organization, one type is described by a senior executive who had faced it earlier in his career. Speaking to a group of executives attending an executive development course, he stated:

If you have not personally experienced the next problem I shall describe, I can assure that you have something in store for you if it ever happens to you. I once inherited, as the overall boss, an organization which had a well-established and well-intrenched informal leader. My division had five branches in it, each under an executive who reported to me. In one of the branches was an older employee whom I soon found had been there longer than any of the branch chiefs, and who exerted an amazing amount of influence over the entire division, including the four branches of which he was not a member. There was no union in the organization, nor was there any reason to believe there would ever be one. I soon became aware of the power of this informal leader when he surreptitiously blocked my announced decision to institute a major change in internal procedures. I was never able to find out how he accomplished this, and I had no evidence whatever which would have held up in any kind of disciplinary action, but several "taps" at the organization grapevine made it clear to me that he was instrumental in blocking the action. (I don't want to give you the details of it, but the changed procedures I had instituted soon "failed" to get the job done, not because they were not good procedures, but because most of the people wanted them to fail.) In the few months that followed, it became crystal clear to me that I was the division chief *only* when my desires coincided with those of the informal leader. When they did coincide, I was highly successful; when they did not, I was highly unsuccessful. I found myself in a situation which was intolerable to me, but which apparently was not so regarded by my two predecessors, who had apparently gone along with the situation. In analyzing the situation, I developed five or six alternative courses of action, weighed them carefully, and finally came up with my decision which to this day I'm not sure was the right one. But I made it.

He did not give his solution, for the purpose of his talk was to give his audience some problems to cope with and to come up with individual solutions in an educational situation. If you had been the executive in the case problem just described, how would you have handled it?

SELF-ANALYSIS

Are you aware of the informal organization(s) within your overall organization? Do you know who the informal leaders are? Are you aware of the grapevine, and the configuration of it, along with its primary communication centers? If the answer to any of these questions is in the negative, you have inflicted this wound upon your organization.

HEAL THE WOUND

Do whatever research or study that is necessary so that you can truly answer "yes" to each of the above questions. This is the first step. Research has shown that one of the determinants of whether the informal organization becomes an asset or liability to the formal organization is the *goals* of the informal organization. If they are aligned with, or similar or identical to those of the formal organization, they represent an asset to the formal organization, and managerial actions should be taken to maintain this situation. If the goals of the informal organization are incompatible with, or in opposition to the goals of the formal organization, it may well be due to the ineptitude of the managers of the formal organization. You must identify the primary causes of this situation, and deal with them in detail to improve the situation. That's as specific as I can be on this one. Finally, read all you can on this subject.

the

BOSS WHO DOES NOT
CARRY the CONSCIENCE
of HIS ORGANIZATION

This boss requires some detailed description to avoid confusion. I am talking about the boss who heads an organizational element of a larger organization. He admits to this fact, especially when it enhances his ego or pride, and does not hesitate to announce that he is part of that larger organization. However, when the larger organization is shown in a bad light, such as in the morals, ethics or efficiency areas, he is the first to announce *his* complete innocence and that of the organizational element he heads. He disclaims any responsibility for the organization as a whole, and further disclaims any responsibility for exerting any influence on individuals higher up in the organization who, in the public eye, are more directly connected with the action or condition which is being criticized. Or, worse yet, he takes the same attitude during the genesis and development of the conditions and/or events which are eventually disclosed, or never disclosed, as the case may be.

This boss has a counterpart at the higher levels of organization, whether he is in the position of the principal executive or a member of the top management team. When unsatisfactory, unethical or immoral conditions or situations are disclosed, he is quick to disclaim any knowledge of or responsibility for the state of affairs.

The concept is this: Every member of an organization *owns and must carry* a portion of the *conscience* of that organization. You may ask, what is the nature of the conscience of an organization? The answer is rather simple in concept, but not so simple in detail. You may argue, how can an *organization* have a conscience? My answer is that, in its own way, an organization *must* create and assume a conscience as it begins and carries on its organizational

300

life. Further, that conscience must stem from, and be the watch-guard of, the fundamental principles for which the organization stands. An organization must have a purpose or purposes, and its stated primary one (e.g., to make a profit, to defend a country, to provide unprejudiced education, and so forth) must have corollary purposes in the field of ethics and moral responsibilities. Finally, if this concept is to work, every member of an organization must share this conscience and take it upon himself to operate his share of that conscience much in the same way he works with his personal conscience. And the operation of his share of the conscience means that not only must he guide his own actions, but he must influence the actions of others in the organization, whether they be subordinates, peers or bosses, immediate or further removed.

Now for some general categories of examples wherein this concept is *not* carried out:

1. The corporation presidents who express surprise and innocence when their organizations are accused and later found guilty of inter-corporation illegal price-fixing.

2. The corporation president and his top management team who show righteous concern when an open secret comes to public light in the form of disclosure that their sales organization is utilizing lavish entertainment and prostitutes to obtain large orders from high-volume customers, such as large distributors.

3. In the same instance, the individuals at lower levels of the organization who know what is going on and disclaim any responsibility for disclosing the information to public authorities, or to attempt to influence responsible members of the organization to discontinue the practice.

4. The delay of individual clergymen and large religious organizations to take a public stand on civil rights in the United States, even though the Document dictating such action had not been revised in nearly two thousand years.

5. The disclaimers so loudly voiced by recording sales company executives several years ago when it was disclosed that their salesmen were giving under-the-table bribes (payola) to disc jockeys to play their records.

6. The government or military officials *above* and *below* the organizational elements and individuals who are violating the overall organizational morals, ethics, and codes.

7. The faculty members of an educational institution who stand idly by and do not resist the president, dean or commandant who attempts to pervert the institution.

There is a rather well-known theory to the effect that an organization's collective conscience is a profound and automatic force which operates as and when necessary, much in the same manner that automatic sprinklers turn on in a building when a small fire erupts near them. While it would be nice to agree with this theory, everything I have ever read, seen or heard in my lifetime causes me to voice emphatic disagreement with it. The expression, "I know of no better way to judge the future than by the past," may be obsolete in the field of technology, but it is still quite true in the prediction of human behavior. Another expression which is still quite true, it seems to me, is the saying that, "The Devil works overtime." Belief in these two concepts prevents, it seems to me, the adoption of the automatic-conscience concept.

In the Spring of 1966, a dramatic case in point gripped the country's interest when General Motors President James M. Roche came to Washington and publicly apologized to, and asked the forgiveness of, a lonely author named Ralph Nader who had had the courage to criticize the giant corporation for manufacturing unsafe vehicles, and who had been ruthlessly harassed by a private investigation triggered by that corporation. The Washington *Post* carried the following news analysis of the incident:

Individual Conscience Scores
GM'S GOLIATH BOWS TO DAVID

When General Motors president James M. Roche asked the forgiveness of auto industry critic Ralph Nader last Tuesday, Goliath was apologizing to David.

It was a rare event on Capitol Hill—a huge corporation acting, through its top executive, like a flesh-and-blood human being.

With candor and grace Roche asked Nader, an intense, 32-year-old lawyer-author who has trouble making ends meet, to accept GM's apology for an investigation into Nader's personal life. The investigation was begun and carried on without Roche's knowledge or consent.

Sen. Abraham A. Ribicoff (D-Conn.), who presided at the confrontation, said he hoped the episode will have "a salutary effect on business ethics" generally.

Sen. Robert F. Kennedy (D-N.Y.) told Nader that his efforts have made "a major impact," and that if it had not been for him and Ribicoff, the subcommittee would not have had auto-safety legislation before it this year.

Near Hopelessness

Although it was submerged by the torrent of news flowing from the 6¼-hour hearing, a central theme in Nader's testimony had to do with the near hopelessness of a lone man grappling with large corporations.

These, Nader said, have vast resources. *They diffuse responsibility and fragment conscience. "People sitting in executive suites," said Nader,* become remote from *"the tremendous carnage"* their decisions may cause.

"I am responsible for my actions," he said, "but who is responsible for those of General Motors?"

Nader said a just social order requires that responsibility rest "where the power of decision rests."

But, he said, "the law has never caught up with the development of the large corporate unit and its "sprawling and indeterminate shelter."

He saw irony in a legal structure that jails corporation executives for price-fixing, but not for marketing products that kill and injure.

Roche's frank, unstinting acceptance of personal responsibility for the investigation of Nader may indicate that the time has come when the irony may become less so.

In what Ribicoff called an "eloquent statement," Nader said he had seen people "decapitated and crushed in highway accidents." He said he asked himself, "What can the genius of man do to avoid this?"

His book, *Unsafe At Any Speed,* laid heavy blame at the manufacturers' doors. Living like an ascetic, he began crusading.

His attacks on the 1960-63 Corvairs, his insistence that they were unsafe because of stylistic and cost-cutting considerations that ignored the reports of GM's own engineers, got under GM's skin.

Its legal department ordered an investigation in which private gumshoes inquired into Nader's sex life, drinking habits, associations—matters unrelated to whether or not Corvairs are safe.

In most men, some blemish might have been found. In Nader's case none was.

He testified that in working on his book, he found that "privacies of a past error, misfortune or human frailty . . . can be exploited to silence criticism and dissent" with investigations and surveillance devices.

He said he found men in the auto industry "in invisible chains" who feared to tell of "neglect, indifference, unjustified secrecy and suppression of innovation concerning the design of safer automobiles."

Needless Death

Progress was delayed for decades, while "needless injury and inestimable sorrow" was endured, he said, because of "an environment that requires an act of courage for a statement of truth."

Sen. Kennedy asked Nader why he was crusading. Nader suggested that the question wouldn't be asked if his concern was the prevention of cruelty to animals.

In his prepared statement, Nader said he had assured, and apparently convinced, GM executives that he was not involved in Corvair litigation. Nonetheless, they persisted in having him investigated.

They are, he said, "blinded by their own corporate mirror-image that it's the buck that moves the man. They simply cannot understand that the prevention of cruelty to humans can be a sufficient motivation . . ."

As to GM, Kennedy produced a December, 1964, letter from an executive of its Research Laboratory saying that then and in the immediate future "safety per se . . . is not likely to be a major concern of our group."

But now, Roche testified, safety has "a priority second to none."

So far as Nader is concerned, a crucial test will be whether GM, at a cost to it "not exceeding $20 per car," recalls its 1960-63 Corvairs for refitting with devices to correct what he considers their principal hazard—a rear suspension that, under certain conditions, causes the rear wheels to "tuck under" and the car to flip over.[1] (My italics.)

If the reasoning expressed in this chapter is logical and valid, it can lead to only one conclusion: There will never be a *Conscience of the Organization* unless every member of that organization desires and accepts a share of its collective conscience, and actively maintains it. This presupposes, of course, that the chief executive and the top management team will first espouse a set of beliefs, purposes, morals and ethics for which the organization stands. This assumption is valid, partly because this is the easy part, because it is popular to do so, but also and most important, people are basically good and want to do the right thing. Having done all this, however, will accomplish nothing unless the concept of conscience-sharing is espoused, enforced and rewarded, and violators punished. Perhaps the military axiom that, "A Commander is responsible for everything that his organization does, or fails to do," could be restated here in the form of, *"A boss is responsible, at least in part, for everything his overall organization does, or fails to do."*

We cannot pass on without asking *you* the question: Are you carrying your share of the conscience of your organization?

SELF-ANALYSIS

First you must determine what the overall organization of which yours is a part stands for in the way of ethics, morals, efficiency, code of conduct, and the like. Then you must ask yourself the honest and searching question whether you are doing your part to maintain the reputation of and carry the conscience of that organization. In order to answer these questions, you must think of examples in which the subject came up and you either chose to ex-

[1] Morton Mintz, "GM's Goliath Bows to David," Washington *Post*, (March 27, 1966). Reprinted by permission of the Washington *Post*.

press yourself on that subject or to remain silent and to not stand up and be counted for your organization. Only by getting down to cases in this manner can you answer the basic question.

HEAL THE WOUND

If, through analysis, you have found that you bear this wound, it will not heal through the mere fact that the wound is also borne by many other bosses in your organization. In this case, there is guilt by association rather than the innocence by association which many would like to assume and you will never heal the wound until you find yourself taking overt action to demonstrate that you are, in fact, carrying the conscience of your organization.

the

CIVIL-WRONGS BOSS

The title of this chapter is self-defining; however, the single sin of prejudice, a human failing which, bad as it is in individual relationships, is far worse when manifested in organizational life. This is true because it works to the detriment of minority groups that exist in any organization, whether or not that group is part of a minority within the population as a whole.

While researching the personnel management policies of a large corporation some years ago, I tried to identify common career patterns of those who had risen to the top ranks within the corporation. The man whom I was interviewing was well informed and had access to confidential personnel records within the organization. When I told him my area of interest, he expressed an opinion that it might be simpler for him to tell me *how not* to rise to executive ranks within that corporation. I shall mention only one, depicted so clearly by his remark:

I will tell you right now that there are not now, and never will be any
_____ * on the top or middle management teams in this organization. We have a company-wide promotion-from-within policy of course, but it's an open secret that members of certain races, colors and religious beliefs somehow never make it past the first or second-line supervisory level. It could never be proven as such, for all eligibles are considered and the final factors affecting actual choices are never made public, which is typical of all organizations, including ours. You might say it is one of our strongest personnel policies, even though you will never find it in any of our policy books.

It is bad enough to discuss this self-inflicted wound in this somewhat abstract manner, but it is far more repugnant when viewed from the standpoint of someone caught in its web. In reflecting on some of the most difficult problems of his executive career, a very senior executive once recounted the personal crisis he faced earlier in his career as he was progressing up the executive ladder.

* His word was one of these, it makes no difference which : Catholics, Jews, Protestants, Negroes, and so forth.

My next problem concerned what you today would probably call "civil rights," but it happened long before the recent trouble in this difficult subject area. On one of my jobs I found myself in an organization which outwardly espoused freedom and fairness of color, race and creed, and inwardly and covertly practiced many kinds of racial, religious and ethnic discrimination. I could take my entire allotted time with this one story, but will only cover it briefly, describing the incident which put me into another personal crisis. I don't even want to identify the religious groups or ethnic groups which had the upper hand, or those which were on the receiving end of the discrimination. From my observation and experience, no group has a corner on this sort of thing, good or bad.

My own crisis came during an overall reduction in personnel, of both salaried and hourly employees. I had been called in by my boss and told that I must select those who would lose their jobs, but was further told that I would be in trouble if those laid off were not members of certain specified ethnic, religious or racial groups. This disturbed me greatly. I found in discussing my problem with a friend, that this often happened in business and industry and, according to him, it was the type of conformity an executive had to go along with, if he were to be successful within the overall organization.

I found further, upon detailed analysis, that I could comply with this unwritten (and, I believed, highly unethical and unfair) policy, without anyone ever being able to prove that I had done so. There were enough people involved and so little known about personal capabilities, with very little documentation as to individual abilities, that it became clear to me that I could carry out this reduction in personnel with only myself knowing the real story behind the layoff actions.

You may feel this fact made my final decision a lot easier, but I can assure you that this was not the case. I knew enough or was capable of learning enough about the employees involved to carry out the reduction based entirely on merit, and in my heart I really wanted to do it this way. I learned enough about my peer bosses' plans to make me believe that they were going to go along with the unwritten pressure, making their layoffs based on ethnic, religious and racial discrimination, even though it would probably never be proven to be such. As the day of my decision approached, my own boss made it quite clear that I might be out of a job if I did not conform. At that time, jobs were not as plentiful as they are now, and the financial needs of my family were quite large. I kept asking myself, 'Must I carry the conscience for this organization?' I don't mind telling you, gentlemen, that this was one of the most difficult decisions I ever made.

You are probably wondering what his decision was. At the risk of annoying you, it will not be stated here, for the reason that we are discussing organizational environment rather than individual actions. You may feel safe in concluding that the *situation* forced the man to make a decision he was inwardly ashamed of. Or, did it really *force* him to? Who is the guilty party here? Only the corporation president? The Board of Directors? The top management team which carries out these discriminatory policies? Can one man buck the system? This book on executive self-analysis can not answer all these questions (although the author feels all must share the blame and shame); however, our question here is the inevitable one: How do you, the reader, score in this regard, notwithstanding the position you hold within the hierarchy of the organization of which you are a member? Perhaps this short chapter will help you clarify your feelings on this subject, and to put them into proper perspective. I hope so.

SELF-ANALYSIS

Do you believe in Civil Rights? If your answer is "yes," do your day-to-day actions reflect your belief? For example, when someone tells an anti-minority story, do you express yourself as disagreeing with the story teller? Do your actions in organization life reflect your basic attitude? For example, when you are hiring and firing do members of minority groups suffer from your actions because they are such? Do you permit pressure from peer bosses to influence you in this regard? Only through deep and soul-searching questions such as these can you determine whether you are a Civil-Wrongs Boss.

HEAL THE WOUND

If you are a Civil-Wrongs Boss it is probably because of a deep-seated attitude on the subject or because you are reluctant to get involved or to stand up and be counted on this subject. The therapy for the one is not the same as the therapy for the other. If you basically believe in civil wrongs (for example that Negroes or Jews are inferior to other people) then you must go through a deep-seated philosophical evaluation, testing this view of the backdrop of your fundamental basic beliefs, including religious ones. If your wound stems from a reluctance to get involved or to stand up and be counted, I suggest that you watch for, or make, an opportunity to express yourself in a group and then to defend yourself from the attacks which will most certainly come your way. Having done this once, you will find it easier to do it again. And you will like yourself a little more, or dislike yourself a little less after each incident.

On the Healing of Wounds

By now, your examination of your executive conscience has included the analysis of seventy-six kinds of self-inflicted wounds. You have probably agreed that one or more of the bosses you have had or observed along the way has incurred each of these wounds. Further, if you have carried out the purpose of this book by looking into the mirror (not in the way the mountaineer did), you have by now identified and located a significant number of these wounds on your executive anatomy. Further still, you are probably asking yourself the final and most important question: "How can I heal these wounds?" Simultaneously, you may have become depressed, somewhat in the manner of the book editor described in the preface who, most agitated, had stated: "I'm no damned good as a boss—I'm doing everything wrong!" If so, don't give up—there is help at hand.

I wish I could give you an easy, magical solution, but I cannot. As a clergyman friend of mine likes to remark, "You are what you have been thinking and doing a long time." You are not going to change overnight, and you are not going to be a perfect boss the day after you complete your reading of this book. However, you have already made progress if you have identified and located your self-inflicted wounds. It has been said that, "A problem well-stated is half-solved." The mere knowledge of the existence of your self-inflicted wounds is a start toward the healing of them. It is something like the statement that virtue is its own reward. You should now be aware of the wounds that you have by following the "Self-Analysis" questions in each chapter. Further, you should be on the road to recovery if you are following the prescription in the "Heal the Wound" sections.

I do have one suggestion for you in the form of a methodical scorekeeping system on yourself as a boss. People like to keep score on things, whether it is a sporting event, a weight reduction program or some other activity. Furthermore, in any self-improvement program, it is the trend that counts. The following chart shows how you can periodically check up on yourself, and

310

score yourself from time to time as a boss, insofar as these self-inflicted wounds are concerned. In this chart, we see that our boss, upon twice examining his executive conscience, found that his trend line was in the right direction, for he scored better the second time than he did the first. The frequency with which you need to conduct these examinations of conscience depends upon you as an individual. I should think the minimum would be every six months, with a more frequent process until you have your trend line well under control. This book was designed so you could keep it in a conspicuous place (e.g. the front part of your top desk drawer), and so you could peruse it quickly from time to time, reading only the first few paragraphs on each wound, if that was all the time you could spare for the exercise.

Having debunked the various principles of management in this book, I would like to offer one which I can *not* debunk. It was written about two thousand years ago, and is often known best by the failure of men to follow it: "Do unto others as you would have others do unto you." Unfortunately, like many principles, it is widely acclaimed and widely violated. Not long ago I came across the profound statement by an anonymous author, "Success is a journey, not a destination." If you and I could just take these two rules to live by, we might not need so many other formulas for living. However, things do not always follow the ideal path, and there may be times when, upon checking out your executive score card, that you are not happy about your progress, nor about the direction of your trend line, and wounds you thought fully healed may have reopened. If this happens, you might do well to remember the encouraging motto of the Christopher Movement: "It is better to light *one* little candle than to curse the darkness." Any progress at all should be a source of satisfaction, and should inspire you further in your difficult program of executive self-improvement.

To close this chapter in a lighter vein, there is one more action you can take to heal those wounds. That action is: You can "LICK 'EM!" For example, I gave some of this material in lecture form in Europe a few years ago, at a gathering of senior executives who had met in a geographically-removed area. After the talk I heard one executive ask another if he were going to return to his home city that week-end. His answer was, "No, I think I'll stay here a few days and lick my self-inflicted wounds." His remarks had a dual meaning, of course, and you can do what he hoped to do. You can lick your wounds like a wounded stag would after a mating season battle, and with continuing attention they may heal and disappear. When this happens, who knows, you may have "licked 'em" once and for all, and your *Anatomy of a Boss* will be healed, healthy and hearty. Try it!

Epilogue
That Unforgiving Minute

By this stage of the game I have become rather uncomfortable and am feeling not a small amount of guilt. I have helped you through the painful process of searching out and locating many wounds of the self-inflicted variety—in fact I have at times seemed to rather sadistically rub salt in those wounds. The therapy has hurt me as much as it has you. In order to relieve my discomfort and to purge myself of guilt, I would like to share with you a formula which, if used properly, will help you keep from going "off your rocker."

Yes, I have a personal, intimate little "system" that I would like to share with you. I have used it in the past five years and have shared it, in lecture form, with thousands of others. In order to lead into the processes of the "system," I must ask you a few rather personal questions.

Do you have that uneasy feeling that you are neglecting some things that you should be doing? Do you have the further uneasy (and frustrating) feeling that you aren't too certain as to what things *are* being neglected, *how much* they are being neglected, and what things (if any) you are giving *too much* of your time? If your answer to either or both of these questions is "yes," you are (I'm reluctant to state) typical of the busy executive, in the world today, whether you are in business, industry, the military, or education.

If your answer to either or both of the foregoing questions is a sincere "no," please *stop* reading this chapter. It was not written for you. However, for those who answered "yes," the paragraphs which follow are devoted to helping you reduce your uneasiness and frustrations.

This may help you decide to read them rather carefully. A prominent professor told me recently that a survey was made not so long ago of a number of executives who had "gone off their rockers." In searching for common aspects of the individual cases, one thing stood out as being more common than all others. It was a "vagueness of goals" in the minds of the individuals suffering from mental disorders. In other words, they were not very aware of the basic reasons *why* they were doing *what* they were doing and, further, they were uncertain as to what they wished to accomplish in life.

My "system" is based on a hypothesis which you may find quite acceptable. That hypothesis is the belief that the non-sleeping

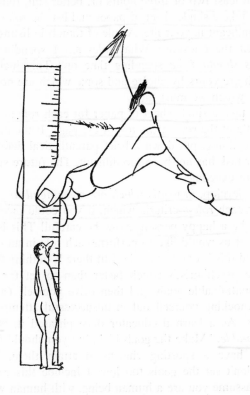

minutes, hours and days which each of us spend are being used in attempting to fulfill the many *roles* we play in life. Take me, for example: I am a *husband;* I am a *father* (and if I had more than one child I would have more than one "father" role); I am a child of God; I am an Army Officer; I am a son of two people (two roles); I am a brother (in my case three roles); I am the head of a family; I am a member of several groups (such as housing area or community groups, parent-teacher associations, and so forth) and so on.

Some of these roles overlap and some of them conflict, but if you agree that yours and my minutes are being spent in carrying out these roles, we are still together and we can go on from there. The next step is to find a few hours of privacy, a difficult accomplishment in itself these busy days. Don't start this step until you have at least two or three hours or, better still, four or five.

Next, take a single sheet of paper and list the *roles* which you feel are significant in your life. A rule of thumb in listing *roles* is to ask yourself the question: What *roles am* I spending time on? What *roles should I be* spending time on? This includes some *roles* which are yours by choice and some which are not. This is a fact of life which we must face.

Next, take a single sheet of paper for each *role* and write the name or title of the *role* at the top of the page. If the name or title is not self-defining, put down a brief parenthetical definition of it. So far your task has not been too difficult. The future steps will be a little more exacting.

Next, develop, *in words which are meaningful to you* a set of criteria for each *role*—criteria which, if you could measure up to, you would be a happy person. Now, be careful! This is a difficult step. Each of us would like to perform each role in an outstanding manner, and this is commendable. But there is nothing that will get you onto a psychiatrist's couch faster than to set for yourself a series of unattainable goals and then drive yourself (and others) crazy by knocking yourself out in unsuccessful attempts to reach those goals. As a learned educator once phrased it, "the project must be *do-able.*" Make the goals high, but you should feel in your heart you have a sporting chance to attain them. One other caution—don't set the goals too low. I include this caution only because I assume you are a human being, with human weaknesses, and today's busy world is a difficult one to live in.

In setting your criteria you should keep in mind that they must provide a basis for being "scored" against. It's something like "par" in golf, but the scoring usually cannot be done with mathematical ease. Generalities, on the other hand, will not be very helpful. For your first set of criteria, select a *role* on which you think you have some pretty firm ideas. Let's construct a partial one first.

to make sure we are together so far. Many of you are fathers. Many of you are fortunate to be the father of more than one child, which we all agree is a blessing, but which we must further agree creates an additional time-demanding role. The following partial list might serve as useful criteria for the *Father role:* (1) Provision for future education, such as college (2) Assistance with planning for and actual help in education, including religious education (3) Availability of father to child (counselling and joint recreation) (4) Sharing with mother in disciplinary problems (5) Recognition of the child's *individual* traits, shortcomings, strengths, and so forth (6) Providing opportunities for the child to meet and know other children (7) Communication of affection to the child; and so on.

If they are good, workable, usable criteria, they will usually lend themselves to the question: "How am I doing in this department?", which brings us to the next step, which is the payoff of the entire exercise.

After you have your *roles* catalogued and have developed your own personal criteria to score against, you should periodically do just that. Here, again, you need a few, perhaps several hours of privacy. I know from personal experience that a weekend spent in a religious "retreat house" is an excellent setting in which to do this *role examination.* A hotel room or a park bench will also suffice, if silence prevails. I urge against trying to do it in your home, unless your family happens to be away for the weekend. *Uninterrupted privacy is a "must," if the system is to work.*

Now for the scoring process, which is not easy, but which is usually gratifying. One reason for this gratification is that most of us are self-critics and rather stern taskmasters in looking at ourselves. We are inclined to remember the few times we "goofed" or fell short (whether or not we're caught at it) much longer than the many, many times we have done well. This scoring process, if we do it well, will help us put the *plus* and *minus* items into proper perspective.

So the first golden dividend you will receive from the system will consist of considerable evidence that you have been doing better than you thought you were. The second golden dividend will be a rather clear indication of where you are falling short of the goals expressed by your criteria, also where you are "overdoing it," so to speak. For example, you may be startled in your *Father role* analysis to learn something your children have known for years—that you are more of a father to one than to the other. In your analysis of your *executive role,* you may suddenly become aware of something your contemporaries have known for years, that you had regarded becoming a vice president or a general officer as a goal rather than as a means toward attainment of a more worthwhile goal, such as individual contribution to the good of the organization of which you are a member.

The frequency or periodicity of the scoring process depends on you, your memory, and yourself as a person. I suggest an "outside limit" of one year at the most, perhaps every six months being more desirable. This should be determined in part by your ability to recall positive incidents, including acts of omission, and to score them against the criteria you developed.

Now, I'm not saying *you* are about to go "off your rocker." But you did answer "yes" to my question(s) in the third paragraph of this chapter. You *did* admit to uneasiness and frustration with the results of how you were spending your minutes, hours and days. So how about giving this system a try? And when you give it the second try don't be discouraged if your score is lower than it was the first time. The chances are (and I'm serious about this) that you have improved in the accuracy of your score-keeping! Don't overwork this view, however, and use it as a crutch.

All of you are familiar with Kipling's famous poem "If," and the last few lines:

> If you can fill the unforgiving minute
> With sixty seconds worth of distance run,
> Yours is the earth and everything that's in it
> And—which is more—you'll be a man, my son!

This system won't give you any more seconds or minutes or hours, but I guarantee you it will make you more knowledgeable as to how you are spending those you have, and it will help you distribute them in ways which make you a less uneasy, a less frustrated and a considerably happier person. Please try it.